TH
JA

Few crimes in history have received such world-wide notoriety as the Jack the Ripper murders in the East End of London in 1888. Even Queen Victoria, in her widowed seclusion at Windsor, took a lively interest in the events, and told the Home Secretary how the killer might be caught.

But the Ripper never was caught.

In this reset and enlarged edition of *The Identity of Jack the Ripper* Donald McCormick sets out to establish who the murderer really was and to name him. 'A classic on a classic case' was the verdict of the *Sunday Times* when the first edition appeared in 1959. Now the author has continued his investigations and unearthed new evidence to support his findings.

Also in Arrow Books by Donald McCormick

Murder by Witchcraft

Donald McCormick

The Identity of Jack the Ripper

ARROW BOOKS

ARROW BOOKS LTD
178–202 Great Portland Street, London W1

AN IMPRINT OF THE HUTCHINSON GROUP

London Melbourne Sydney
Auckland Johannesburg Cape Town
and agencies throughout the world

*

First published by Jarrolds Publishers (London) Ltd 1959

This new and revised edition
published simultaneously by
John Long Limited and Arrow Books Ltd 1970

*Made and printed in Great Britain
by The Anchor Press Ltd.,
Tiptree, Essex*

ISBN 0 09 003740 5

Contents

	Author's Preface	9
1	Two-weaponed murder	15
2	Polly of Thrawl Street	28
3	Dark Annie	40
4	Leather Apron	52
5	Bernard Shaw poses a question	64
6	An autumn of terror	74
7	The correspondence of Jack the Ripper	93
8	Inspector Abberline makes a discovery	113
9	Grand Guignol in Miller's Court	128
10	Sir Charles Warren resigns	140
11	Clay Pipe Alice and Carroty Nell	155
12	The case of the drowned barrister	169
13	Dr. Jekyll or 'Mrs.' Hyde?	187
14	The barber from Warsaw	203
15	The search for Dr. Pedachenko	217
16	The end of the quest	232
	Bibliography	249
	Index	253

Illustrations

Between pages 128 and 129

Attempted murder by Jack the Ripper—*(Radio Times Hulton Picture Library)*

Sir Melville Macnaghten—*(Elliott & Fry)*

The first notice circularised to householders in the East End

Spitalfields prostitutes outside a doss-house—*(Cassell and Company)*

'Clay Pipe Alice'—*(Radio Times Hulton Picture Library)*

'Clay Pipe Alice.' A sketch drawn after her murder—*(Radio Times Hulton Picture Library)*

29 Hanbury Street—*(Frazer Wood)*

Bucks Row—*(Radio Times Hulton Picture Library)*

Kitchen of a typical doss-house—*(Cassell and Company)*

The Ripper letter sent after the murder of Catherine Eddowes—*(Professor F. E. Camps and 'The Criminologist')*

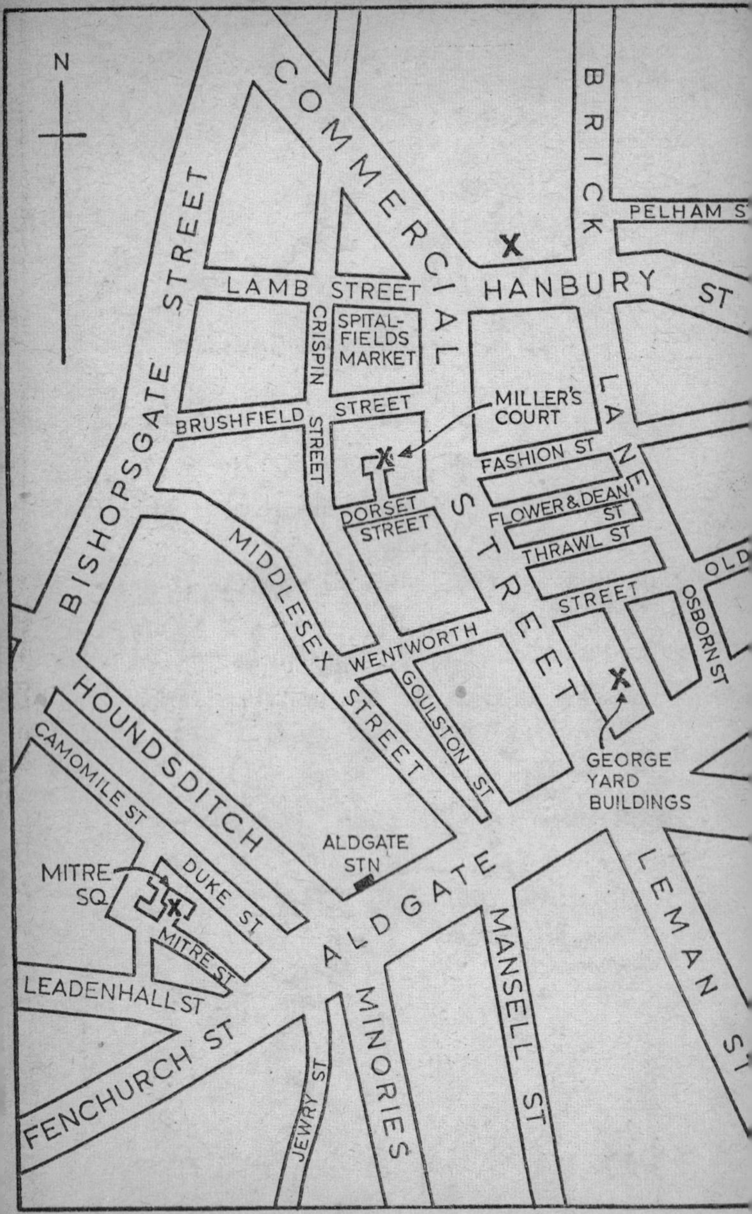

The crosses mark the sites of the Ripper murders

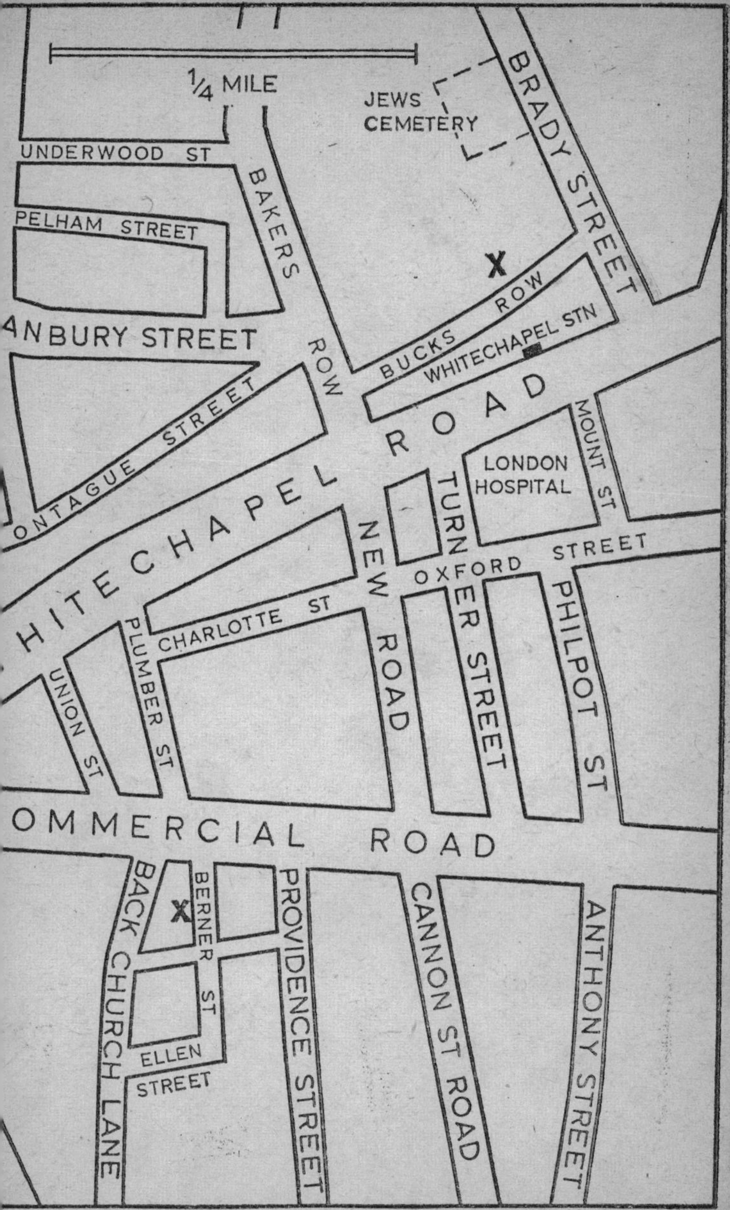

1/4 MILE
JEWS CEMETERY
UNDERWOOD ST
PELHAM STREET
BAKERS ROW
BRADY STREET
ANBURY STREET
BUCKS ROW
WHITECHAPEL STN
ONTAGUE STREET
HITECHAPEL ROAD
LONDON HOSPITAL
MOUNT ST
TURNER STREET
NEW ROAD
OXFORD STREET
CHARLOTTE ST
PLUMBER ST
UNION ST
PHILPOT ST
OMMERCIAL ROAD
BACK CHURCH LANE
BERNER ST
ELLEN STREET
PROVIDENCE STREET
CANNON ST ROAD
ANTHONY STREET
X
X

Author's Preface

There is no real-life murder story quite so intriguing as an unsolved one and the Jack the Ripper crimes, which terrorised London in 1888, are no exception to this rule.

Much has been written about these ghoulish murders; they have formed the basis of novels and films and ingenious theories by amateur criminologists. Yet no serious attempt had previously been made to establish the identity of the murderer until my original version of *The Identity of Jack the Ripper* was published by Jarrolds in 1959.

Perhaps this was because others who had investigated the mystery had become more interested in the motive for the crimes than in the person who committed them. But it is not essential to find a motive in order to catch a murderer. When the crimes are of a sexual nature the quest for a motive may actually obscure the truth.

However, when my book was originally published it not only produced a quite extraordinary quantity of correspondence, but prompted three other people to start their own investigations. Daniel Farson carried out considerable research into the Ripper crimes for a programme entitled *The British as Murderers* which was televised by Associated Rediffusion in 1959, and in which I took part. As a result of this, Farson evolved his own theory as to who the Ripper was.

Then in 1965 two more books on the subject were published. Robin Odell in *Jack the Ripper in Fact and Fiction* concentrated more on the motive for the murders and on a psychological explanation for them. Tom Cullen in *Autumn of Terror* produced evidence which he claimed pointed to the

Ripper being a young barrister and someone quite different from the person I had named as the killer.

Thus when it came to bringing out a new edition of my own book it was quite obvious that it needed to be a completely revised and up-to-date work which paid attention to and examined in detail not only the correspondence on the subject which I have received over the past ten years, but the findings of Messrs. Farson, Cullen and Odell.

In writing this new version I have kept to the framework of my original book, but have added in a good deal of new information and the results of further research. I have examined as objectively as possible not merely all available evidence produced since my book was first published, but the theories of more recent investigators of the crimes. I have not deviated from my original view as to the identity of the Ripper, but have introduced new evidence to support my claim. In connection with this I acknowledge most gratefully the assistance I have been given by the Dowager Lady Aberconway and the permission she has given me to quote from the notes of her late father, Sir Melville Macnaghten, formerly of Scotland Yard.

Such was the controversy aroused by the Ripper murders that even Queen Victoria from her seclusion at Windsor sent to the Home Secretary of the day a forthright memorandum of her views on the subject. The crimes spotlighted the appalling conditions of poverty and vice which abounded in the East End of that period; they touched the social conscience and resulted in genuine attempts to clean up what had become a district of degradation and hopelessness.

In trying to recapture the atmosphere of the period and of the neighbourhood of the crimes I have in several chapters used first-person narratives which, some critics may say, is not in keeping with a serious assessment of the facts and might be construed as a fictional reconstruction of the incidents.

To this criticism there is an answer. The first-person narratives which are recorded are based on (and in most cases litrally transcribed from) statements actually made by the persons concerned either to the police, at inquests on the victims, in cross-examination, or in diaries, letters and newspaper reports. Fortunately, from the viewpoint of a student of these crimes, the newspapers of the 'eighties recorded in far greater detail than today the statements of witnesses: in most newspapers, including *The Times*, these were given verbatim.

Thus the conversations of the soldiers in the first chapter are taken from statements made to the police and are not a fictional trick thought up by the author. The narrative of the labourer Hutchinson, who claimed to have seen the Ripper with his last victim, is an entirely factual reconstruction of what he said in his statement. Even the mistakes made by witnesses have been included in the narrative dialogue—for example, Mrs. Maxwell's reference to a 'macaroon shawl' when she meant a 'maroon shawl'.

I

Two-weaponed murder

It was an uproarious and bibulous Monday night in the Prussian Eagle tavern in Wellclose Square in London's East End on 6 August 1888. The bawdy singing of the drunks, the hornpipes of the sailors and the shrieks of laughter which greeted the clumsy attempts of the obese Teutonic dance hostesses to dance the can-can and the cheers which rang out at intervals all suggested something of a special occasion.

Yet in fact all that these cheerful, if rowdy, people were doing was to celebrate August Bank Holiday in the traditional East End manner. In the philosophy of that most delightful Cockney of all—Mr. Doolittle—this meant putting a finger to the nose at all depressing influences and conjuring up that 'little bit o' luck' which brings gaiety to the drabbest surroundings. High days and holidays were infrequent enough in this part of the Metropolis in the 'eighties and to the great mass of East Enders a Bank Holiday was an excuse for drowning their inhibitions. It was one of the few chances in the year when the sordid, dreary struggle for a mere existence could be forgotten for a single day in a non-stop orgy of eating, drinking, singing and dancing.

At least, it was an orgy for those who had a few shillings to spare. The rest either borrowed or stole, or hoped to scrounge the odd drink from someone better off than themselves.

A party of soldiers from the garrison at the Tower of London had decided to have a night out. They started off at Aldgate, went on to the Prussian Eagle, where there was music most nights and always dancing on a Bank Holiday. On these occasions the 'ladies of the cabaret' sought to gather in the harvest of Bank Holiday gaiety and translate it into free drinks and hard cash. Perhaps because the adjective Prussian was included in the title of this hostelry the landlord thought that to be logical his cabaret girls should be of the German race. If so, he certainly chose those who represented the brawnier and more muscular of the Teutonic fair sex and made no attempt to use the yardstick of Venus in assessing their attractions.

The soldiers sat quietly drinking their beer, gazing in mild astonishment at these fat-legged, heaving bosomed specimens of Amazonian femininity. Some of the sailors on leave were already sufficiently mellow to dance uninhibitedly with the hefty harridans, but the soldiers soon tired of the spectacle and one of them suggested a move to Limehouse.

This was some years before Charlie Brown had established his reputation at the Railway Tavern as the 'uncrowned king of Limehouse'. Nevertheless the East End's Chinatown was sufficiently gay and unusual to attract the casual sightseer. Indeed Limehouse, even in the 'eighties, was not quite the sinister neighbourhood so beloved in the imagination of melodramatic novelists who had already begun to portray it as a district of opium dens, secret societies, villainous Chinese bandits and kidnappers. In all probability it was the most sober and law-abiding part of the East End, for the Chinese inhabitants were in the main an honest, hard-working, kindly, but self-effacing community.

The parish of Limehouse extended from the waterfront of the Thames to Ropemakers' Fields, Three Colt Street and the borders of Poplar. Perhaps two or three opium parlours could be found in alleys off Ropemakers' Fields, but they were mostly patronised by the Chinese themselves, or by Lascar seamen. The Chinese community consisted chiefly of men who had settled down off West India Dock Road, in Pennyfields and Limehouse Causeway. In the year that this story begins there were possibly a hundred such men in all, yet, by setting up home alongside one another, by the Chinese lettering and designs on their shop fronts and restaurant windows, they gave the impression of a far larger population.

Usually they either married Englishwomen or girls of Anglo-Chinese parentage; hardly ever did they bring Chinese wives to London with them.

There were no Chinese down in the Two Brewers where the soldiers joined the sailors in singing:

'Dear old Limehouse,
Jolly old Limehouse,
Good old Limehouse Town.
Full of jollity and frivolity,
Passing up and down.'

For the Chinese Limehouse was a place in which to earn a living. For the seamen it was the gateway to London and somewhere to spend the cash which had accrued to them after a long voyage. And the girls who haunted this tavern instinctively fluttered over to the seamen like moths round a candle, knowing that Jack, when ashore, brought a wad of money with him, while Private Tommy Atkins probably had no more than a shilling to last him the night.

One of the soldiers from the Tower tried on several occasions to attract the attention of the girls without success. Then, finishing off his beer, he announced his intention of looking for a partner elsewhere.

'I'm fed to the bloomin' teeth wiv these gels. Not time for anyone but a matelot. Let's go somewhere else.'

'Wot baht cuttin' back on our tracks and goin' to the City Road. We could pop in the Eagle and 'ave one and then go an' see this rorty gel wot sings "My Soldier Laddie".'

He was referring to the Eagle in the City Road, the tavern which inspired the famous ditty

'Up and down the City Road,
In and out the Eagle,
That's the way the money goes,
Pop goes the weasel.'

In brief, a visit to the Eagle with its Grecian Theatre on

the first floor was not infrequently followed by an urgent call at a nearby pawnbroker's.

'We ain't got enough for the Eagle,' replied another soldier. 'All the same I would like to 'ear that Bella Delmere agin.'

'Bella Delmere? She's dropped that name now. Marie Lloyd she calls 'erself today.'

There was an argument for a few minutes; it ended in the soldier who was so anxious 'to find a gel' leaving his pals and going off in the direction of Commercial Road. His comrades did not see him again after that, but an hour later at least two other people saw him in the public bar of the Angel and Crown near Whitechapel Church, drinking with a woman who was known to some as Martha Tabram and to others as Martha Turner.

No one took much notice as Turner, unlike the girls in the Two Brewers, made a habit of striking up chance acquaintanceships with soldiers. A married woman, living apart from her husband, she was a notorious local prostitute who usually solicited her custom in the vicinity of the Tower of London.

It was just after midnight and those East Enders who had made their favourite Bank Holiday jaunt—out to Hackney Fields or Epping Forest in a four-horse wagonette—were beginning to return for the last few drinks before turning in. The Refreshment Houses Act of 1865 had imposed a closing hour of 1 a.m., but this legislation had not appreciably decreased the drinking habits of the people. It merely meant that between midnight and 1 a.m. the public houses, especially those in the East End, were fuller than usual, with all present intent upon drinking against the clock.

During this last feverish hour of drinking the lowest class of prostitutes descended into the taverns in hordes, bent upon finding men sufficiently fuddled to overlook their drab, sluttish appearance and to fall like ripe plums into their greedy, scraggy arms. Earlier in the night the more successful members of their profession had already paired up with the likeliest and more prosperous customers, but between midnight and 1 a.m. it was a two-fold procession of drabs and little girls who held the stage. Perhaps the most appalling feature of this traffic in sex was the victimisation of young children. The sale of little girls was a regular traffic in Hackney, Dalston, Whitechapel and along the Mile End Road. It was pathetic to see children of eleven and twelve, with rouged faces, kicked out of their homes by an irate and penniless father and told to stay out until some monster of a man would give them a couple of shillings.

Also in the Angel and Crown that night were Mr. and Mrs. Mahoney. They, too, had dropped into the public house for a last drink before returning to their home at No. 47, George Yard Buildings, after a day out in Epping Forest. This was the nearest the Mahoneys ever got to the English countryside, and the drive back along the hot and dusty roads had given them a thirst.

So for a few minutes they joined in the choruses of the traditional East End songs in the Angel, where there was standing room only at this late hour. Market porters, labourers, soldiers, sailors, women suckling their babies and prostitutes huddled together over their beers, ports and hard liquor.

It was 'Knees up, Mother Brown' for the women, as with skirts held high, they waddled and high-kicked their way around the crowded bar, occasionally knocking someone's pint over and starting a fiery altercation. For the men it was usually something a little more robust, with a marked preference for the horrific rather than the pornographic. With a pint pewter mug balanced on his head, remaining remarkably steady considering that at least five other pints had been emptied down his throat that night, a short, squat man, his cap half over one eye, sang:

'Oh, my name it is Sam Hall, Samuel Hall.
Oh, my name it is Sam Hall, Samuel Hall.
Oh, my name it is Sam Hall,
And I hate you one and all;
You're a gang of muckers all—
Damn your eyes!

'Oh, they say I killed a man, so they said.
Oh, they say I killed a man, so they said.
For I hit him on the 'ead with a bloody great
lump of lead.
Oh, I left him there for dead,
Damn 'is eyes.'

Shrieks of mirth and shouts of encouragement greeted this bloodcurdling ballad. The swing doors of the public bar crashed open as late-comers arrived, some to join in the raucous saraband of Mother Brown, others to sing the chorus of 'Samuel Hall'. In the end, doubtless because of the deafening baritone of the man with the pint pot on his head, the devotees of Samuel won . . .

'Oh, they put me into quod, into quod.
Oh, they put me into quod, into quod.
Oh, they put me into quod all for killing of that sod,
They did—so 'elp me Gawd—
Damn their eyes!'

Presumably the baritone knew Martha Turner quite well. At any rate he ensured that those in the bar would recollect her presence afterwards by substituting her name for Samuel's mistress, Molly, in the song . . .

'I sees Martha in the crowd, in the crowd,
I sees Martha in the crowd, in the crowd.
I sees Martha in the crowd, so I hollered out aloud
"Now ain't you bleedin' proud,
Damn your eyes."'

There was more mirth at this sally, which produced a drunken laugh from Martha and a blush of embarrassment from the young soldier. Shortly afterwards they both left the Angel together.

The Mahoneys departed at closing time and reached their home shortly before two o'clock in the morning. Both Mrs.

Mahoney and her husband were quite emphatic that as they climbed the stone staircase in George Yard Buildings there was nobody and certainly nothing unusual to be seen there.

'My hubby felt a bit peckish when we got in,' said Mrs. Elizabeth Mahoney, 'so I said I'd run along to the shop on the corner and get two ha'porths each of fish and chips. And I remember when I was buying them the man in the shop called out: "Ten past two, Maggie. Time to shut up."

'As I came back up the stairs there was nobody about. We had our supper and went to bed. And we heard nothing more that night.'

But about 3.30 a.m. Albert George Crow, a cab driver, who lived at No. 35 in the same buildings, noticed somebody lying on the first landing as he came up the staircase. 'I didn't stop to look any closer,' he said. 'It was nothing unusual to see somebody lying drunk, or asleep in the stairway, so I just passed on to my room and went to bed.'

John Saunders Reeves had a room at No. 37 in George Yard Buildings. He got up early on that morning of 7 August. It was about 5 a.m. when he left his room, intending to look for a job at one of the markets. As he turned a corner in the staircase he saw the body of a woman lying in a pool of blood. He noticed that she was huddled up on her back, with her bodice torn open and wounds in her breasts.

Without stopping to examine the corpse, Reeves ran for the police.

Sometime between 2.20 and 3.30 that August morning a murder had been committed in the stairway of George Yard Buildings.

No one at first paid much attention to the violent death of Martha Turner. There had been a considerable increase in the numbers of murders committed in London in the previous twelve months and, in the East End at least, a wave of crime had swept over Spitalfields, Whitechapel and Stepney throughout 1888. People had become, if not indifferent, at any rate apathetic to crimes of violence ending in death. And in the case of Martha Turner no one came forward to mourn her demise. Any family ties had been irrevocably severed when she went to ply her sordid trade in the alleyways of the East End. Thirty-five years of age, according to police records, she looked at least forty; her mode of life had taken the inevitable toll of her looks. Little was known of her except that she lived at No. 4, Star Place, off Commercial Road.

Indeed, this might have been dismissed as just another crime of violence, but for the report of the surgeon who examined the dead woman. Dr. Timothy Robert Keleene was himself amazed when he carried out the post mortem. There were no fewer than thirty-nine wounds on Turner; nine stab wounds in the throat, seventeen in the region of the breasts and thirteen in the abdomen. This was no ordinary murder, no sudden fit of violence after a drunken brawl, but the work of some frenzied maniac.

It was not long before the police learned from various people that Turner had been seen in the Angel and Crown and in an alleyway not far from that tavern with the soldier who had left his comrades at the Two Brewers. No one could fix the exact time they had been seen together, but it must have been sometime between midnight and 2.30 a.m.

The soldier in question was quickly traced to the garrison in the Tower of London, and the local police, convinced that the wounds must have been caused by a bayonet, felt sure they had found the culprit. All the troops from the Tower were put on an identity parade the next day, but nothing came of this and the chief soldier suspect was able to establish that he had rejoined his comrades before 1.30 a.m. Later it transpired that after seeing the soldier Turner had returned to the Angel and stayed there until closing time.

So the police, baffled by this turn of events, were left without any further clues. The surgeon's report was examined once more and Dr. Keleene was asked many questions. He felt sure that a bayonet was not the weapon used by the murderer, but he was quite positive that the wounds were inflicted not by one weapon, but by two, which made this killing even more unique. No, he added, he could not be certain what weapons had been used, but he thought one was a long-bladed knife and the other possibly a surgical instrument. In his opinion the murderer was not a soldier, but someone with at least an elementary knowledge of surgery. 'Whoever it was, he knew how and where to cut.'

Why should the killer use two weapons? That was the poser which the police asked themselves in vain. The obvious deduction was that the murderer was ambidextrous: certainly he could deliver blows as effectively with one hand as with the other. The police thought it was just possible he wished to give the impression that he was left-handed. If so, he cannot be said to have succeeded.

It is also important to note that in this murder the woman's throat was not cut, nor were any organs removed from the body. Nor did there appear to be any deliberate or systematised mutilations of the body. Later it was suggested that the killer was disturbed in his gruesome task, possibly by the arrival of Albert Crow, and that therefore he had no time to complete his ghoulish operations. The full significance of these features of the crime will be seen later.

Very little publicity was given to the murder in the press. There was no reference to the affair until Mr. George Collier, the Coroner, opened the inquest on 10 August. A verdict of murder against some person or persons unknown was returned.

This proved to be the beginning of the worst series of murders which Britain has ever known.

For years it was a subject of intense speculation and controversy how many of these murders were committed by the same person, and which of them provided his first victim. How these crimes came to be universally known as the 'Jack the Ripper' murders will later be apparent, but it is sufficient now to assert quite positively that Jack was not responsible for all of them. Naturally in the bars of the East End rumour and exaggerated talk credited him with anything from a dozen to twenty victims. Even criminologists have asserted with an air of finality that he slew more than a dozen unfortunate women. This reflects not only the boasts of bar chatterers, but the hysterical state of public opinion at the time. The moment a newspaper-seller went round hollering 'Another 'orrible murder!' so people jumped to the conclusion that the Ripper had struck again.

Sir Melville Macnaghten, who joined the Criminal Investigation Department at Scotland Yard in June 1889 as an Assistant Chief Constable, became Chief of the C.I.D. in 1903. He wrote: 'At one time or another fourteen murders were attributed to Jack the Ripper—some before and some after 1888. Suffice it to say that the Whitechapel murderer committed *five* murders and no more.'

Not all experts, even including police chiefs, agreed with Sir Melville as to the number of killings which could be attributed to Jack. But this is not the point at issue at the moment. What we have to try to establish is which was his first murder. To do this it is necessary to eliminate the charge, often made by police and coroners, that the first Ripper crime was the killing of Emma Smith on 3 April 1888.

There were certain similarities between this case and that of Martha Turner. Both crimes were committed on a Bank Holiday Monday, Smith being killed on Easter Monday. Smith, who was forty-five years old, was also a prostitute, living in George Street, Spitalfields, and her death occurred in the same neighbourhood. She was going past Whitechapel Church about 4 a.m. when four men followed her up Osborne Street, attacked and robbed her. She managed to stagger back into the house where she lived and to give a description of the four men before she died in hospital from severe abdominal injuries.

But here the similarities end. In Turner's case no motive was apparent; with Smith the crime followed an act of robbery. And, though Smith's assailants were never caught, there were grounds for believing that they were members of the notorious Old Nichol Gang, which in the last quarter of the last century terrorised the East End of London. The mean streets of this quarter were often the scene of gang fights between the Hoxton Market Gang and the Old Nichol Gang, named after Old Nichol Street, Bethnal Green, which had been a centre of organised crime for a hundred years. The Nichol Gang used thugs to beat up and rob women of the streets, while their rivals sent out children at nightfall to steal from shops or snatch from passers-by. The meaner streets of the area would give food in exchange for any stolen object.

If London's East End was not quite so bad in the 'eighties as in Dickens' day, it certainly made an appalling commentary on Victorian 'civilisation'. At this time the first of Russia's revolutionaries came and settled in the East End, and if to-day one is sometimes surprised to read Soviet descriptions of this area of London because they sound reminiscent of the era of Fagan and Bill Sykes, it must be remembered that they are often based on narratives of the 'eighties provided by revolutionaries who were still alive in the 'twenties of the present century.

Crime was so rampant in the East End then that John Reeves, in *Recollections of a School Attendance Officer*, wrote: 'I have seen men examining burglars' tools on window sills and practising robbery from upper windows. . . . The life of the people was chiefly occupied in deception and concealment. There was scarcely a family but appeared to have some reason for fearing the police.'

It was a case of too many people chasing too few jobs in an overcrowded area where there was no industry and very little money available even for those who could get work. In such an environment robbery became the chief trade of whole families and prostitution the only industry open to many of the womenfolk. In the filthy, broken-down, rat-infested hovels, disease, immorality and violence were rife. The ignorance of the masses was appalling. Few, at least of the English population (the foreigners were far superior), could read or write. Fewer still had any conception of right or wrong. Ninety-eight per cent of the lower classes did not attend any church. There were churches everywhere, but most of them were empty on Sundays and the parsons and their assistants had to find non-ecclesiastical work with which to justify their existence. To their credit, they did what they could to point the way to a community spirit among their parishioners and helped to foster an example of charity and tolerance. But it was uphill work with little reward and plenty of kicks and jeers.

Soup kitchens, social evenings and boxing clubs were organised by the parsons and the Vicar of St. James the Great at Bethnal Green raised a fund to enable his parishioners to be married for as little as sevenpence instead of the usual fee.

Before this most of the East Enders, even those who were nominally Christians, lived in sin rather than indulge in the luxury of a marriage ceremony for which they could not afford to pay. The result of this vicar's enterprise was that he found himself inundated with requests to 'splice us'. Whereas in the past he had performed not more than thirty such ceremonies in a year, he now found himself confronted with a thousand couples clamouring for marriage—often from other parts of London.

But the real tragedy of the East End was that it had become beyond the resources and ability of the police to keep its crime under control. A police force, particularly if it is unarmed, is useless if it cannot count on the co-operation and goodwill of the public. And the East Enders as a whole were, if not openly hostile to the police, at least determined not to co-operate with them. Such a state of affairs tended to demoralise the force. Quite a few of the constables and sergeants secretly allied themselves with known criminals, others not only ignored the prevalence of street-walkers, but took bribes from brothel-keepers. In Shadwell and Wapping it was too dangerous for policemen to walk singly at night and they were warned to keep away from the rows of brothels in the mean streets where sailors were robbed and beaten up with impunity. The highest frequency of police casualties in London was ascribed to a block of buildings in Limehouse Cut, nicknamed the 'Fenian Barracks', which was inhabited by violent Irishmen.

For the Irish question dominated the politics of the day. Gladstone was out of office, but in opposition was fulminating almost daily against the 'Coercion' policy of the Marquis of Salisbury's government. And the Irish, whether in Ireland or London, were not merely vocal in their condemnation of the English, but anxious to show by deeds of violence their open contempt for the Anglo-Saxon race.

Not unnaturally where there was so much ignorance and total illiteracy, superstition was rife. That part of the county of Essex which borders on the East End was notorious for its many witch trials and even as late as 1886 cases of witch-baiting were recorded here.

Of all types of murder that of the sexual maniac, where no obvious motive is apparent, is always the most difficult to solve, and when the victim is a prostitute, accustomed to furtiveness and with her acquaintances nearly always people unknown to her, it is sometimes well-nigh impossible to track down the killer. This is true today; in the East End of London in 1888, where people sullenly refused to help the police, the difficulties were even more apparent. In this period forensic science was quite unknown. Fingerprints in connection with crime detection had not been heard of in London. Foreign criminals were able to enter London with ease: the benefits of Interpol, the modern organisation which enables exchanges of information between various national police forces, were unavailable. Post mortems were often carried out in inadequate premises and performed with a degree of casualness which would appal any modern pathologist. If the doctor was conscientious and competent, the police had something to work on. More often the post-mortem reports were hastily composed and lacking in essential details, leaving the investigators completely in the dark.

The fact that the police at first believed that Martha Turner was killed with a bayonet reflects little credit on their preliminary investigations and suggests that the first examination of the body was a cursory one. It was not until Dr. Keleene was questioned after the identification parade at the Tower of London that it transpired that the murderer had used two weapons.

A number of other suspects were questioned by the police and one man was actually detained, but they all established foolproof alibis and so the killer of Martha Turner was never positively determined.

2

Polly of Thrawl Street

Vice inevitably flourishes where there is either too much or too little money, and in the East End of London it was the one industry which enabled many of the women—and, tragically enough, even girls of tender age—to exist at all.

Thrawl Street was the centre for hundreds of these dregs of humanity—sluts who knew no other way to live, cast-off wives and impoverished widows, dipsomaniacs and the 'slaves' of out-of-work labourers. Here existed so-called lodging houses, where these women herded together, paying fourpence a night for the privilege of sleeping on a bug-infested bed consisting of little more than a blanketed board in a room that might accommodate as many as sixty at a time.

The appalling conditions of Thrawl Street would have sapped the morale of the stoutest heart. Sanitation arrangements were even more primitive than those of an Arab kasbah, but the squalor and filth were far worse as the East Enders did not possess elementary ideas of hygiene whereas the poorest Arab has learned the health code as propounded by Mahomet from childhood. If the East End of London was a disgrace to any civilised country, it is not altogether surprising, for sanitation throughout Britain was far from satisfactory in this period: even Buckingham Palace's drains stank in hot weather.

Many of the houses in Thrawl Street backed directly on to other houses; sometimes defective drains resulted in the sewage seeping into basements, bringing diphtheria and typhoid fever in their trail. Many houses were built over old rubbish dumps, building laws often being completely ignored. When the rubbish decayed, the vegetable matter decomposed and emitted gases which penetrated into the tenements. As a rule a single tenement lavatory served several homes; nobody was responsible for cleaning it and it would be out of repair and reeking with filth for months at a time.

'Where humans could hardly survive,' says Robert Sinclair in *East London*, 'caged songbirds (a relic of the Huguenot tradition) were nurtured until they could be sold. The nearest other approach to wild life was at Limehouse where, round the dwelling houses after an early morning shower, the rats came out by thousands.'

A typical inhabitant of Thrawl Street was Mary Ann Nichols, who lived at No. 18, and was more popularly known as Polly. For such a woman the adjective 'popular' may seem slightly out of place, but Polly was generally liked even by her own sex and by those who competed against her for the dubious and trivial favours of men. 'She had no enemies', was one tribute paid to her; 'you couldn't 'elp likin' 'er' was another.

Polly had been born forty-two years before the events of this chapter. Her father was Edward Walker, a blacksmith, of Maidswood Road, Camberwell. She had married a decent enough man—a printer's machinist named William Nichols, but her slovenly habits and fondness for drink had caused them to separate in 1881, by which time she had borne him five children. For a short time after their separation Polly had lived with her father, but once again her addiction to alcohol was the cause of trouble. After an altercation with her father, following one of her drinking bouts, the prodigal daughter walked out of the house.

From that day her decline was swift. For a time she lived with a man named Drew, another blacksmith, who had a house and shop in York Street, Walworth. Then she spent several weeks in Lambeth Workhouse where she made friends with another 'Mary Ann' whose surname was Monk. When she left the workhouse she took a job as a servant at Wandsworth Common. But Polly's craving for drink meant that she required more money than that provided by the miserable pittance of a servant's wages. She stole three pounds from her employer and absconded. Then, as a fugitive from justice, she emigrated to the East End, joining her friend, Mary Ann Monk. For some months she had resided at No. 18, Thrawl Street, seeking a precarious living as a prostitute, sometimes battening on to a single man for a few weeks until, disgusted at her habits and perpetual state of drunkenness, even he would shake her off. But more often she walked the streets, content to find any man who would pay her the price of a berth on the floor and buy her a few drinks.

'The code of immorality in the East End was unabashed in its depths of degradation,' wrote Sir Melville Macnaghten in *Days of My Years*. 'A woman was content to live with a man so long as he was in work, it being an understood thing that, if he lost his job, she would support him by the only means open to her.'

Polly had drifted lower than most of her class. So low, in fact, that she had even been turned away from 18, Thrawl Street, on one occasion. Late one night she arrived there the worse for drink, if not actually drunk, and was refused admittance.

'Never mind,' she laughed, adding with a touch of bravado, 'I'll soon get my doss money. See what a jolly bonnet I've got now.'

Drunk or sober, there was something pathetically likable about Polly. She was never aggressive when drunk, only rather noisily gay. And that night she was wearing a new hat, at least it was certainly one she had not been seen wearing before.

At 2.30 a.m. on Friday, 31 August 1888, she was seen by another friend, Emily Holland, at the corner of Whitechapel Road and Osborne Street. As they had often slept side by side in the same Thrawl Street lodging house, they stopped for a chat.

'Any luck tonight?' asked Emily Holland.

'Nothing at all,' replied Nichols tipsily and disconsolately. 'Where have you been these last nights since Thursday?'

Hiccoughing and reeling on her feet, Nichols managed in halting sentences to convey to her friend that she had been staying at a common lodging house at Flower and Dean Street.

'It's better than Thrawl Street. They sleep men as well as women there,' she added, sniggering.

'Then why ain't you there now?'

'I've been turned out because I ain't got me rent money,' was the reply.

Nichols then waved a drunken farewell to her friend and staggered off down Osborne Street. That was the last occasion on which anyone admitted to seeing her alive.

Three-quarters of an hour later William Cross, a carter, was walking down Bucks Row, Whitechapel, on his way to work when he noticed on the opposite side of the road something that looked like a tarpaulin.

Had his occupation been any other than that of a carter, it is probable that Cross would not have troubled to walk over the road to examine it. But, thinking that somebody had lost a tarpaulin from a truck, he sensed a useful find.

When he came close to the object and saw the form of a woman he was not particularly disturbed or surprised. He assumed that she was simply a street-walker who had fallen down in a drunken stupor and gone to sleep. While he was gazing down at her, wondering whether he should give her a shake, another man named John Paul appeared.

Paul took one look, snorted, gave the sprawled-out figure a kick and commented: 'She's dead drunk. Come on, mate, let's get her on her feet.'

In the darkness both men groped down to get a hold of the woman. As they did so an involuntary cry burst from Cross's lips:

'Blimey! She's bleeding from the throat.'

Paul turned round and looked closer.

'Strewth, mate, you're right. She's not just bleeding, she's perishing well dead!'

As they turned the body over they saw a pool of blood beneath where her neck had lain.

'Gawd help us!' said Paul, 'it might have been one of us. Her legs are so warm she can't have been dead many minutes.'

They dropped the body and instinctively jumped back a few steps, carefully looking around the dark and unlit street.

'Think the bloke who done her in is still lurking around?' asked Cross.

'It ain't no time for bloody silly questions, mate. Come on, let's clear out of this and fetch the police.'

The two men, terrified out of their wits, sprinted down Bucks Row to the corner of Brady Street, built on the site of a pool, long since dried up, which was once the ducking-stool pond for local wives who h'ad erred. It was ironic that Mary Nichols—for it was her dead body the men had found—should meet her end in such a place.

At the corner of Brady Street the two men ran straight into Police Constable Haine, who was patrolling the area. They told him what they had seen and he immediately blew his whistle to summon another policeman who had only left him half a minute previously.

'You'd better come back with me,' said P.C. Haine, adjusting his lantern as he strode briskly in the direction of Bucks Row. And at that moment all three of them saw the flashing signal of another policeman's lantern coming from Bucks Row.

For by this time Police Constable Neil, an officer of more than twenty years' experience in the force, had also discovered the crumpled up body of Mary Nichols. His beat took him about twelve minutes to cover and, even allowing for stops *en route*, he reckoned he must have passed the very spot where Nichols was lying about half an hour at the most before he discovered her. On that occasion he had neither seen nor heard anything unusual.

'Well, I've seen nobody my way,' said P.C. Haine, 'and I'm quite certain no one could have come out of Bucks Row into Brady Street without my seeing him. Which way did you come?'

'I've come up from Old Montague Street,' replied Neil. 'And nobody passed me. What about you fellows?'

Both Paul and Cross agreed that they hadn't seen anybody, nor heard any cries.

'Well, it doesn't make sense,' said Neil. 'This body's as warm as a toasted crumpet and whoever killed her must have done it during the last half-hour.'

'There's beginning to be too many of these murders in Whitechapel,' was Paul's comment. 'It ain't safe for decent folk abroad.'

'And who said it was murder?' inquired Neil a little truculently, obviously offended at the implied aspersion on the police. 'I haven't said it was murder yet. Maybe it's suicide.'

'Blimey! You don't think she'd cut her own throat, do you? Take a look at her.'

'I'll thank you to leave me to examine the—er—deceased in my own time. This is a job for the surgeon and no one's to touch the corpse before he arrives.'

'Tell you what, Constable. The Jewish Cemetery lies at the back of there,' said Cross, jerking his thumb over his shoulder. 'I suggest you have a look around the graves. Probably some sneaking Yid who wouldn't pay for 'is fun, then she cut up nasty like and he did her in.'

P.C. Haine cut this unproductive conversation short by suggesting the murder was the work of the Old Nichol Gang, who were known to blackmail prostitutes. P.C. Neil, feeling no doubt that an argument between his subordinate and the other two was highly undesirable from the point of view of police discipline, peremptorily ordered Cross to go to Whitechapel police station for assistance, while Paul was told to fetch Dr. Ralph Llewellyn from his surgery nearby.

Perhaps the doctor was annoyed at being aroused from a deep sleep, or perhaps he was too anxious to return to his bed, but he certainly made the most perfunctory examination of the dead woman. When he arrived at Bucks Row he merely felt her pulse and pronounced life extinct. Beyond cursorily glancing at her body he made no attempt to examine her properly.

'She's quite obviously dead,' Dr. Llewellyn told P.C. Neil. 'And I should say she has been dead for not more than half an hour. You had better have her taken along to the mortuary at Old Montague Street Workhouse. If you want me later, you will find me at the surgery.'

As in the case of Martha Turner, so no one saw or heard Mary Nichols' killer. What was even more remarkable was that five men—P.C.s Haine, Nizen and Neil, Cross and Paul—all approaching Bucks Row from different directions, probably within twenty minutes at the most of the actual time of the killing, saw not a single person. Three-quarters of an hour previously Mary Nichols had been seen and spoken to in Whitechapel Road at the corner of Osborne Street, a distance of slightly less than a quarter of a mile from where she was found dead. Whatever happened to her must have occurred within minutes of her leaving Emily Holland.

One must assume that the murderer either hid in the shadows when he heard any of these people coming his way, or that he knew the vicinity so well that he was able to escape down some side alley. P.C. Neil estimated that whoever it was must have passed along his actual beat and escaped into the Whitechapel Road either through Brady Street, or a passage through Queens Buildings.

Three night watchmen were on duty close to Bucks Row, but they heard no cries or sounds of a scuffle. Similar testimony was given by three other men employed in a slaughterhouse within earshot of Bucks Row. Mrs. Emma Green, who lived at New Cottage, which was within a few yards of the place where the body was found, declared she had heard no one talking or calling out. 'I was awake at the time. I couldn't sleep. If the woman had screamed, I must have heard her.'

It was astounding and amounted to little less than culpable negligence that neither the police nor the doctor realised the extent of the dead woman's injuries before she was removed to the workhouse mortuary. That was bad enough, but surely it was a major blunder that the mortuary attendant was allowed to handle the corpse before the post mortem was carried out and that the bloodstains in Bucks Row had been washed off before Detective-Inspector Abberline, of Scotland Yard, arrived.

It was a policeman who first saw the savage wounds inflicted on Mary Nichols. It was his first experience of murder and, as he lifted up her clothes, he saw to his horror that she had been disembowelled. He reeled back and vomited; then, distraught and white-faced, ran all the way from the mortuary to the surgery where an impatient Dr. Llewellyn had to give him first aid.

'Your first murder, is it?' said the doctor. 'Well, I'm afraid you've got to get used to this sort of thing in the East End.'

'But this . . .' cried the policeman. 'This wasn't just murder. It was butchery. Just wait till you see the corpse. She was just ripped up, ripped from her throat to her belly. If that's murder, I hope I never see another one.'

At the inquest, conducted by Mr. Wynne E. Baxter, the question was posed—why were the savage mutilations of the body not noticed at first? Did the police not realise that by removing the body to the workhouse before a thorough examination had been made vital clues might have been destroyed?

It was then learned that the mortuary attendant who was left in charge of the body was not even a professional mortuary-keeper, but a pauper from the workhouse named Robert Munn, who obviously had little knowledge of police requirements. He had stripped the body and washed it down before the post mortem was carried out.

For the police the excuse was made that 'clearly the gutter of a public thoroughfare was no place to make a detailed examination'. Perhaps not, but the crowd could have been cleared away and screens set up.

The Coroner questioned Robert Munn.

'When you undressed and washed the body, were the police present?'

'No. There was nobody there, only me and my mate, Hatfield.'

'Did the police tell you not to touch the body?'

'No, they said nothing.'

'Then you did all this entirely on your own and without receiving any instructions?'

'Well, sir, I did what is usual in these cases.'

'But you surely realised that this was a case of murder?'

'Oh, yes, sir. I shut up the mortuary and went off to have my breakfast. Then I came back and me and my mate undressed her afore we cleaned her up a bit and made her tidy.'

'Do you recollect if her clothes were torn?'

'They were torn and cut, sir.'

But the police were not sure on this point. They were under the impression that the clothes had not been tampered with to any great extent. They were equally emphatic that they had told Munn not to touch the body.

Nichols' clothes provided the first clue to her identity, as the skirt of one petticoat and the band of another article bore the stencil stamp of Lambeth Workhouse. The only articles in her pockets were a comb and a piece of looking glass.

Mary Nichols' body was identified by various people, including her father and her husband. It was quickly established that neither could have had anything to do with the crime. Both the father and the husband insisted that she was 'not fast', but that drink was her main failing.

'Many's the hard words I've said about her,' remarked William Nichols solemnly, when he stood over her body in the mortuary. 'But I forgive her for everything she did now I find her like this.'

The police's first theory was that Nichols was the victim of a blackmailing gang. They noted that the killings of Emma Smith, Martha Turner and Nichols all occurred within 300 yards of one another. They were certain that Smith was murdered by the Nichol Gang and, because of this, assumed—wrongly—that the other two women had also met their fate at the hands of these ruffians.

But Detective-Inspector Abberline quickly rejected this theory. He was confident that this was the work of a lone killer and for this reason ruled out any connection between the deaths of Turner and Nichols with that of Emma Smith. The post-mortem findings revealed essential differences between the murder of Nichols and Turner, although there were also similarities. Turner's throat had not been cut, but Nichols had been slit from ear to ear. In the case of Turner there had been no systematic or deliberate mutilations, whereas Nichols had been slightly mutilated, though no part of the body was missing or severed. But in this murder, as in the one which preceded it, the wounds inflicted were numerous and savage. They suggested that the killer was either in a frenzy of maniacal rage or a cold-blooded and particularly revolting sadist.

Because no cries had been heard it was at first thought that the murder had been committed elsewhere and the body deposited in Bucks Row. But nothing substantiated this theory. Though the blood-stains had been washed away by the police before Detective-Inspector Abberline arrived, P.C.s Haine, Nizen and Neil were able to testify to the relatively small quantity of blood in the street, bearing in mind the extent of the wounds. This might, it is true, suggest that the body had been dumped in Bucks Row, but the absence of any trail of blood proved that the body could not have been dragged to where it was left.

Nor were there any marks of wheels in the roadway, no hint that a cab, a trap or a cart could have carried the body. And Dr. Llewellyn's report stated: 'There was very little blood round the neck and there were no marks of any struggle, or of blood, as though the body had been dragged.'

This time there was no evidence of two weapons having been used. Dr. Llewellyn expressed the opinion that the injuries were 'from left to right and might have been done by a left-handed person. All were done by the same instrument.'

Was the murderer the same in each case? This was by no means certain and expert opinions differed. Detective-Inspector Abberline thought the same man had killed both Turner and Nichols. Sir Melville Macnaghten insisted that Turner was not a victim of the Ripper because 'her throat was not cut and nothing in the shape of mutilation was attempted'. He asserted that the first Ripper victim was Mary Nichols.

Sir Robert Anderson, Assistant Commissioner of the Metropolitan Police, claimed that Turner was the first.

On the post-mortem reports of the two victims it is impossible to say with certainty whether the Ripper killed Turner, but in the case of Nichols his bestial handiwork—the mutilations—was clearly evident. It is possible that the killer was disturbed when he murdered Turner—possibly by Albert Crow shutting the door of his room—and that he had no time to carry out the mutilations. On the other hand, as will be seen later, the other indication of the Ripper's technique was the straight, ear-to-ear slit with which he cut the throats of his victims, and this was not evident in the murder of Turner.

The problem of how the Ripper approached his victims was not easy to solve because of conflicting evidence. The police thought he must have cut Nichols' throat from behind and that he took her completely unawares: this theory fitted in with the fact that no shrieks were heard.

But Dr. Llewellyn disagreed with this view. A bruise on Mary Nichols' face could, in his opinion, have been caused by the putting of a hand on her mouth to silence her. But he did not think her throat had been cut by a man standing behind her. The weapon used, he said, was 'an exceptionally long-bladed knife—possibly a cork-cutter's or a shoemaker's knife'.

The mutilations of the lower part of the abdomen were extensive and 'deftly and fairly skilfully performed'.

The savage nature of Mary Nichols' death revealed for the first time that a sadistic and cunning killer was at large. The fact that there was no obvious motive strengthened this theory. It was the lack of motive which gave rise to the wave of terror which began to sweep the East End. There was a feeling that this silent killer would pounce indiscriminately: no one had yet realised that he would confine his attentions solely to women of the streets.

No longer was there apathy about the murder and violence in East London. Public opinion began to rouse itself and a surprised police force found that persons who had hitherto been hostile to anyone in a blue uniform were actually volunteering information and offering to help catch the killer.

Nor was this all. In streets where murder had been committed an almost middle-class respectability manifested itself even in the meanest homes. It was not the dirt, the squalor or the stinking drains to which they objected, but the fact that their street was one in which a prostitute had been done to death.

Bucks Row prided itself on being more respectable than most in this neighbourhood. Even *The Times* laid stress on this. And it was here that the residents were most vocal in demanding a clean-up of the whole area and urging a drive against prostitutions in the streets.

Perhaps ill-timed jests caused some resentment. There was a postman who took a ghoulish delight in knocking on doors, handing over letters and saying: 'Number Three, Killer's Row, I believe.'

The residents had an answer to all this. They agitated for the name of their street to be changed and, as a result of a petition signed by nearly everyone who lived there, Bucks Row had its name changed to Durward Street by the civic authorities.

3

Dark Annie

Two murders had now been committed in the East End without the police having had a single worthwhile clue as to the identity of the killer. More than a dozen people had been detained and questioned, but each one provided a satisfactory alibi.

The Times in those days regaled its readers with a superabundance of gory detail and bloodcurdling fact which would have done credit to *The News of the World* today. This august and respectable journal published two and sometimes three columns a day of closely packed paragraphs in the smallest type concerning the Whitechapel murders. Indeed, the standard of crime reporting in *The Times* was quite as good as anything in the popular newspapers of the 'thirties and certainly superior to anything published in the daily papers of today. The reader was taken behind the scenes of the crime in a fascinatingly frank manner and he was spared nothing of the most sordid details. And who said the Victorians were squeamish? Nobody complained because *The Times* saw fit to devote three columns to the Whitechapel murders.

The earliest hint of a clue contained in its columns was the suggestion that the police were looking for a man known as 'Leather Apron', who was believed to have been seen with Mary Nichols and who, according to various women, had attempted to assault a number of prostitutes.

This statement is, however, confusing to any serious student of the Ripper crimes. The name of 'Leather Apron' recurs with monotonous regularity throughout the history of these cases. It became as much of an obsession with the women of the streets as was King Charles' head to Mr. Dick, while junior police officers quoted the name so often that Detective-Inspector Abberline finally declared in justified exasperation: 'Never mention that blasted nickname again.'

'Leather Apron' was more a phrase than a real person. Or perhaps that is not quite correct. Rather should one say that 'Leather Apron' was the title given to a whole series of suspects and could never be applied positively to any one of them. Probably what started the story of this mysterious character was that Nichols was thought to have been killed by a shoemaker's knife and 'Leather Apron' was the nickname sometimes applied to men of this trade.

But not only shoemakers wore leather aprons. Many men of other trades wore them, too. Thus anyone seen wearing a leather apron immediately came under suspicion. It is the considered opinion of many experienced police officers, not to mention doctors and psychologists, that women are remarkably prone to hallucinations and that sex in its more Freudian forms is the cause thereof. At any rate a surprisingly large number of women claimed to have been threatened, raped or assaulted by men in leather aprons.

Then, only eight days after Mary Nichols' body had been found in Bucks Row, the silent killer struck again. Shortly after 6 a.m. on Saturday, 8 September 1888, Inspector Joseph Chandler was walking along Hanbury Street, close to Spitalfields Market, when he saw several men running in his direction. One, who was shouting 'Police! Police!', nearly knocked him over.

At first the inspector, imbued with that innate suspicion which his work made inevitable, thought they were fugitives from justice.

'Murder! Come quickly. It's something horrible,' shouted another man. He was hardly coherent.

'Now just tell me quietly what's happened,' said Inspector Chandler, whose thoughts were on the bacon and eggs he hoped shortly to consume and certainly not attuned to the idea of murder just before breakfast.

'Come on quick, for Gawd's sake. My missus is all alone and who knows but what the killer mayn't be hiding somewhere.'

'What's the address?'

'Twenty-nine, Hanbury Street.'

Inspector Chandler sighed heavily and trudged wearily alongside the babbling men. Gradually he began to piece their story together. Two men, James Kent and James Green, workmen in Bailey's yard in Hanbury Street, had been hailed by John Davies, a porter at Spitalfields Market, about 6.10 a.m. He had told them to come and look in the yard of No. 29; they had gone and what they had seen was ' 'orrible, 'orrible'.

If the inspector was sceptical, he was swiftly to be disillusioned. Hanbury Street extended from Commercial Street to Bakers Row, the end of which was close to Bucks Row. No. 29 was a house rented by a Mrs. Emilia Richardson and let out to some sixteen people, all of the poorest class. The passage of the house led from the front door, which was wide open, past the door of the front parlour to another door which gave access to a small backyard, about four feet below the house level and reached by two stone steps. As Chandler descended the steps he saw the body of a woman lying close against the wall.

Even then he did not suspect murder. 'It's only a drunk,' he told the men.

'You go close and have a look.'

Chandler took a few steps forward and looked. His back stiffened and he drew in his breath between clenched teeth. The woman lay flat on her back with her clothes disarranged. He could see that her head was nearly severed from her body and that she had been stabbed in the most brutal manner.

Then the frightened man told his story. John Davies lived with his wife in the top room of No. 29. He got up as usual about 5.30 a.m. to go to work, said goodbye to his wife, and, before leaving the house, went out into the backyard. . . .

'It must have been about five minutes to six. I'm certain of it, because I heard Spitalfields Church clock strike the hour just after. And then I sees this. It was enough to scare any man.'

'I must say,' said Inspector Chandler, now fully sympathetic, 'it fair puts me off my breakfast. Now, you'd better leave this to me. I mustn't leave the premises. You'd better go to Commercial Street police station and tell them what's happened.'

Davies needed no second bidding. He ran all the way to the police station.

Inspector Chandler's thought processes may have been somewhat slow, but he was thorough and not one to lose his head. While he was waiting he made a close inspection of the yard. He noted that there were a few blood-stains on the wall close to the body, but nothing larger than a sixpenny piece, and relatively little blood in the yard itself. At first he thought that the body must have been dumped there. Surely, he argued, with so many stab wounds, there must have been more blood if the murder had been committed in the yard.

But he retraced his steps along the passage and found no blood-stains or other incriminating marks. He assumed that the woman's clothes must have absorbed most of the blood.

A search of the yard did not reveal much, but a few slender clues were provided. Two brass rings, a few pennies and two farthings were neatly laid out in a row at the woman's feet: it was quite obvious that they had been deliberately placed in this fashion and not dropped haphazardly. An examination of the woman's hands showed that the rings appeared to have been wrenched off the middle finger of her left hand. In another corner of the yard was a portion of an envelope, stained with blood, and bearing the crest of the Sussex Regiment. The postmark was 'London, 28 August 1888', but the part of the envelope containing the address was missing with the exception of the letters 'M' and 'Sp' in writing. Two medicinal pills, wrapped up in paper, were also retrieved by the observant inspector.

None of the woman's clothing appeared to be torn. The only other article of interest—and it goes without saying that this interested the inspector very much—was a leather apron saturated in water, though containing no blood-stains.

By this time the other inmates of the house had appeared and Chandler questioned them closely. The porter Davies had told him that the front door of No. 29 and the door leading into the yard were never locked; they were either left open or on the latch. The front door was frequently left wide open all night. And Davies was certain that it was open when he came down that morning.

Mrs. Richardson said she lived with her son in the house. She was awake about 3 a.m., but she 'heard nothing unusual like'. After that she dozed off again. A Mr. Thompson, a carman, his wife and adopted daughter, occupied the second-floor front room of the house. At a few minutes to four o'clock Mrs. Richardson gave Mr. Thompson a call. Afterwards she heard him leave the house, but she was sure he didn't go into the yard.

'Who else lives here?' asked Chandler.

'Well, there's an old woman named Sarah Cox in the back room on the third floor, and there's a Mr. and Mrs. Copsey, who are cigar-makers, on the second-floor back room. The front parlour is let to a Mrs. Hardman who uses it as a shop to sell cat's meat.'

'Where does she sleep?'

'Oh, she sleeps in the shop, all along with the pussy-cat's grub, and her son dosses down in the same room.'

'So the body couldn't have been carried through the passage without disturbing Mrs. Hardman and her son.'

'Oh, no, I don't think that's possible.'

'Who lives in the back room of the first floor, the one that overlooks the yard?'

'A Mr. Alfred Walker and his father.'

But neither of these had heard anything; nor had anyone else in the house. Mrs. Richardson agreed that the front door and the yard door were left open day and night.

'But aren't you afraid of a robbery? Do you mean to say you've left these doors open even after these murders in the East End?'

'Well, I trust all the people in the house. They're good folk, and we've never had a robbery. Oh, except once, a while ago, from the cellar, and since then my son's put a padlock on the cellar door.'

'Nothing else unusual has happened?'

'Well, about a month ago I heard a man on the stairs about 3 a.m., but I never knew who it was.'

By the time Dr. Bagster Phillips, the police divisional surgeon, had arrived to inspect the body, a crowd of about a hundred people had gathered outside the house. The body was then removed to the mortuary.

On the Monday morning *The Times* declared: 'It is evident that the murderer thought he had completely cut the head off, as a handkerchief was found wrapped round the neck as though to hold it together.'

This murder evidently caused far more of a sensation than those which had preceded it. 'During the whole of Saturday morning and yesterday,' added *The Times*, 'a large crowd congregated in front of the house in Hanbury Street and the neighbours on either side did much business by making a small charge to persons who were willing to pay it to view from the windows the yard in which the murder was committed.'

Certainly on Saturday night there was some panic in the East End. A rumour that the murderer had been caught sent a crowd rushing round to Spitalfields Market intent on lynching the man if they could lay their hands on him. But it turned out to be only a wretched blind man who had been arrested on a warrant to answer a charge of stabbing. But throughout Saturday night several persons were questioned and later detained at various East End police stations.

It was not long before the police identified the killer's latest victim. They rounded up various common lodging-house-keepers, and one of these, Timothy Donovan, of 35, Dorset Street, recognised the body as that of a woman whom he knew by the name of 'Dark Annie'. He had seen her in the kitchen of the lodging house in Dorset Street as late as 1.30 to 2 a.m. on Saturday. She was a prostitute who frequented the streets of Stratford.

Dorset Street, which ran parallel with Spitalfields Market, was a notorious area. It was full of lodging houses where the dregs of humanity were crammed into beds that practically touched one another, even the cellars and attics being used for this purpose. It was also well known that men and women were admitted into these lodging houses and often slept in the same rooms together.

Donovan said that when he saw Dark Annie he asked her for the money for her lodging. She replied: 'I haven't got it. I am weak and ill and have been in the infirmary.'

'Well, you know the rules,' replied Donovan. 'No money, no bed.'

Thereupon she said she would go out and 'find the money somehow'.

The only other clue that Donovan could provide at this stage was that Dark Annie was also known as Annie Sievey, but he didn't know whether that was a nickname or not.

But other people knew Dark Annie. Some of them told the police they had seen her with a man in a public house the night before, but there was no confirmation of this. Apparently she had suffered from ill health for some months, during which time she had been in and out of infirmaries. Before this she had lived with a sieve-maker in the area, hence the nickname of 'Annie Sievey'.

Bit by bit her story was pieced together. Of all the Ripper's victims she was the only woman with a respectable middle-class background. The fact that she had 'known better days' did not endear her to some of the other prostitutes and she seems to have made a few enemies among them because of this. Her real name was Annie Chapman. She had formerly lived at Windsor, where she was married to an Army pensioner, Fred Chapman, who was also a veterinary surgeon. Whether her husband was to blame for her downfall, or whether her fondness for drink was responsible, is not clear. Certainly Chapman himself seems to have descended in the world, for latterly he was employed as a coachman. Four years before she was found dead, Annie left her husband, though he continued to make her an allowance of ten shillings a week until he died some two and a half years later. There were two children of the marriage, a boy, who was deformed, and in a cripples' home, and a girl who was in some institution or school in France. It was not clear who supported these children, or how the girl came to be sent to France. But it is clear that Annie Chapman's meagre and haphazard earnings could not support them.

After her husband died Annie Chapman's struggle for existence was marked with singularly little success. She was forty-seven, not more than five feet in height, plump and well proportioned, with blue eyes and wavy, brown hair. But alcohol—she was frequently the worse for drink—and ill health had taken toll of her looks and she gave the impression of being at least eight years older than she was. It has been suggested by some writers that she was a 'one-man' woman and not 'a regular street-walker'. But this is not true. Her liaison with the sieve-maker was brief and, on the evidence of Donovan and others, she frequently took men back to the common lodging house in Dorset Street.

Occasionally she supplemented her income by doing crochet work and selling flowers, but as Amelia Farmer, one of her acquaintances, said:

'She was not very particular what she did to earn a living and she stayed out at all hours of the night looking for men who would pay her the price of a bed.'

Inspector Chandler's problem was to try to trace her movements in the hours immediately preceding her death. Donovan said she was wearing three brass rings when he last saw her. But Chandler felt sure the murderer had not mistaken these for gold and intended to steal them. If robbery was his motive, he would hardly be likely to take the rings from her finger and lay them out in a neat pile. Nor would he take one ring and leave the other two.

Donovan had mentioned that on the previous Monday night Annie Chapman had had a quarrel with another woman, who had mauled and kicked her. Amelia Farmer, who last saw Chapman at 5 p.m. on Friday, testified that Chapman had bruises on her temple and breast.

'You know who did this,' said Annie, and named a woman known to both of them.

Apparently Chapman had met this woman and a man named Harry Hawkins in a public house in Commercial Street. Hawkins, who was drunk, had slapped a florin down on the bar counter, and, when he wasn't looking, the other woman had picked it up and replaced it with a penny. Chapman intervened and told Hawkins what had happened, and that started a fight between the two women.

'Annie looked real ill when I last saw her,' said Amelia Farmer. 'She said she wasn't well and thought she would go into the casual ward for a day or two. She had had nothing to eat or drink that day—not even a cup of tea. I gave her twopence, saying, "This is for a cup of tea, but don't have rum." I knew she couldn't keep off the drink, if she had the money, and she was always the worse for drink at week-ends.'

Annie's last words to her were: 'I must pull myself together and go out and get some money, or I'll have no lodgings.'

John Evans, the night watchman at the lodging house in Dorset Street, frequented by Chapman, confirmed the story of the fight with a woman named Eliza. He last saw the unfortunate Annie at 2 a.m. on Saturday. When she left she entered Paternoster Court. He understood she had been to visit one of her sisters who lived in Vauxhall during Friday night.

The only other possible clue to Annie's last hours was provided by a woman named Darrell, who told the police that at 5 a.m. she saw a man and woman talking outside No. 29, Hanbury Street. She did not know Chapman personally, but she identified the body as that of the woman she had seen.

The more Chief Inspector Abberline considered the case, after he had talked with Chandler, the more he felt convinced that the man they were looking for was one who knew the district and every alleyway in it. Either the murderer, or Chapman, or both of them, must have known that the door of No. 29 was always open and that it was possible to creep quietly into the yard. Possibly Chapman had used the yard before for assignments with men.

If the murder was committed between 5 and 6 a.m., it meant that the killer would have to take the risk of walking in streets already full of men going to work at the market. In that case it seemed odd that nobody had noticed a man with blood-stains on his person, or his clothes, for the murderer could hardly have avoided covering himself in blood. How, then, did he escape detection?

Abberline's view was that the killer must know the district well enough to wend his way through the labyrinth of alleyways and side passages where he would be unlikely to meet anyone. But even this seemed risky. If he were a respectably dressed man, he might pass unsuspected, as, though poverty abounded in the East End, the well-to-do and the poor often lived side by side. Many of the foreigners living in Whitechapel and elsewhere were relatively well-to-do. On the other hand the killer could be a man who changed his lodgings each night and who, when he had committed a crime, slipped into a nearby lodging house, where he already had a bed booked, washed the blood off his hands in the communal sink and disappeared before the police made their routine search.

All these devices for escaping detection were, however, far from foolproof, and Abberline was convinced that the man they were dealing with was clever, cunning and cautious—at least, possessing sufficient of these qualities to commit three murders without leaving a real clue.

When the inquest opened the police had an unhappy time. The Coroner, Mr. Wynne E. Baxter, complained that they had not provided him with a plan of the locality. 'If country police forces can do this for a Coroner, why cannot the Metropolitan Police Force?' he asked.

Then Henry Holland, one of the witnesses (he had been called by the porter, Davies, to the scene of the crime), said that when he ran for a policeman, the latter 'refused to come. I told him there had been a murder done, but he said he couldn't come and I must find another constable. But I couldn't find one. Yet the policeman was standing by himself and not doing anything.'

In vain did Inspector Chandler explain that the policeman spoken to was on duty in Spitalfields Market and not supposed to leave his post. As the Coroner severely pointed out, 'murder was murder'.

Dr. Bagster Phillips, who performed the post mortem, protested bitterly about the 'great difficulties' under which he carried out his examination. 'I raise my protest as I have previously done that members of my profession should not be expected to perform such duties in inadequate circumstances.'

The Coroner agreed that the body should have been taken to a proper mortuary and not to a shed. 'In the East End, where mortuaries are required more than anywhere else, there are far too few of them. But in this case, where murder had been done and a proper examination of the body was required, the corpse should not have been taken to a shed.'

And once again the doctor complained that the body had been stripped and washed before he could perform his post mortem.

It was obvious from his findings that the same killer had been at work, but that this time he had provided more evidence of his brutality and ferocity. In the first murder the throat had not been cut, in the second it had been slashed from ear to ear and in this third case he had done his job so thoroughly that the head was almost severed from the body.

A singular coincidence about the corpse was that there were two front teeth missing, as in the case of Mary Nichols. Incisions into the skin, both in the throat and the back, indicated that they were made from left to right. There were two distinct, clean cuts on the left side of the spine; these were parallel with one another and separated by about half an inch. These had obviously been made so that a kidney could be removed.

The tongue was swollen and there were recent bruises on the chin and the sides of the jaw, suggesting that the murderer had clapped his hand over his victim's mouth to stop her from calling out. The woman had been savagely mutilated and the removal of a kidney and the ovaries 'showed indications of anatomical knowledge'. It was true that there were some jagged incisions, but, added Dr. Phillips, 'if there was a lower degree of skill in some of the mutilations, this was only to the extent to which one would expect when someone was working with great haste'.

There were no signs at all of any struggle before death, nor was the clothing torn. The murderer must have used 'a very sharp knife with a thin, narrow blade. It would have been at least six to eight inches in length and probably longer. The weapon could have been a bayonet, or sword bayonet, or an instrument such as a doctor would use for surgery'.

A little girl, who lived at No. 25, next door but one to No. 29, had noticed peculiar marks on the wall and on the ground of the backyard of her home. These were at first thought to be blood-stains, and the police assumed that the murderer had climbed over the dividing fences between Nos. 29, 27 and 25 to make his escape. But Dr. Phillips rejected this theory: the marks were definitely not blood-stains, he reported.

Dark Annie was not completely forgotten after her death. Some relatives came to claim her body and were present at her funeral which they arranged at Manor Park Cemetery.

4

Leather Apron

Within two days of Annie Chapman's murder the inhabitants of Spitalfields decided that it was time they banded together to resist the devilry of the unknown killer.

A meeting of some sixteen local tradesmen was held on 10 September and a Vigilance Committee was formed, with a Mr. J. Aarons as secretary. They issued the following statement:

'Finding that, in spite of murders being committed in our midst, the police force is inadequate to discover the author or authors of the late atrocities, we, the undersigned, have formed ourselves into a committee and intend offering a substantial reward to any one, citizen or otherwise, who shall give such information as will be the means of bringing the murderer or murderers to justice.'

In addition, Mr. S. Montagu, a local Member of Parliament, offered £100 for the capture of the killer.

The police received hundreds of letters from all parts of the country, offering suggestions on how to catch the Ripper. Many people wrote that for a modest financial consideration they would be prepared to act as 'special detectives' and were quite sure that their own remarkable talent as amateur criminologists would lead to a swift capture. Cranks suggested that the killer was a 'saint with supernatural powers', chosen by Almighty God to rid the world of prostitution.

A 'country doctor' wrote to *The Times*:

'I would suggest that the police should at once find out

the whereabouts of all cases of homicidal mania which may have been discharged as "cured" from Metropolitan asylums during the last two years.'

Mr. L. Forbes Winslow, M.B., of Wimpole Street, followed up with another letter which stressed the 'method shown in the gradual dissection of the body'. He felt sure that the murderer was to be found 'in the upper classes of society'.

Inspector Abberline began to think that this theory might well be the right one. But as information began to filter through to the police the evidence at first pointed to members of the working classes.

Soon after the murder was discovered a woman reported to the police that a man had accosted her in Spitalfields early on Saturday morning. She tried to avoid him, but he caught up with her and knocked her about. When she screamed he ran off.

These tactics seemed far too clumsy for the Ripper. And when the police questioned the woman further she admitted that he had tried to palm off on her two brass medals for half-sovereigns. The wages of sin in the East End did not realise one half-sovereign let alone two and the woman's story sounded highly improbable. In any case her description of her alleged assailant was far from clear.

But the great time-waster for the police in these early stages of the inquiry was the problem of the mysterious Leather Apron. Within forty-eight hours they were looking for at least three men said to answer to this nickname. One story was that Leather Apron had disappeared from his usual haunts, that he had heard all about the hue and cry raised for him and had stayed away from Spitalfields.

A young woman named Lyons said that at 3 p.m. on the day Chapman was killed she had met a strange man in Flower and Dean Street. He had asked her to have a drink with him at the Queen's Head at 6.30 p.m. While they were talking and drinking Lyons noticed that the man had a large knife protruding out of a trousers pocket and she drew the attention of another woman to this.

This gesture by Lyons had not passed unnoticed by the

man. Smiling somewhat enigmatically, he bent forward close to her face and said slowly and deliberately:

'You are about the same style of woman as the one that's just been murdered.'

'What do you know about her?' asked Lyons, startled.

'Ah,' replied the strange man, 'you are beginning to smell a rat. Foxes hunt geese, but they don't always find 'em.'

At which parting shot the man hastily finished his drink and left the public house. Lyons followed him until he was close to Spitalfields Church when, turning round and seeing he was being followed, he ran round the corner into Church Street and was lost to view.

The description of the man tallied with that of Leather Apron, but the police felt sure he was merely a mildly lunatic hoaxer. He was never located.

The same evening at about seven o'clock in Grove Street, Deptford, a man entered a newsagent's shop and asked for 'any special editions on the Whitechapel murders'. He seemed 'particularly agitated', said the newsagent, 'threw down a penny and ran off down Emily Place'.

This man was of ruddy complexion, stout build, with a slight moustache and wearing an old felt hat with his coat collar turned up. Afterwards he was traced to a tram which ran from Deptford and Southwark to Tooley Street. The tram conductor thought he seemed 'rather odd' and noticed that he appeared to be in a great hurry.

It was quite a novel experience for the police to be getting so much assistance from the public, but the amount of information they were receiving was also somewhat of an embarrassment. Very little of it proved to be of any use. An arrest was made in Deptford that night, but the man was quickly able to establish an alibi.

Thieves came forward to pledge themselves to capture the killer. Inspector Chandler was confronted by six notorious jail-birds who swore solemnly that, though they hated the sight of the police, they wouldn't rest until they found the monster and handed him over to justice. 'But,' they added, 'we don't promise you he'll be alive.'

Shortly before 8 a.m. on that Saturday night Detective-Sergeant Thicke had a tip-off that Leather Apron had been found. With three other officers he went to 22, Mulberry Street and knocked at the door. It was opened by a Polish Jew named Pizer, who was immediately arrested on the grounds that he was concerned with Chapman's murder.

Pizer, a thirty-three-year-old bookbinder, was taken to Leman Street police station. Meanwhile his house was searched and Detective-Sergeant Thicke took possession of five sharp, long-bladed knives used in his trade, and several old hats. Several women who had known Pizer had said he was in the habit of wearing different hats.

But Pizer and his friends protested that he knew nothing about the murder and that he had not been out of his house since Thursday night. Pizer also denied that he was known as Leather Apron. But, despite these denials, Detective-Sergeant Thicke was able to establish that Pizer was not only known by this nickname, but in the habit of wearing a leather apron.

Pizer, a short man with black whiskers, but a shaven chin, was paraded with other Jews at Leman Street police station while various women were asked to identify the man they referred to as Leather Apron. They all failed to do so.

But the case which the police had built up against Pizer was not demolished quite so swiftly. Emmanuel Violenia, a man who was half Spanish and half Bulgarian, presented himself at the police station. His story was that he had tramped with his wife and two children from Manchester to London, intending to emigrate to Australia. They stayed at a lodging house in Hanbury Street while waiting for a ship. Then, in the early hours of Saturday morning, Violenia went for a walk alone in Hanbury Street. Why he did so was not satisfactorily explained. In that street he saw a man and woman quarrelling, the former threatening to kill the latter. And though Violenia could not identify the deceased as the woman he had seen, he swore that Pizer was the man. But under closer cross-examination Violenia's story proved to be full of contradictions which finally discredited his evidence.

So Pizer was released. He eventually admitted that he knew

of the suspicions against him and that after he heard of Chapman's murder he thought it prudent to stay at home and keep out of sight of his accusers until the uproar died down. Detective-Sergeant Thicke was satisfied that Pizer was not the man he wanted and, in fairness to the thoroughly frightened Pole, he was called to give evidence at the inquest and was formally cleared by the Coroner.

Sir Robert Anderson, in *The Lighter Side of My Official Life*, declared that the Ripper was 'a sexual maniac of a virulent type. The conclusion we came to was that he and his people were certain low-class Polish Jews and it is a remarkable fact that people of that class in the East End will not give up one of their number to Gentile justice.

'If the police here had the powers such as the French police possess, the murderer would have been brought to justice.

'Having regard to the interest attaching to this case I am almost tempted to disclose the identity of the murderer. But no public benefit would result and the traditions of my old department would suffer. I will merely add that the only person who ever had a good view of the murderer unhesitatingly identified the suspect the instant he was confronted with him, but he refused to give evidence against him.

'In saying that he was a Polish Jew I am merely stating a definitely established fact.'

We will need to examine this statement of Sir Robert Anderson later. At this stage, however, two comments on it must be made. In the first place Sir Robert Anderson must have known that Pizer was one of the original suspects—indeed the most publicised of all of them—and to talk vaguely of 'a Polish Jew' without exonerating Pizer is not only unfair, but makes a mockery of his feigned respect for the traditions of his service.

If on the other hand Anderson disregarded the view of the police force and persisted in believing Pizer was the killer, he was either indulging in ridiculous anti-semitism or was quite unfit to hold the post he did. No other police chief supported this view. But the probability is that Sir Robert had someone else in mind.

Inspector Chandler regarded John Richardson, the son of the tenant at No. 29, as a witness who had not explained everything satisfactorily. Why, he wondered, if Richardson lived at 2, John Street, did he call in at No. 29 on his way to work at Leadenhall Market? Then again there was the leather apron which had been found in the yard of No. 29; Mrs. Richardson had said it belonged to her son. He decided to ask Richardson a few questions.

'Well,' replied Richardson in answer to his first query, 'I've made a habit of popping in to No. 29 of a morning between 4.30 and 5 a.m. You see, my mother had trouble sometime back. Somebody broke into the cellar. So I generally go along of a morning to see the padlock I put on the cellar door hasn't been tampered with.

'And I always make a habit of looking in at the yard as we get whores and tramps who kip down there for the night. But I saw nothing suspicious. I'm sure there was no body there. Even though it was dark, it wasn't that dark I shouldn't have noticed.'

'Have you ever found people in the yard?'

'Oh, yes, lots of times, and I've turned 'em out.'

'Your mother tells me that the leather apron I found in the yard is worn by you. Is that so?'

'Yes, that's right.'

'What did you do after you'd been in the yard?'

'As far as I remember I went indoors again before going to work.'

Inspector Chandler produced a tiny piece of leather.

'Does this mean anything to you?'

Richardson looked bewildered and puckered up his eyes. 'Oh, I suppose that came off my boot?'

'How do you mean?'

'Well, I remember now: on the way back into the house I stopped on the steps of the yard and trimmed a bit of leather off my boot.'

'Oh, you did, did you? And what did you trim it with, may I ask?'

'My knife. Why, blimey, copper, you ain't suggesting . . .?'

'I'm suggesting nothing. But I'd like to see that knife, all the same.'

Chandler might be slow, but he was remarkably painstaking. He carefully examined the knife which Richardson brought for his inspection. It was about five inches in length, very sharp and in good condition, but contained no bloodstains.

Chandler took it away for examination, but Dr. Phillips was emphatic that it wasn't long enough to be the knife the killer had used.

So once again the police found themselves in an impasse. Richardson and Pizer had been cleared, so had at least six other suspects. The only hope seemed to be to question all the witnesses again. Chandler decided to start with Donovan, the lodging-house-keeper.

Chapman had brought various men to Dorset Street; could Donovan identify any of them. No, he didn't think he could. There were many of them and most were casual acquaintances of Annie Chapman—'pick-ups, if you like'. But, come to think of it, there was one 'particular bloke—a reg'lar, you might call 'im. On Saturday nights she used to bring this chap back to the lodging house.' He was a man of military appearance and Donovan believed he was a pensioner, though he had heard he worked as a dock labourer.

'Did this man come to Dorset Street on the Saturday before her death?' asked Chandler.

'Yes, I remember now, he did. And Dark Annie paid eightpence for the two beds.'

But though a description of this man was obtained, it did not prove easy to find him. Probably the news of the murder had scared him out of the district.

Donovan also said he knew Leather Apron well. But it was certain that the man who answered to this nickname was not the same as Pizer. Chandler, like his superiors, was getting weary of hearing the name Leather Apron. The man Donovan knew was about five feet four inches in height, 'rather wild-looking' and he wore a double-peaked deerstalker's hat. Some months previously Donovan had ordered him out of the lodging house because he had threatened women on the premises with violence.

Circumstantial evidence is something one instinctively expects to find in fiction rather than in life. Yet, just as one instinctively rejects it in fiction, so in life one finds it difficult not to accept. Naturally, for the police, whose job it is to unmask criminals, circumstantial evidence is even harder to reject, and who can blame them? The Whitechapel murders —more perhaps than any other series of crimes—provided frequent examples of the dangers of circumstantial evidence and more than one man suffered as a result. But it must be conceded that when these cases collapsed the police did their best to make amends and openly admitted their errors. Unhappily, because in the earlier murders they fell into so many of these traps of circumstantial evidence, so later on they often stayed their hands for fear of repeating their errors.

The Sunday night after the Chapman murder provided a typical example of the risks of circumstantial evidence. News came from Gravesend that Leather Apron had been found. A man named William Henry Piggott had been detained by the police after being located in the Pope's Head public house in that town and was being brought by train to London Bridge.

Detective-Inspector Abberline was at first extremely dubious about the new suspect. 'There are scores of men nicknamed Leather Apron,' he said. 'I think you are wasting your time.'

'Gravesend police seem convinced they have a strong case against him, sir,' said Chandler.

Abberline rushed over to London Bridge to meet the train and commandeered a four-wheeler cab to take the new suspect to Commercial Street police station. And, as the story from Gravesend was unfolded, it did indeed seem as though they had at last found the killer. The suspect had first attracted attention because he was wandering about in a dazed condition, there were blood-stains on his clothes and his hands showed traces of recent wounds. An examination at the police station revealed that blood appeared to have been wiped off his boots recently and that two shirts, drenched in blood, were in a bundle he had been carrying.

Piggott was a native of Gravesend, aged fifty-two, unkempt, decidedly peculiar in his manner, furtive and shifty, apparently without any visible means of support. Yet only eight years earlier he had been a prosperous publican at Hoxton.

Piggott's own story was rambling and incoherent, but even so it largely confirmed the police's suspicions. By dint of patient cross-examination they learned he had been in Whitechapel and Spitalfields in the early hours of Saturday morning. While walking along Brick Lane, Whitechapel, at 4.30 a.m. he saw a woman fall down in what he thought was a fit. He stooped to pick her up and she bit his hand. Exasperated at such a churlish response to his good nature, Piggott—in his own words—'clouted her good and proper'. Then, seeing two policemen arrive on the scene, he ran away.

Under further questioning he altered his story somewhat. The woman who bit him was 'in a yard at the back of a lodging house' when she was seized with a fit. Piggott would not explain how he came to be in the yard. He 'didn't remember'. On the Thursday night he had slept at a lodging house in Osborne Street, but on Friday night and throughout the early hours of Saturday he was walking the streets of Whitechapel. He had no sleep and walked on to Gravesend on Saturday.

Detective-Inspector Abberline summoned all the women who claimed to be able to recognise Leather Apron, including a Mrs. Fiddymount, who said she had seen him at the Prince Albert on Saturday night. An identification parade was held, but the women were unanimous that Piggott was not the man they knew.

Despite this, the police regarded Piggott's actions as suspicious and his story as highly improbable, and a further check on his movements was made while he was held in custody. Finally they were convinced that he could not have done the murder, though he was found to be insane, certified and put in an asylum.

Having eliminated so many suspects, Abberline's task was to try to get a clearer picture of the murderer. At first, with so many conflicting statements, this seemed an impossibility. But Abberline knew that in the two previous murders the police had been hopelessly handicapped because no description of any suspect was forthcoming. Difficult as it might be to reconcile various witnesses' statements, the detective-inspector felt that this was the only line of approach left open to him.

The best clue seemed to be that provided by the woman Darrell, who had reported seeing a man and woman talking outside No. 29 at 5 a.m. on the day of the crime. Darrell had identified Chapman as the woman she saw, and her description of the man tallied in some respects with that given by another person who claimed to have seen him alone in Hanbury Street at 2 a.m.

A Mr. Cadoche, who lived in the next house to No. 29, had gone into the backyard of his premises at 5.20 a.m. on the morning of the murder and heard a woman say 'No, no'. After that there was a scuffle and a sound as though someone had fallen against a fence. But Mr. Cadoche had not been sufficiently inquisitive to find out what had happened, so his evidence wasn't of much use.

Thomas Ede, a signalman employed by the East London Railway Company, was walking down Cambridge Heath Road that same morning when, opposite the Forester's Arms, he saw a man who 'appeared to have a wooden arm, as it was hanging by his side. A long-bladed knife was sticking out of his trousers pocket'.

Ede's description of the man was fairly comprehensive, for by this time—it was after 6 a.m.—it was daylight. 'Must have been about five foot eight tall, with a dark moustache and whiskers. He wore a double peak cap, dark brown jacket and overalls over dark trousers. The overall was quite clean.'

Elizabeth Long, the wife of a park-keeper, of Church Row, Whitechapel, was able to substantiate Darrell's evidence to some extent, though there was a difference of half an hour in their assessment of the time. She was on her way to Spitalfields Market at 5.30 a.m. when she saw a man and woman outside No. 29. The woman she identified as Chapman. The man was 'about forty, a little taller than the woman, and he wore a dark coat and had a shabby, genteel appearance'.

Mrs. Long heard the man say, 'Will you?'

The woman replied: 'Yes.'

'I should say from the way he spoke he was a foreigner,' Mrs. Long told Abberline.

From these statements Abberline worked out a timetable:

2 a.m. A man seen alone in Hanbury Street.

4.50 a.m. (if one accepted John Richardson's evidence) The body was not in the yard.

5 a.m. A man and woman seen outside No. 29 by Darrell.

5.20 a.m. Cadoche heard sounds of a scuffle in the yard of No. 29.

5.30 a.m. Mrs. Long saw a man and woman outside No. 29.

5.55 a.m. Davies discovered the body.

If these times were exact, then the murder must have been committed some time betweeen 5.30 and 5.55 a.m. But Abberline doubted whether all the estimates of time were accurate. There was also the testimony of Dr. Phillips who first of all insisted that Chapman must have been dead since at least 4.30 a.m., though afterwards he admitted it might have been later.

On the strength of the information received by all these people the following notice was issued to all police stations:

'Description of a man who entered a passage of a house where the murder was committed of a prostitute at 2 a.m. on 8 September. Age 37, height 5 ft. 7 inches. Rather dark beard and moustache; dress—dark jacket, dark vest and trousers, black scarf and black felt hat. Spoke with a foreign accent.'

This was the first, but by no means the last, description of a wanted man in connection with this series of murders. In many ways it was a vague and unsatisfactory description; its lack of detail would make it hard indeed for anyone to identify the murderer, and it might apply to hundreds of men—especially in the East End where a foreign accent was not unusual. Whitechapel was full of *émigré* Poles, Russians and Letts, not to mention a fair sprinkling of other races.

Abberline's motive in putting out this slipshod description may have been to impress public opinion that the police were doing something at a time when they were under a barrage of criticism. Or he may have done this to soothe the frightened East Enders into believing that they were hot on the killer's trail. At the same time he genuinely believed that if they could narrow down a list of suspects by means of applying the test of a lowest common denominator of all descriptions received, something would be achieved.

For this reason he eliminated all mention of a deerstalker's hat, mentioned by some witnesses. But it is odd that he should describe a man seen alone at 2 a.m. rather than a man seen with a woman by two different witnesses at between 5 and 5.30 a.m.

Meanwhile the missing pensioner was located. He admitted having consorted with Chapman on various occasions—the last time being on the Sunday prior to the murder, 2 September, between 1 and 3 p.m. His movements were checked and he was proved not to be implicated in the death of Dark Annie.

Eliza Cooper, the woman who had quarrelled with Annie Chapman and beaten her up, was also found. She insisted their quarrel was 'all over a bar of soap'. But she was not able to help the police much: the sum total of her evidence was that Chapman bought the three brass rings which she wore from a black man.

5

Bernard Shaw poses a question

If the readers of the popular press in the 'eighties did not have a crusading columnist to castigate their particular *bêtes noires*, at least there was George Bernard Shaw to find them scapegoats.

Shaw, then a dramatic critic in London and already noted for his witty satires and verbal tirades against Authority and Capital, found time to write a letter to *The Star* on 24 September 1888, which appeared under the heading of 'Blood Money to Whitechapel':

'Now that the Whitechapel murderer has been so successful in calling attention for a moment to the social question. . . . Less than a year ago the West End press were literally clamouring for the blood of the people—hounding Sir Charles Warren to thrash and muzzle the scum who dared to complain that they were starving—heaping insult and reckless calumny upon those who interceded for the victims—applauding to the skies the open class bias of the magistrates and judges who zealously did their worst in the criminal proceedings which followed, behaving, in short, as the propertied class always does behave when the workers throw it into a frenzy of terror by venturing to show their teeth.

'. . . The riots of 1886 (*during the Dock Strike*) brought in £78,000 and a People's Palace. It remains to be seen how much these murders may prove worth to the East End *in panum et circenses*.

'Indeed, if the habits of Duchesses only admitted of their being decoyed into Whitechapel backyards, a single experiment in slaughterhouse anatomy on an aristocratic victim might fetch in a round half million and save the necessity of sacrificing four women of the people.'

This typical Shavian extravaganza infuriated the police and magistrates, but, as letters in *The Times* and other newspapers revealed, the murders had focused attention on the appalling conditions in the East End and especially on the brothel-keeping activities of slum landlords. Meetings were held at various working men's clubs to condemn the existence of organised vice in the heart of Whitechapel and Stepney. The Rev. Samuel Barnett, of St. Jude's Church, Commercial Street, suggested that philanthropists might buy up some of the houses of ill-fame, convert them into homes for the poor 'even if this meant accepting a lower profit than the present owners get'.

And the Victorians being touchy when their morals were called into question, a few philanthropists wrote offering to do just this—with what results we are not told. The significant fact is that the Ripper murders not only focused attention on the social evils of the East End, but marked the beginning of a positive attempt to control them. This area had changed little since Henry Mayhew twenty years before had written:

'Shadwell, Spitalfields and contiguous districts are infested with nests of brothels as well as Whitechapel. Brothel-keeping is a favourite mode of investing money in this neighbourhood. Some few years ago a man called James was prosecuted for having altogether thirty brothels, and although he was convicted, the nuisance was by no means in the slightest degree abated, as the informer, by name Brooks, has them all himself at the present time.'

Until 1888 practically nothing had been done for more than forty years to tackle the problem of organised vice. When the Bishop of Exeter asserted that the number of prostitutes in London exceeded 80,000, the City police pooh-poohed this cleric and claimed there were no more than 8,000.

Mayhew's own researches revealed how profitable vice could be even to its meanest exploiters in the East End. He told of a woman renting a miserable hovel in Victoria Place, running out of Bluegate, who 'paid five shillings a week rent and charged the prostitutes who lodged with her four shillings a week for their accommodation'.

For the police this was an unhappy period. If the proletariat of the East End were at last offering their co-operation —only in so far as it meant helping to capture the Ripper, of course—the public generally and the politicians, with an eye for cheap popularity, were openly attacking the alleged incompetence of the Metropolitan Police.

Certainly the police made many blunders, mainly through crass leadership. When the adjourned inquest on Mary Nichols was held, Inspector Helston admitted that after her murder he hadn't called at *all* the houses in Bucks Row.

The foreman at this inquest, doubtless recalling that 'it's the rich wot gits the pleasure, it's the pore wot gits the blime', commented:

'A substantial reward would have been offered if a rich man had been murdered. But nothing has been done in this case. I myself would be glad to give five pounds for the capture of the murderer.'

This must surely be unique in the annals of jurymen.

Forty years later an elegant young author named Michael Arlen, delving into the Shaw letter already quoted, decided that here was material for a new novel. The result was *Hell! said the Duchess*, in which the theme of the Whitechapel murders was transplanted into the West End in a contemporary setting, but with the difference that the victims were young men and the Ripper an exquisitely groomed and exotically perfumed duchess.

Local tradesmen not only formed vigilance societies, but furnished their own patrols for guarding the streets in which their shops were situated. But the unlit, drab alleys where the prostitutes congregated remained unwatched except for the policemen on their beat. Shaw must have snorted at this East End example of putting property before the lives of the people.

False alarms and futile arrests also brought the police under further ridicule. Apart from the examples of these mentioned in the last chapter there were at least two other occasions when premature arrests resulted in the police being made to look extremely silly.

Charles Ludwig, a German who lived in The Minories, was charged at Thames police court with being drunk and threatening to stab another man with a penknife. The police made further inquiries about the German, having noted that his description was similar to that of the man in the double-peak cap whom Thomas Ede saw. He had been heard to threaten women with violence and, according to his landlady, had twice returned home to wash blood from his hands. Some particularly stupid police officer told the press that the Ripper had been found and so hopes were falsely raised again. They were quickly dashed to the ground when it was learned that the police had absolutely no evidence against Ludwig.

Then one night a man walked into Wandsworth police station and said: 'I am John Fitzgerald. I want to give myself up for committing the murder at Hanbury Street.'

He was arrested and put in a cell. When the police surgeon arrived he surmised that Fitzgerald was drunk. It subsequently proved that he had been drinking to excess for days and was suffering from delirium tremens.

Because Bucks Row was close to a slaughterhouse it was thought that a slaughterman or a butcher might be the killer. Every slaughterhouse from Aldgate Shambles to Stepney was searched. L. Forbes Winslow, the specialist in mental diseases who spent 'day after day and night after night in the Whitechapel slums', trying to find the Ripper, said detectives were disguised as slaughtermen in an effort to solve the mystery. Lieutenant-Colonel Sir Henry Smith, head of the City of London police, recorded that he 'visited every butcher's shop in the City'.

Indeed, for a time, the quest for butcher suspects developed into a form of witch-hunting. A story was circulated that the murderer was a butcher who wore blue overalls and, of course, the inevitable leather apron. A Jew named Jacobs, who worked in a slaughterhouse, attracted attention because he answered the description of this man. Jacobs was perfectly harmless and entirely innocent, but people made life unbearable for him after the police had questioned him. For weeks he was pointed out as 'the East End killer' and more than once he had to run helter-skelter to the nearest police station to take refuge from an enraged crowd who threatened to lynch him. Eventually this unhappy man became demented and finally lost his reason altogether.

A man at Holloway who made a habit of carrying long butchers' knives was arrested. He, too, was found to be insane and was put in an asylum.

The young David Lloyd George had not yet been elected to Parliament, but he was already a political force and in the constituency which he was nursing he made some caustic attacks on the police for 'harrying the poor dockers and denying the rights of strikers, while failing miserably to find the brute who kills the poor women of the East End'.

Whether in quest of ammunition for more polemics of this nature, or out of morbid curiosity, we are not told, but Mr. Frank Owen in his biography of Lloyd George describes how the young Welshman made an excursion into East End night life.

'One Saturday night, with a fellow Welshman, the late Sir Alfred Davies, and a Caernarvon-born superintendent of the Metropolitan Police, he made an expedition to the scenes of Jack the Ripper's recent operations,' writes Mr. Owen. 'The Radical Press attacked the incompetent Tory Home Secretary. So it was with a sense of excitement that Lloyd George met his friends that evening at nine o'clock at Aldgate Underground Station, which was within a couple of hundred yards of Jack the Ripper's first murder.

'. . . In the dim-lit sawdust bars they saw dockers in rags drinking with their drabs the cheapest liquor which their wretched wages could just afford, while their wives hung around outside the doors, abusing them, calling them home and being clouted and kicked in return. They heard hungry children whimpering. They then turned into the squalid alleys and backyards of the fourpenny doss-houses, climbed the rickety stairs and pushed their way into the crowded dens where tramps and thieves lay in dozens on the floor.'

Lloyd George and Bernard Shaw were not alone in criticising the police for paying more attention to the demonstrations of the dock workers and strikers in Trafalgar Square and elsewhere than to finding the killer. In the East End it was being whispered that the police were being paid to harry the people, not protect them.

Grossly unfair as this criticism may seem, it was not so ill-founded as might be supposed. When the police arrested suspects against whom there was the flimsiest evidence, the victim was invariably one of the poorer classes. Yet, when, on at least four occasions, constables wished to detain members of the middle and upper classes, upon much stronger grounds, station superintendents declined to take action.

The organisation of the Metropolitan Police force left much to be desired and the objectives of its chief were confused and confusing. General Sir Charles Warren, the Commissioner of the Metropolitan Police, had been summoned from his Royal Engineers' command in Africa to take up this post. A most unsuitable choice for the office, he was in manner and mentality the nineteenth-century counterpart of Colonel Blimp.

Unimaginative, authoritarian, incapable of assessing any problem except in military terms, he upset the entire police force by his tactlessness and antagonised the Criminal Investigation Department by his scant regard for that body. Nor was this the sum total of his shortcomings. He was a source of intense irritation and annoyance to the luckless Home Secretary, Mr. Matthews.

Warren's main contribution to the reorganisation of the Metropolitan Police was the appointment of five military officers and a large increase in the numbers of inspectors and sergeants. This policy is said to have marked the origin of the phrase 'all generals and no privates', the apt comment of a Cockney police constable on 'Warren's Rabbits'.

In short, his term of office amply justified the criticism that soldiers are failures as heads of the Metropolitan Police, the more so as his megalomania led him to challenge the civilian control of the Home Office, an error of judgement which was too much even for the remarkably complacent Mr. Matthews to swallow.

Sir Charles' annual reports omitted all reference to crime statistics in London, but devoted considerable space to the question of boots and saddles for the police. Monro, the Assistant Commissioner, resigned because it was impossible to work with Warren.

Sir Robert Anderson has referred to 'the foolish ways of the Home Office' and how the 'officers of the C.I.D. were demoralised by the treatment accorded to their late chief, Munro'. It was under these conditions, with the C.I.D. seething with discontent, that Sir Robert was appointed Assistant Commissioner of the Police and Head of the C.I.D. in September 1888.

'After one week in Scotland Yard, because of ill health, I went on holiday to Switzerland. The second of the Whitechapel murders had been committed the night before I took office,'* wrote Sir Robert.

When, after further murders, he was urgently ordered to return to London by the Home Secretary, he promptly complied, although still a sick man.

'We hold you responsible for finding the murderer,' was Mr. Matthews' greeting.

'My answer was,' added Sir Robert, 'to decline the responsibility. I went on to say that the measures I found in operation were, in my opinion, wholly indefensible and scandalous, for these wretched women were plying their trade under definite police protection.

'Let the police of that district [Whitechapel] receive orders to arrest every known street woman found on the prowl after midnight, or else let us warn them that the police will not protect them.

'Though the first course would have been merciful to the very small class of women affected by it, it was deemed too drastic and I fell back on the second.'

If Sir Charles Warren was awkward and unimaginative, Sir Robert Anderson seems to have allowed hysteria to inter-

* *The Lighter Side of My Official Life*, by Sir Robert Anderson.

fere with his judgement. He certainly gave the impression of a man whose health had failed him at the very moment of his appointment and who was without any practical solution to the problem of the Ripper.

Throughout his term of office Sir Charles Warren blundered from crisis to crisis. When the riots staged by the unemployed occurred in 1887 and the constant disturbances by dockers and others in Trafalgar Square the same year created a problem, he certainly repressed them with military vigour. But his actions, far from being a deterrent, only served to inflame the unemployed still more, provoking increasing disturbances and a good deal of political agitation.

Then came the celebrated Cass case which caused a major political furore and some feverish criticism in the House of Commons. On Jubilee Night in 1887 a young single woman named Cass was arrested for soliciting in Regent Street. She was taken into custody and charged. Subsequently the woman was found to be highly respectable and completely innocent of any such charges, but the case did considerable harm to the reputation of the police.

Again Warren blundered. He showed very bad grace and made no apologies. Within a few months of this event he was disputing the right of the Home Secretary to apply the Official Secrets Act to the Commissioner or any member of the Metropolitan Police force.

But, as will shortly be seen, it was during the Ripper murders that Warren made his biggest blunders and forfeited the few remaining shreds of faith which his harassed superiors had in him.

Meanwhile the inquest into Annie Chapman's death lasted for several days. Dr. Bagster Phillips, who was recalled by the Coroner, protested that he did not wish to give more evidence in public. 'The medical evidence,' he said, 'is totally unfit for publication.'

But the Coroner was insistent and Dr. Phillips had to comply with his instructions. When he did so, he stressed the 'deliberate, successful and apparently scientific manner in which the poor woman was mutilated. The murderer showed great anatomical knowledge. I myself could not have performed such surgery, even working at top speed, in under a quarter of an hour. If I had acted deliberately and with the greatest care in removing the organ from the body, it would have taken me the best part of an hour.'

The Coroner's summing up smacked of Lyceum melodrama. 'Perhaps with Judas-like approaches the wretch must have seized the deceased. He pressed her throat and while this prevented the slightest cry, at the same time it produced insensibility and suffocation. Even in these preliminaries the wretch seems to have known how to carry out his nefarious work efficiently.

'There is no evidence of any struggle. The clothes were not torn. Her throat was then cut in two places with savage determination and the injuries to the abdomen were inflicted. All this was done with cool impudence and reckless daring.

'No unskilled person could have done this. It must have been someone used to the post-mortem room. The conclusion that the desire was to possess the missing abdominal organ seems overwhelming.'

But the Coroner, having dramatised Chapman's death in phrases worthy of a thriller-writer, left his most sensational observations to the end. He gave the impression of having savoured every moment of this inquest and of delighting in keeping his choicest revelations until the last possible moment.

'*There was a market for that missing organ*,' he observed, pausing to allow his words to seep into the consciousness of the shocked but bovine jurymen.

'Within a few hours of the news of the medical report given in the earliest stages of this inquest being published, I received a communication from an officer of one of our great medical schools.

'It was to the effect that he had information which might help. I attended this school and was informed by the subcurator of the Pathological Museum that some months ago an American had called on him and asked to procure a number of specimens of the organ which was missing in the deceased.

'This American said he would give twenty pounds apiece

for each specimen. He said his object was to issue an actual specimen with each copy of a publication on which he was working. He was told that it was impossible to comply with his request, but he still urged that the organs be given to him. 'He wished to preserve these specimens, not in spirits of wine, but in glycerine in order to keep them in a flaccid condition and then he wished to send them direct to America. He repeated his request at another institution where he was also refused.'

This information, added the Coroner, had been passed on to Scotland Yard. His purpose in referring to the matter at the inquest was in the hope that publicity might bring forth some further clue.

But it didn't. All that followed was a pompous letter to *The Times* from a West End specialist who protested against 'this gross and unjustifiable calumny on the medical profession'.

Members of the medical profession are ever *touché* and this letter from Mr. J. R. Bennett was followed by others which attacked the police and the Coroner for daring to suggest that any doctor could possibly be a criminal, or a party to criminal proceedings.

'Boots and saddles,' Sir Charles Warren had said, 'were very important.' If so, he might have paid more attention to detail. For, said Chief Constable Wensley, in those days a junior officer, as a result of the Ripper crimes 'we nailed to our clumsy regulation boots strips of rubber, usually bits of old bicycle tyres, so that we could patrol silently'.*

Quite the most sensible suggestion put forward in *The Times*, and one which might usefully have been adopted, but wasn't, read:

'I beg to suggest the organisation of a small force of plain-clothes constables mounted on bicycles for the rapid and noiseless patrolling of the streets and roads by night.'

Such a plan would have been far more sensible than Sir Robert Anderson's sick-bed inspiration of a curfew for Whitechapel whores.

* *Detective Days,* by F. P. Wensley.

6

An autumn of terror

'No one who was living in London that autumn will forget the terror created by these murders,' wrote Sir Melville Macnaghten. 'Even now I can recall the foggy evenings and hear again the raucous cries of the newspaper boys: "Another horrible murder, murder, mutilation, Whitechapel."

'No maidservant deemed her life safe if she ventured out to post a letter after ten o'clock at night.'

The lurid cries of the newspaper vendors must have unnerved some people, for a letter to the *Daily Telegraph* complained:

'Can nothing be done to prevent a set of hoarse ruffians coming nightly about our suburban squares and streets yelling at the tops of their hideous voices: "Whitechapel! Murder!"?'

But presumably the newspaper salesmen had their imitators, mischievously bent on disturbing the tranquillity of West End squares after dusk, causing chattering panic and dropped teacups in the servants' quarters and choleric anger in the drawing rooms.

In Whitechapel the landlord of the Star and Garter went bankrupt and blamed it all on the murders: 'People aren't going out at night any more,' he claimed. 'Since the killings I hardly get a soul in here of a night.'

Yet there was little need for anyone outside the East End to worry and, judging by the selection of his victims, no cause for respectable women to be alarmed. For the killer, with reckless daring—or so it seemed—concentrated his attention on an area of little more than a square mile between the City and Spitalfields. His victims unwittingly gave him most aid: they may have been terrified in continuing to pursue their sordid trade, but whether from sheer necessity, or an obstinate belief in their ability to defend themselves, the East End whores remained in the darkest corners and most deserted alleys where least protection could be afforded them.

There was a pathetic fatalism in their attitude. On one occasion Sir Melville Macnaghten made a tour of East End doss houses. In a common lodging house he saw an unemployed man toasting bloaters. 'When his "lady" returned he asked her if she "had had any luck".

'She replied: "No —— luck." When asked about Jack (the Ripper) she said: "Well, let him come—the sooner the better for such as I." '

It was in the early hours of the last night of September 1888 that the Ripper scare reached its zenith. Two murders were committed within three-quarters of an hour; the victims were found within a quarter of an hour's walk of each other.

The scene of the first of these crimes was a narrow court in Berner Street, a quiet thoroughfare running from Commercial Road down to the London, Tilbury and Southend Railway. At the entrance to the court were a pair of large wooden gates; in addition to these was a small wicket gate for use when the former were closed. High walls on each side of the court blotted out all light except for a faint glimmer from the windows of the International Workers' Educational Club at the furthest end. This club was an offshoot of the Socialist League and a rendezvous of Russians, Poles and Jews.

On Saturday nights members of this club met for debates and on September 29, which was a Saturday, there had been a discussion on 'the necessity for socialism among Jews', followed by a concert at 11 p.m.

Louis Diemschutz, who by day was a hawker and by night the steward of this club, was returning to Berner Street with his pony and cart about 1 a.m. The gates of the court were still open, but, despite this, he had some difficulty in guiding his pony through the entrance. It appeared that for some reason the pony was determined to avoid the right-hand wall of the court and it refused to budge any further than the entrance.

Diemschutz dismounted, thinking there must be some obstruction which he could not see. He poked about the court with his whip and discovered the body of a woman, huddled up close to the right-hand wall.

With a cry of horror, the steward did not stop to investigate: he knew instinctively that the East End killer must have struck again and he rushed into the concert hall of the club to tell them what had happened.

Zozebrodski, a member of the club, accompanied him when he returned to the court. The body was still warm, the clothes were wet from rain, but the ground underneath the body was completely dry. Obviously the murder must have been committed only minutes before Diemschutz returned to the club.

The woman was gaunt and scraggy. She wore a jacket made of black diagonal cloth with feather trimmings, a black skirt, velveteen bodice, crêpe bonnet, spring-side boots and white stockings. In her right hand she clasped a bunch of grapes and in her left some sweets. In the pocket of her dress were two handkerchiefs, a brass thimble and some black darning worsted. The clothes were not disarranged, though her bodice was open at the top.

No one in the vicinity had heard any cries or unusual noises, though they agreed that these might have been drowned by the singing in the club. William West, overseer of a printing works which also occupied part of 40 Berner Street, said he attended a meeting at the club until about 12.30 a.m. when he went out into the court. He noticed that the gates were still open, but was sure there was no body in the court then.

The club was immediately searched by the police and names and addresses of all members were taken. Morris Eagle, a club member, said he left Berner Street about midnight and returned at 12.40, but saw nothing unusual in the court. Likewise a Russian named Joseph Lave passed through the court about a quarter of an hour before the body was discovered and was positive he could not have missed the corpse had it been there then. 'It was very dark, and because of this I groped my way along the right hand wall. Had there been a body, I must have stumbled over it.'

Three doctors were called to examine the body—Drs. Bagster Phillips, Kay and Blackwell. Dr. Frederick Blackwell arrived in the court at 1.15 a.m. and estimated that the woman had been dead for not more than half an hour and possibly only twenty minutes. Though her throat had been cut and the murder revealed the Ripper's normal technique the body had not been mutilated, and it seemed possible that the arrival of Diemschutz in his cart, which must have been heard at quite a distance, disturbed the killer who ran away before completing his surgical operations.

A large crowd quickly assembled in Berner Street notwithstanding that it was the middle of the night and about sixty people ghoulishly followed the body on its journey to the mortuary.

Early on Sunday morning Sir Charles Warren himself and Major Smith of the City Police visited the scene of the crime. For both of them the previous twelve hours had been like a nightmare. Within an hour of the discovery of the body in the court off Berner Street had come news of another killing—this time within the precincts of the City of London. This occurred in Mitre Square, and for years afterwards the site of this murder was known as 'Jack the Ripper's Corner'.

Lieutenant-Colonel Sir Henry Smith (Major Smith as he then was) stated in *From Constable to Commissioner*: 'The night of Saturday, September 29, found me tossing about in my bed at Cloak Lane police station, close to the river and adjoining Southwark Bridge. The smell of fur skins made sleep impossible . . . then the bell rang, and . . .

'"Another murder, sir. This time in the City."'

In a hansom cab, with three detectives hanging on behind, Major Smith went down to Mitre Square.

He was an energetic and conscientious officer, refused to be bound by bureaucratic regulations and often quite daringly employed unorthodox tactics, sometimes with remarkable success. In the six years since he had joined the City of London Police force he had risen to the position of Commissioner.

Major Smith never forgot the night of September 29–30. Not only was there the sensation of two murders committed within three-quarters of an hour in the same area, but the galling experience of learning that failure to carry out his instructions had ruined the best chance the police had yet had of capturing the Ripper.

For the woman who was found with her throat cut and her body horribly mutilated in Mitre Square was Catherine Eddowes, *who had been under arrest at Bishopsgate police station only a few hours previously*.

Indeed, Major Smith went on record as declaring that Eddowes was in custody 'twenty minutes before she was murdered'. This is not quite correct. Eddowes was released on bail at 1 a.m., and from Bishopsgate police station to Mitre Square is a distance of about twenty-five minutes' walk. It must be assumed that sometime during this walk she was accosted by the murderer and presumably detained for a few minutes. It was 1.45 a.m. when her body was found.

Despite the fact that she was horribly mutilated about the face, Eddowes was identified by her sister, Eliza Gold, of Thrawl Street. Forty-three years of age, Eddowes was so ravaged by alcohol and loose living, so emaciated by poverty, that she looked more like sixty-three. She seems to have had a number of aliases. For seven years she had lived with a labourer named John Kelly, to whom she was known as Kate Conway, the wife of Thomas Conway. But, as far as could be ascertained, she had never been married, and had eked out a day-to-day existence by selling articles in the streets and, more frequently, by prostitution. 'Emily Birrell' and 'Anne Kelly' were names found on pawn tickets in her pocket, and, when arrested at 8 p.m. on 29 September, for being drunk and incapable in the gutter, she told the police she was 'Kate Kelly' and gave an address in Fashion Street.

Eddowes and Kelly had been down in Kent hop-picking and had only returned to London on the previous Thursday. Notwithstanding the fact that they had been working, both of them were literally penniless and so spent the Thursday night in the casual word in Shoe Lane. On Friday afternoon Kelly earned sixpence and Eddowes said to him: 'You take fourpence and go to the lodging house. Give me twopence and I'll go to the casual ward.'

Just how utterly destitute this couple were may be judged from the fact that on the Saturday morning Eddowes pawned John Kelly's boots for half a crown to buy some food.

The orders which Major Smith had given to the men in his force were to 'account for every man and woman seen together in suspicious circumstances'. He had put nearly one-third of the force into plain clothes with instructions to 'do everything which, under the circumstances, a constable should not do. It was subversive of discipline, but I had them well supervised by senior officers.' Smith had insisted that his men should shadow every whore known to frequent dark passages in the City after dark, and it is clear from his instructions that Eddowes should have been followed after her release from the cells.

Though she had had time to sober up, Eddowes could have been in no fit condition to wander about the streets at 1 a.m., and it was crass stupidity to have let her go before daylight. Not to have shadowed her after she had been set free was an act of the utmost folly.

'The "beat" of Catherine Eddowes was a small one,' said Smith. 'She was known to a good many of the constables, but, known or unknown, she was in the streets late at night and must have been seen making for Mitre Square. Had she been followed, the murderer would have been caught.'

Eddowes must have left the police station just after the murder in Berner Street had been committed, and the killer must have gone straight from there to Mitre Square. This murder could certainly not have been premeditated. Probably, infuriated at being disturbed during his first crime, and his mind crazed with blood lust, the maniac was determined to strike again at the first opportunity which presented itself.

Police Constable Watkins, of the City Police, was on his beat at 1.45 a.m., when, turning his lantern upon the darkest corner of Mitre Square, he saw the body of Eddowes lying in a pool of blood. He was certain the body could not have been there more than a quarter of an hour, for he had timed himself to work his beat in from ten to fifteen minutes.

A man named Morris, the night watchman at Kearley and Tonge's premises in Mitre Square, had been on duty inside the warehouse with the door open. He had neither seen nor heard anything until P.C. Watkins called him outside.

'I was here in the square at 1.30,' Watkins told Morris, 'and there was nobody here then.'

'I reckon that the killer was watching you and waited until you nipped off before coming into the square,' replied Morris.

There were two blunders by the police that night. Apart from the failure of his men to carry out Major Smith's instructions, Sir Charles Warren himself was responsible for the most lamentable error of all.

'It would scarcely be believed that the Metropolitan Police held the clue to identification of the murderer in their own hands and deliberately threw it away under the personal direction of the Commissioner of Police, who acted in the belief that an anti-semitic riot might take place if a certain damning piece of evidence were permitted to remain on the walls.'*

Before leaving Mitre Square the murderer had torn off a piece of the apron which Eddowes was wearing. Making his way towards Whitechapel, he had had the audacity to stop in a close off Dorset Street where he washed his hands in a sink. Major Smith who, in his own words, 'wandered around the City and East End until six o'clock that morning', actually saw the blood-stained water before it had been drained out of the sink.

Then, anxious to get away from the vicinity of the crime as speedily as possible, the Ripper wiped his hands on the piece of apron as he hurried eastwards. Possibly he was disturbed while rinsing his hands in the sink, for there were a few blood-stains on the fragment of apron when it was found at 2.55 a.m. in the doorway of a house in Goulston Street,

* Statement by Major Smith.

parallel to Commercial Street, about a third of a mile from Mitre Square and not far from Petticoat Lane.

This was the first real clue the police had. P.C. Alfred Long, who made the discovery, went inside the doorway and noticed on the wall of the passage leading to a staircase the following words hastily scrawled in white chalk:

'The Jewes are not the men to be blamed for nothing.'

An ambiguous statement and it is conceivable that it did not refer to the murders. But as the writing on the wall had not been there at midnight and as the fragment of Eddowes' apron was found nearby, the police were convinced that the killer had done this, especially as some of the words appeared to be slightly smudged by blood-stains.

When Sir Charles Warren came down to the East End he gave instructions for the words to be wiped off the wall immediately. Inspector MacWilliam demurred and told Sir Charles this would be 'a grave mistake'.

However, whether the police removed the writing, or whether Sir Charles, incensed at his instructions being queried, personally carried out this task, the one possibly vital clue was destroyed before anyone had a chance to follow it up. Major Smith believed that 'Warren wiped out the words with his own hand'. He added that 'the words may have been written by the murderer, or may not. To obliterate the words that might have given us a most valuable clue, more especially after I had sent a man to stand over them till they were photographed, was not only indiscreet, but unwarrantable.'

Altogether it was an unhappy day for Major Smith. Twice he had been frustrated by other men's blunders.

Years later Sir Robert Anderson, of the C.I.D., had this comment to make on the incident:

'The night on which the murder was committed I was on my way home from Paris and great was my indignation when, next day, I heard of what was an act of crass stupidity. But the Scotland Yard men were in no way responsible for it. It was done by the officers of the uniformed force in the division upon an order issued by one of my colleagues.'

It was hardly surprising that when a crowd of a thousand

gathered in Victoria Park that Sunday afternoon under the chairmanship of Mr. Edward Burrow, not only were there highly critical speeches against both the Home Secretary and Sir Charles Warren, but a resolution was passed stating that it was 'high time both men should resign from office'.

Throughout the East End people were highly indignant at the conduct and direction of the police. Four other meetings were held during the day on Mile End Waste, where similar resolutions were passed.

'Sir Charles Warren,' declared one speaker, 'is the enemy of the working classes. He has hounded us incessantly during the past two years. And he has got away with it. This is our chance —perhaps our only chance—to pull this monster down. He must not be allowed to stay in office. If he comes to the East End again, we will string him up on the nearest lamp-post.'

The Whitechapel Vigilance Committee sent a petition to the Queen asking for the offer of a large reward for finding the murderer.

But if the Metropolitan Police were chary of making any such offer, the City Police had no inhibitions about it. The square mile of the City of London was policed by a force of its own, quite independent of Sir Charles Warren's jurisdiction, and the fact that a murder had been committed within their boundaries gave them the excuse to act. After consultation with the Lord Major the City Police issued this notice:

'A reward of £500 will be paid by the Commissioner of Police of the City of London to any such person (other than a person belonging to the Police Forces in the United Kingdom) who shall give information leading to the discovery and conviction of the murderer or murderers.—(Sir) James Fraser, Colonel, Commissioner, City of London Police.'

This appeal was fully backed by the Lord Mayor and the City fathers.

The editor of the *Financial News* sent this letter to the Home Secretary:

'In view of your refusal to offer a reward out of Government funds for the discovery of the perpetrator, or perpetrators, of the recent murders in the East End of London, I am instructed on behalf of several readers of the *Financial News*, whose names and addresses I enclose, to forward to you the accompanying cheque for £300, and to request you to offer that sum for this purpose in the name of the Government.'

It was a waste of time. A Home Office official, on the instructions of Mr. Henry Matthews, promptly returned the cheque.

But this did not deter other private offers of rewards being made. Colonel Sir Alfred Kirby, Officer Commanding the Tower Hamlets Battalion, offered £100 on behalf of himself and his officers, saying he was ready to place fifty members of his corps at the disposal of the authorities, to be utilised in assisting them in 'any way they may consider desirable for the protection of the public'.

If the generosity of private citizens did not move Sir Charles Warren, the mention of bloodhounds was sufficient to stir his martial blood. And within two days of the murders of 30 September scores of people were writing to the newspapers urging that bloodhounds should be used to catch the killer.

'As a breeder of bloodhounds, I might help,' wrote one scribe. 'I have the very sagacious bloodhound which would do the job for you,' stated another. The Master of Foxhounds of a Sussex hunt suggested that he should be given *carte blanche* to conduct operations in the East End, optimistically guaranteeing that he would soon 'root out this dastardly fiend'.

The Times, anticipating the banality of subject matter, if not the delicacy of style of latter-day 'Fourth Leader' writers, ponderously observed: 'Twelve years ago a murder at Blackburn was traced out by the help of a bloodhound, and, thanks to the sagacious instinct of the dog, the murderer was convicted. The experiment which was successful at Blackburn might once again be of avail.'

One can imagine Sir Charles Warren, bemused and bewildered, utterly unconscious of his own shortcomings, reading his *Times*, slapping it down on his desk, ringing a bell and barking at a subordinate: 'Get me a pack of bloodhounds!'

This is exactly what he did. Being a Royal Engineer, he

knew nothing about these animals. Senior police officers blanched, realising only too well the fatuity and futility of using bloodhounds. But Warren was not to be deterred. This, he told them, was where he took charge of operations and he was quite certain he would succeed where others had failed.

He obtained his bloodhounds from a Mr. Edwin Brough, of Wyndyate, near Scarborough, and promptly called for a trial in the 'most convenient open space'.

'It should have been obvious,' said Sir Melville Macnaghten, 'that bloodhounds were useless in Whitechapel. I cannot conceive of a more impossible locality in which to expect hounds to work.

'A highly placed police official [*this is certainly a reference to Warren*] arranged to be hunted himself by bloodhounds in Hyde Park. He had begun to think that the police were on the way to becoming the masters.'*

What happened on the occasion of this remarkable Gilbertian harlequinade in the park we are not told except for a report in *The Times*, which confirms the experiment and suggests it was ruined by a hoar frost. But at a later trial at Tooting Common the bloodhounds lost themselves, and, to make matters worse, the police lost trace of them, too. A message had to be sent to all police stations directing that a watch be kept for them. This produced some unwelcome publicity for the police force in the popular press and nothing more was heard about using bloodhounds. The mirth of Cockney London effectively stifled Warren's one and only brainwave, or brainstorm as some ribald police officers more aptly termed it.

Meanwhile the quest for the killer was conducted more orthodoxly on a lower level. Few new clues appeared to take the place of the one which Warren had so rashly destroyed. But in Whitechapel Road a blood-stained knife, the blade of which was ten inches long, was found. But Dr. Bagster Phillips doubted whether it was the weapon the killer had used.

The woman found dead in Berner Street was identified as Elizabeth Stride, a gawky, elongated wanton of forty-five,

* *Days of My Years*, by Sir Melville Macnaghten.

known in the locality as 'Long Liz'. Like the Ripper's other victims, she was a prostitute and lived in that notorious hive of harlotry, Flower and Dean Street.

Her husband was supposed to have been a ship's carpenter named Thomas Stride. Several witnesses in the area insisted that Elizabeth was a Swede; some said they had heard her talking Swedish, but whether or not this was the language she often used, all testified that she spoke a foreign tongue.

A clerk to the Swedish Church in the East End said that she was born Elizabeth Gostsdotter at Forslander near Gottenburg. He first stated emphatically that she was married to a man named Stride, then admitted that she was registered as an unmarried woman. He supposed she had told the clergyman she was married, while agreeing there was no proof of this. Stride had told people in the neighbourhood that she had nine children and that some of them were in the 'Swedish School', but the clerk had never heard of any children belonging to her.

Various men came forward and admitted to having lived with her at different times. Two of them knew her under the name of Annie Fitzgerald. She had told most of her acquaintances in the district that she was the mother of nine children, two of whom she lost, together with her husband, when the pleasure steamer *Princess Alice* sank in the Thames on 3 September, 1878, after colliding with a cargo vessel. Most of the 500 passengers, including many women and children, were drowned on that occasion: Elizabeth Stride claimed she was one of the few to be rescued.

There was no corroboration of this story and indeed it is almost certainly untrue, even though Stride herself might have been one of those aboard the boat. She certainly had no children, as far as can be ascertained. But this was her hard luck story to explain the cause of her downfall. She claimed that it affected her so severely that she started drinking heavily. Her craving for hard liquor had driven her on to the streets to seek the means to purchase it. Records showed that she had frequently been convicted of drunkenness at Thames police court.

But Mrs. Mary Malcolm, the wife of a respectable tailor, of Red Lion Square, told a very different tale. She was quite sure that the dead woman was Elizabeth Watts, her own sister. She recognised her by a black mark on her leg, where she had been bitten by an adder many years ago.

Elizabeth Stride, according to Mrs. Malcolm, was in reality the wife of a Mr. Edward Watts, a wine and spirit merchant of Bath. 'My sister left home because she brought disgrace on her husband. He caught her with a porter.'

Every Saturday, claimed Mrs. Malcolm, her sister used to call on her and she gave her two shillings. Once her sister left a naked baby on her doorstep: 'I had to keep the babe till she fetched it away. She told me that some policeman was the father.'

Which revelation did not please the police at all, and they were eager to disprove Mrs. Malcolm's statement. But her evidence was given with diffidence and sincerity, not at all in the manner of a sensation-seeker, and she appeared genuinely distressed at the disgrace brought upon her family by the story she had to tell.

There was a dramatic moment in the inquest when Mrs. Malcolm told the Coroner she had had a 'presentiment' of her sister's death. 'About 1.20 Sunday morning I was lying on my bed when I felt a kind of pressure on my breast, and then I felt three kisses on my cheek. I also *heard* the kisses; they were quite distinct.'

Michael Kidney, who claimed to have lived with Stride on and off for three years, to some extent corroborated Mrs. Malcolm's evidence. 'Mrs. Malcolm is very like her,' he said, and he added that Stride had told him about a policeman she used to meet in Hyde Park 'before she was married to Stride'.

At 12.45 a.m. on the Sunday Stride had been seen with a man in Berner Street. William Marshall, a labourer, told the police that 'the man was kissing her, and I heard him say, "You would say anything but your prayers"'.

Police Constable Smith had noticed them, too. He recalled that Stride had a red rose and some maidenhair fern fastened on her right side.

The *Police Gazette* published the following descriptions:

'At 12.35 a.m., 30 September, with Elizabeth Stride, found murdered on the same date in Berner Street at 1 a.m., a man, age 28, height 5 feet 8 inches, complexion dark, small dark moustache; dress, black diagonal coat, hard felt hat, collar and tie; respectable appearance, carried a parcel wrapped up in a newspaper.

'At 12.45 a.m., 30th, with the same woman in Berner Street, a man, age about 30, height 5 feet 5 inches; complexion fair, hair dark, small brown moustache, full face, broad shoulders; dress, dark jacket and trousers, black cap with peak.'

The probability, indeed almost the certainty, is that these were two slightly differing descriptions of the same man. It is hardly likely that Stride was with two different men within a period of ten minutes in the same place, and, as she was found murdered fifteen minutes after being seen with the man with the black cap with peak, this person was almost certainly her killer. No two people ever give the same description of someone they have seen briefly only once, especially when that person is in a dimly lit street. There are sufficient similarities in the two descriptions to suggest there was only one man with Stride during this period.

Mrs. Mortimer, of 36 Berner Street, which was only four doors away from where Stride's body was found, had stood at the open door of her house 'sometime between 12.30 and 1 a.m. to get a breath of air'. She heard 'some sort of a row', but thought it was in the International Workers' Club.

'It wasn't like an argument, though there was something like a stifled cry, or an angry voice. Then there was a bump; it must have been the body falling.

'Leastways, now I come to think about it, I suppose that's what it was. Didn't strike me that way at the time. Before I could properly tell what it was I saw a young man carrying a black shiny bag, walking very fast down the street. He looked up at the club, then went round the corner by the Board School.'

But this time the police had other descriptions to work on.

For someone had seen Catherine Eddowes with a strange man, too. This was recorded by the *Police Gazette* in the following terms:

'At 1.35 a.m., 30 September, with Catherine Eddowes, in Church Passage, leading to Mitre Square, where she was found murdered at 1.45 a.m., same date, a man, age 30, height 5 feet 7 inches, or 8 inches; complexion fair, moustache fair, medium build; dress: pepper and salt colour, loose jacket, grey cloth cap with peak of same material, reddish neckerchief tied in knot; appearance of a sailor. Information respecting this man to be forwarded to Inspector MacWilliam, 26 Old Jewry, London E.C.'

It is easy, of course, to assert that the last mentioned description is entirely different from the other two. Yet the height is about the same, so, too, is the estimate of the age; the moustache this time is 'fair', but nevertheless a moustache is what the three descriptions have in common. The 'grey cloth cap with peak' could easily be the 'black cap with peak'. The most marked difference is the 'reddish neckerchief tied in knot' and the suggestion that the man seen with Eddowes had the appearance of a sailor.

But what of the 'shiny black bag' carried by the young man whom Mrs. Mortimer saw walking away from Berner Street? Could this have been the killer? Only one other witness claimed to have seen anyone like him that night. This was Albert Backert, who got into conversation with a man in the Three Nuns Hotel in Aldgate on the Saturday night.

Backert and the stranger had a few drinks together and in due course the latter hinted that he was 'looking for women'.

'He wanted to know what sort of loose women used the public bar of the Three Nuns and where they were in the habit of going afterwards. It seemed rather odd to me,' Backert told the police.

'He was a queer character, shifty, and up to no good, I should say. He was shabby, but a genteel sort of fellow, with black clothes, a black felt hat, and carried a black bag. We came out of the pub together at closing time [midnight] and I left him outside Aldgate Station. I am not certain, but I think he followed an oldish woman who had been in the Three Nuns selling matches. I got the impression that he was in the habit of hanging around railway stations at night looking for women.'

It is highly improbable that anyone as cunning as the Ripper would risk drawing attention to his quest for women, and Backert's testimony would be hardly worth mentioning, but for two coincidences. First, there was the fact that Mrs. Mortimer saw a similar man with a black bag, and, secondly, the revelation made in 1937 by a former member of the Metropolitan Police force that he not only saw a man with a black bag that same September night in 1888, but actually arrested him.

On 16 March 1931 the *Daily Express* published a letter from Mr. Robert Clifford Spicer, of Saville Row, Woodford Green, Essex, in which he claimed that as a uniformed constable, aged twenty-two, he 'had the pleasure of capturing Jack the Ripper and taking him to Commercial Street police station after he had committed two murders'.

Police Constable Spicer was on duty in the East End on the night of 29–30 September. It was past 2 a.m. and the news of the Ripper's two crimes had already been passed by word of mouth to all the police on their beats. There was a theory at the time that the killer must know all these beats, where they left any side street or alley uncovered, and the exact timetable of the constables on duty. For this reason it was suggested that the police might occasionally vary their routine and even work their beats differently.

P.C. Spicer decided he would work his beat backwards. He had left Brick Lane and entered Henage Street. About fifty yards down this street was a narrow alley known as Henage Court. At the bottom of the court was a brick-built dustbin.

It was very dark, but the light from the constable's lantern revealed two pairs of legs at the end of the court. Spicer drew closer and, seated on the dustbin, he saw 'both Jack and a woman (Rosy) . . . She had two shillings in her hand, and she followed me when I took Jack on suspicion. His shirt cuffs had blood on them and he had the proverbial bag with him.

'As soon as I saw the man in that dark alleyway I felt sure he was the Ripper. The woman to whom he was talking was a notorious character, of the class to which all the Ripper's victims belonged.

'He evaded my question when I challenged him. "That's none of your business," he replied when I asked him what he was doing.

'"Oh, isn't it?" I said. "Then you come along with me," and I marched him along to the Commercial Street police station, with the woman following.'

This man was remarkably cool and unperturbed. He made no attempt to run away and merely shrugged his shoulders and accompanied the constable quietly. He wore a high hat, a black suit with silk facings and a gold watch and chain. He was about five feet eight inches, 'weighed around twelve stone, had a fair moustache, high forehead and rosy cheeks'.

Though it was nearly three o'clock many families in the East End were awake and dressed. Some had never gone to bed, others had been aroused from their slumbers by shouts of 'Murder!'; the news that two more murders had been committed that night had scared away all thought of sleep. Someone looking out of an upstairs window near Commercial Street police station saw P.C. Spicer with the man and woman and immediately shouted: 'They've got him! The killer's been caught!'

The shout brought innumerable heads to the bedroom windows. Women peered out and screamed or cheered, according to their temperament. Some were so excited that they ran half-naked into the street and followed Spicer and his suspect to the police station.

As he entered the station the young constable felt highly elated. Confident that he had captured the very man for whom every policeman in London was looking, it was with real pride that he told his story to the station inspector. There were eight other inspectors at Commercial Street Station that night—all engaged on the hunt for the killer—and Spicer could hardly be blamed if he cherished hopes of rapid promotion.

His elation was short-lived. Instead of being warmly welcomed and slapped on the back, as he had expected, he was met with chill indifference and grim silence. It was quickly obvious that the station inspector did not share his enthusiasm.

The woman, Rosy, made no complaint about the man with the black bag and her attitude seemed to decide the issue. So convinced were the inspectors that this wasn't the Ripper that they didn't even ask him to open his bag. A few questions were asked and it was quickly established that the man was a highly respected doctor with an address in Brixton.

'You have no evidence against this gentleman,' Spicer was told. 'You deserve a reprimand for arresting him. He is a respectable doctor and can establish his identity. You should have known better than to do this.'

'Then, sir,' asked Spicer, posing a very pertinent question, 'what is a *respectable* doctor doing sitting on a dustbin in a dark and dirty alley at this hour of the morning with a common prostitute? It doesn't make sense.'

Nor did it. But nobody attempted to answer Spicer's query. The station inspector had had severe reprimands himself for making arrests prematurely on earlier occasions. In Metropolitan Police headquarters there was a suspicion that the police had made fools of themselves too often by raising false hopes of a solution of the mystery and then finding they had been deceived. In addition there had been quite a few cases of members of the public fooling the police. Only the night before a well-dressed man had called in at Bishopsgate police station and anounced that he was 'the Whitechapel murderer'. It soon transpired that he was another inebriated practical joker.

Nor was this an isolated instance. A man in Islington was seen writing 'I am Jack the Ripper' on a street wall; he was pursued, but ran away. At least half a dozen other persons 'confessed' to one or other of the murders. One of them, William Bull, was charged at the Guildhall, and, having been proved hopelessly drunk, he promised the magistrate to 'take the pledge here and now never to touch a drop again'.

At this time, too, it was not known that the Ripper had

retraced his steps eastwards after the Mitre Square murder, the assumption being that, having headed westwards from Berner Street to the City, he had continued in a westerly direction or headed north to Finsbury.

'I was so disappointed when the man was allowed to go that I no longer had my heart in police work,' said Spicer. 'The case was taken out of my hands by the detective branch, but I am sure I would have been able to prove my suspicions if the matter had been left to me. I left the force five months after the suspect had been released. Yet I saw the man several times after this at Liverpool Street station, accosting women. I would remark to him: "Hello, Jack! Still after them?" He would immediately bolt.

'Whenever I saw him afterwards—always on the prowl for women—he was dressed the same and carried his little bag.'

This incident reflects the justification of a complaint made at the time by the Rev. Daniel Greatorex, an indefatigable worker on behalf of the vigilance committees. He alleged that policemen were switched from one beat to another too frequently in the East End, with the result that 'most constables didn't get to know the people in their district. They had no time or chance to get to know them.'

Certainly P.C. Spicer had not seen this doctor before. It is noteworthy that he did not see him again until he, too, was switched to another beat.

7

The correspondence of Jack the Ripper

In his portrait of Wainewright, the art critic, poet and poisoner—*Pen, Pencil and Poison*—Oscar Wilde studied the psychology of a murderer through a perusal of his writings. '*Janus Weathercock, Egomet Bonmot* and *Van Vinkvooms* were some of the grotesque masks under which he chose to hide his seriousness or to reveal his levity,' wrote Wilde. 'A mask tells us more than a face. These disguises intensified his personality.'

It is true both in literature and in the correspondence columns of newspapers that a pseudonym often reveals more than a genuine name. Anonymity preserves individuality; indeed, it does more—it is the means of creating it. And though Jack the Ripper was no Boz, or George Eliot, nor even a Janus Weathercock, he was certainly a prolific and entertaining letter-writer, with a keen, if misplaced, turn of humour and a superb sense of timing, while as a poet he was somewhat above the level of anonymous scribblers on walls. It is important that his correspondence and verse should be studied, if not with the fastidious and critical eye of an art critic, at least with more serious attention than that bestowed by most of his contemporaries.

Nor should this digression be regarded as a mildly satirical aside. But for the correspondence of Jack the Ripper, his name would never have been handed down to posterity and in all probability the crimes he committed would have long ago been forgotten. For it was he who created this 'grotesque mask', under which he contrived most effectively to 'hide his seriousness and reveal his levity'.

There are three questions which require an answer in this chapter: (1) was Jack the letter-writer the East End killer?; (2) was he a practical joker?; (3) does his correspondence provide any clue to his identity?

The name of Jack the Ripper was never mentioned either by the police or the newspapers until after the two murders committed on the night of 30 September. Then it was revealed in the press that a letter signed Jack the Ripper, referring to the murders, had been received by the editor of the Central News Agency.

The letter, which bore a 'London East Central, September 28' postmark, had been passed on to Scotland Yard, where it was at first regarded as the work of a hoaxer. The legend that the letter was written in the blood of one of the killer's victims is sheer fantasy which even the writer himself did not try to substantiate. The text of this extraordinary epistle was as follows:

'Dear Boss,

'I keep on hearing the police have caught me, but they won't fix me just yet. I have laughed when they look so clever and talk about being on the right track. The joke about Leather Apron gave me real fits.

'I am down on whores and I shan't quit ripping them till I do get buckled. Grand work, the last job was. I gave the lady no time to squeal.

'How can they catch me now? I love my work and want to start again. You will soon hear of me and my funny little games. I saved some of the proper red stuff in a ginger beer bottle over the last job, to write with, but it went thick like glue and I can't use it. Red ink is fit enough, I hope. Ha! Ha!

'The next job I do I shall clip the lady's ears off and send to the police officers, just for jolly, wouldn't you? Keep this letter back till I do a bit more work, then give it out straight.

'My knife's so nice and sharp, I want to get to work right away if I get a chance. Good luck,

'Yours truly,

'Jack the Ripper'

A postscript added: 'Don't mind me giving the trade name. Wasn't good enough to post this before I got all the red ink off my hands; curse it. No luck yet. They say I am a doctor now. Ha! Ha!'

The murders in Berner Street and Mitre Square forced the police to reconsider this remarkable letter in more serious vein. For in Berner Street the killer had obviously been disturbed and thwarted from carrying out his systematic mutilations. Was it an unsatiated blood-lust or a desire to fulfil his promise to post the police 'a pair of ears' that caused him to abandon his normal caution and seek another victim that same night? The doctors who performed the post mortem on Catherine Eddowes supplied a partial answer: all testified that 'the lobe of the right ear was obliquely cut through'. And Dr. Bagster Phillips stated that the lobe of Stride's left ear was torn.

Again, however, the Ripper must have been interrupted, for he did not finish off this self-imposed task. It seems certain that he had calculated exactly how long it would take before the policeman on patrol arrived back in Mitre Square, for the mutilations were much more hastily performed than was usually his practice.

Did he then retrace his steps into Whitechapel with the object of finding a third victim that night—a victim who would provide him with a pair of ears? And was that victim to have been the 'Rosy' whom P.C. Spicer saw sitting with the doctor on the dustbin?

But before the police had had time to consider these new posers a further letter was received from the Ripper. This time he wrote:

'I was not codding, dear old Boss, when I gave you the tip. You'll hear about Saucy Jack's work tomorrow. Double event this time. Number one squealed a bit. Couldn't finish straight off. Had not time to get ears for police. Thanks for keeping last letter back till I got to work again.'

Note the economy of phraseology in this communication compared to the previous one. It is the work of a man in a hurry. This letter was written and posted on 30 September.

Now this day was a Sunday and nothing was published in the press about the double murders until the Monday. It is true that anyone living in the East End would have heard about the murders on the Sunday, but he could not have obtained anything like the detail which appeared in the press the following day. Unless Jack the Ripper was the killer how could he have known that Elizabeth Stride had 'squealed a bit' (the 'stifled cry' heard by Mrs. Mortimer), or that an attempt had been made to clip off the ears?

Facsimiles of the two letters were sent to the newspapers and were reproduced on public notice-boards, calling for anyone who recognised the handwriting to report to the police. There was no response to this, but the publicity effectively labelled these East End crimes as the Jack the Ripper murders for all time.

When the body of Catherine Eddowes was examined by Dr. F. G. Brown, the police surgeon, he discovered that the left kidney and entrails had been removed. Some days afterwards what purported to be that kidney was posted to Mr. George Lusk, a builder of Alderney Road, Mile End, who had been prominent in the Vigilance Committee activities. This revolting object was packed in a cardboard box which contained a note:

'From Hell. Mr. Lusk, sir, I send you half the *kidne* I took from one woman, *prasarved* it for you, *tother* piece I fried and ate it; was very nice.'

Dr. Openshaw, pathological curator of the London Hospital Museum, examined the object and declared it was 'a portion of a human kidney (a "ginny" kidney, that is to say, the kidney of someone who drank heavily). I should say it belonged to a woman aged about forty-five and had been removed from the body within the last two weeks.'

A Dr. Reed made almost identical observations on the kidney, and in the view of both doctors this incident was not a practical joke.

'Both kidney and note were forwarded to me,' drily commented Major Smith. 'Unfortunately, as always happens, some clerk or assistant in the office was got at and the whole affair was public property next morning.'

But the letter-writer continued his bantering mood. 'Old Boss,' he wrote to Major Smith, 'you was *rite* it was the *lift kidny*; i was goin to hopperate again close to your ospittle—just as i was goin to drop my *nife* along of er bloomin throte them cusses of coppers spoilt the game but i guess i will be on the job soon and will send you another bit of innerds. Jack the Ripper.

'Oh have you seen the devle
with his mikerscope and scalpul
a lookin at a kidney
with a slide clocked up.'

Note the mixture of spelling in these epistles. Kidney is spelt 'kidne', 'kidny' and 'kidney'.

Newspapers and public alike scoffed at 'a new hoax on the police'. 'The kidney was that of a dog. Anyone can see that,' wrote one journalist. 'It was evidently taken out of a corpse after a post mortem,' said another. 'A medical student's prank,' was the comment of a third.

J. Hall Richardson, a correspondent of the *Daily Telegraph*, who was himself engaged in reporting the East End murders, complained that newspapermen during the Ripper crimes were constantly up against the inventions and fictitious stories of competitors in journalism.

'The Jack the Ripper letter, which is preserved in the Police Museum at New Scotland Yard, is the creation of an enterprising London journalist,' stated Sir Robert Anderson. But, just as this chief of the C.I.D. claimed to know the identity of the killer but declined to reveal it, so he refused to say who the letter-writer was. 'No public benefit would result and the traditions of my old department would suffer.'

For years two specimens of the Ripper's letters were kept in the Black Museum of New Scotland Yard, and privileged visitors were shown the smudge of red ink and told it was a blood-stain. Perhaps the authorities decided that the visitors were being hoaxed in an unseemly manner, or perhaps some less credulous visitor complained that it was ridiculous to pretend that red ink was blood when a simple scientific test would prove otherwise. At any rate the official police view was that the correspondence was a complete hoax and unworthy of a place in a serious crime museum. The letters have long since been removed, now being preserved in the Metropolitan Police's Central Registry files.

I find the hoax theory unsatisfactory. It is far too glib a method on the part of the officials to explain away something for which they had no solution. If Sir Robert Anderson knew the identity of the 'London journalist', why was he not prosecuted for causing a public mischief? Why for so long were the letters given a prominent position in the Black Museum—immediately on the left of the door as one entered? Why at no time during the period in which the crimes were committed did the police not issue a statement to the effect that the correspondence was the work of a practical joker with a warped sense of humour? They had every reason to do so as the Ripper's letters accentuated panic and gave the public the impression that the killer was totally unafraid of all measures to trap him.

It is irritating to pose rhetorical questions if one is not prepared to answer them. This I shall try to do. First, let it be admitted that there were many letters sent to the police, to the newspapers and to various individuals concerning the murders—probably at least 2,000 over a period of years. This does not take into account a dwindling, but still steady stream of letters, including many bogus 'confessions', until as recently as 1969.* Of this correspondence the bulk was of anonymous authorship; there were more than one hundred letters or cards signed Jack the Ripper, Jack or The Ripper. A fair percentage of these were obviously imitations of the original Jack and in a totally different handwriting.

According to the police the letters signed Ripper were de-

* The author was informed of a letter to a Sunday newspaper stating that the writer's father, 'when a boy of fifteen', was 'Jack the Ripper'! Name, address and death certificate of the father were given.

finitely not in the same handwriting as that of the originals. And at least one epistle signed Jack the Ripper was a fake. At Bradford Borough police court in October 1888, 'a respectable young woman named Maria Coroner, aged twenty-one' was charged with having written certain letters tending to cause a breach of the peace: they were signed Jack the Ripper. Thus it is correct to say that some of the correspondence was the work of imitators and hoaxers.

But the correspondence of the original Jack the Ripper is not so easily dismissed. There is no evidence that any single journalist benefited to the extent of a scoop as a result of these letters: had such a journalist wished to benefit himself he would hardly have sent his communications to the editor of a news agency, knowing that the information would eventually be passed on to all newspapers. And it hardly seems feasible that a London journalist would have taken the trouble to travel up to Liverpool to post a letter signed Jack the Ripper.

On 29 September this assiduous scribe wrote from Liverpool:

'Beware, I shall be at work on the 1st. and 2nd. inst. in Minories at twelve midnight, and I give the authorities a good chance, but there is never a policeman near when I am at work.

'Yours,
'Jack the Ripper'

Some time later this was followed by another brief missive:

'Prince William Street, Liverpool.
'What fools the police are. I even give them the name of the street where I am living.

'Yours,
'Jack the Ripper'

One police chief did not dismiss the correspondence as a hoax. Major Smith was sure that the writer had at least some detailed knowledge of the crimes. Despite the guffaws of his colleagues, he asked for a medical report on the kidney which had been sent in the post.

Meanwhile he studied the police surgeon's report on the mutilation of Eddowes' body and the kidney left in the corpse. This stated that 'the renal artery is about three inches long; two inches remained in the corpse, one inch was attached to the kidney. The kidney left in the corpse was in an advanced stage of Bright's disease.'

Major Smith compared these two reports together with those submitted by Drs. Openshaw and Reed and made this significant comment: 'The kidney sent to me was in an exactly similar state. Of more importance Mr. Sutton [one of the senior surgeons at the London hospital and an authority on the kidney and its diseases] said he would "pledge his reputation" that the kidney submitted to them had been put in spirits within a few hours of its removal from the body—thus effectively disposing of all hoaxes in connection with it.

'The body of anyone done to death by violence is not taken to the dissecting room, but an inquest is held first.'*

Presumably Major Smith was certain that the kidney was from the body of Catherine Eddowes, but wished to stress that no medical student or hoaxer could have had an opportunity of removing it from the corpse so soon after the murder.

There was another letter to Mr. Lusk:

'Say, Boss, you seem rare frightened. Guess I like to give you fits, but can't stop long enough to let you box of toys play copper games with me, but hope to see you when I don't hurry too much. Goodbye, Boss.'

Jack did not always confine his literary efforts to prose. Occasionally he made sallies in verse:

'I'm not a butcher,
I'm not a Yid,
Nor yet a foreign skipper,
But I'm your own light-hearted friend,
Yours truly, Jack the Ripper.'

* *From Constable to Commissioner,* Sir Henry Smith.

'The above queer verse was one of the first documents which I perused at Scotland Yard, for at the time the police post-bag bulged large with hundreds of anonymous communications on the East End murders,' wrote Sir Melville Macnaghten.

Butchers, Jews and skippers of coastal craft had all been under suspicion and Jack was ever ready to show how keenly he followed the police's investigations.

'Up and down the goddam town
Policemen try to find me.
But I ain't a chap yet to drown
In drink, or Thames or sea.'

This was a reference to a suggestion that the East End killer had committed suicide by jumping in the Thames.

'I've no time to tell you how
I came to be a killer.
But you should know, as time will show,
That I'm society's pillar.'

The last verse is perhaps the most enigmatic of all Jack's ventures in rhyming. It is surprisingly well phrased and the simplicity of its construction in no way detracts from its merits. It may seem odd that the man who could write such drivel as that contained in the first letter to the Central News Agency could compose anything like this. The phrase 'that I'm society's pillar' has a subtle suggestion of understatement about it. This is not the language of a sexual megalomaniac who believes he has been detailed by the Almighty to destroy harlots. Yet in more economical language it fits in with the writer's earlier diatribe—'I am down on whores and shan't quit ripping them till I do get buckled.'

Obviously Jack had as many 'masks' as Wainewright. From the point of view of a crude moron who had a 'down' on whores, he could swiftly switch to that of a self-righteous arbitrator who saw himself as a defender of society against the scourge of prostitution. Yet the emphasis is all important: he was '*society's* pillar', not an instrument of divine vengeance.

The man was such an incorrigible joker that one could never be sure whether he had his tongue in his cheek all the time. It was the jocularity of Jack which caused the police to believe he must be a hoaxer. Subconsciously, the Victorian psychological viewpoint manifested itself; that is to say, they could not imagine a mad man making a joke about his crimes. A maniac, they argued falsely, must be a person without a sense of humour.

Mr. L. Forbes Winslow, a specialist in mental and nervous diseases, however, took a very different view both of Jack the writer and Jack the killer. He devoted considerable time to analysing the psychological implications of the East End murders, and, to use his own words, he 'gave heart and soul to the study of the mystery'. He was convinced that the murderer was 'not a wild-eyed maniac, but an insane monster, possessing both shrewdness, caution and intelligence, yet alert to the consequence of being captured, and cunning as all lunatics are'.*

Mr. Forbes Winslow believed that in crimes of this kind the influence of the moon was important and he stressed that the murders were either committed when the new moon rose, or when it had entered upon its last quarter. Certainly this pattern of events is true in the case of some murders, but it could equally and more usefully be shown that invariably crimes were committed during a weekend—between Friday night and Sunday morning.

Views such as these irritated the police and they tended to look upon Mr. Forbes Winslow as an unmitigated nuisance and a hindrance. All the detectives working on the cases knew him and at one time his ubiquity at the scene of the crimes caused them to check up on his movements. There was, of course, not the slightest evidence to link him with the murders.

The theory that this specialist developed was that the killer was a homicidal maniac of religious views, who believed he had a divine mission to fulfil in killing as many whores as

* *Recollections of Forty Years,* by L. Forbes Winslow.

possible. The only way to catch so cunning a fiend, he argued, was to draw him off his guard by expressing sympathy with his motives. For this purpose he proposed to publish in all London newspapers the following Personal Column notice:

'A gentleman who is strongly opposed to the presence of fallen women in the streets of London would like to co-operate with someone with a view to their suppression.'

Scotland Yard refused to entertain the idea. One can hardly blame them: any such notice would have drawn a heavy post-bag from cranks and fanatical reformers, not to mention ribald jokers, without being in the least likely to lure so wily a person as the Ripper into being indiscreet.

Possibly Mr. Forbes Winslow was impressed by the remark overheard by William Marshall in Berner Street: 'You would say anything but your prayers.'

On 19 October came a letter from the mysterious Jack, stating that 'the next murder will be on 9 November'. As will be seen later, the next Ripper crime occurred on this date. Mr. Forbes Winslow asserts that this letter was 'in the same handwriting as that found under the archway'. Presumably he is referring to the wall in the entrance to the staircase on which the message 'The Jewes are not the men to be blamed for nothing' appeared. Though this writing was washed off the wall by orders of Sir Charles Warren, Mr. Forbes Winslow, who was nearly always at the scene of the crime shortly after the police arrived, may have seen the message before it was removed. He had kept facsimiles of the Ripper's letters and was skilled in copying other people's handwriting. At the same time too much attention should not be paid to his judgement.

There is, however, some corroboration for his statement. Dr. Thomas Dutton, who at the time was living in Westbourne Villas, Bayswater, compiled over a period of sixty years three volumes of handwritten *Chronicles of Crime*, based on his experiences as a doctor. Prior to the East End murders he had been a leading figure in the Chichester and West Sussex Microscopic Society and had specialised in micro-photography.

'I made micro-photographs of 128 specimens of the alleged correspondence of Jack the Ripper to the police and other institutions and individuals. Of these at least thirty-four were definitely in the same handwriting. This is not to assert that all the remaining letters and verses were fakes, or written by other persons. Some undoubtedly were, but the authentic letter-writer was, to judge from the micro-photographs, deliberately disguising his true method of calligraphy, and, in doing so, he not unnaturally fell into the error of frequently forming his C's, H's, R's and T's in a variety of ways.

'Some letters appeared to be in a different handwriting when looked at with the naked eye. It was only by comparing a large number of letters and noting the frequency with which certain letters were formed differently and by examining the micro-photographs that one could detect positively minute similarities in writing which, superficially at least, seemed as though it could not have been the work of the same man.

'I often thought that the police paid too little attention to these letters, and it is certain that, had the crimes been committed today, our highly specialised detective force would have made more of them. They assumed that several hoaxers were at work and therefore regarded every new letter or warning received as of no significance.

'The fact that there was more than one letter-writer does not detract from the importance of the thirty-four which were in the same handwriting. And thirty-four were the minimum number of letters which Jack wrote. Micro-photography in the 'eighties was still in its infancy, and I was only an amateur at it. But I dare say that modern methods would have shown many more to be the same man's work.

'The writing was disguised to appear to be that of an uneducated man on some occasions; on others it was that of a painstaking clerk. The same with the phraseology. But even that was marked by "lapses" into literacy, especially in Jack's effective essays into verse. To quote one example:

"Eight little whores, with no hope of heaven,
Gladstone may save one, then there'll be seven.
Seven little whores begging for a shilling,
One stays in Henage Court, then there's a killing.

Six little whores, glad to be alive,
One sidles up to Jack, then there are five.
Four and whore rhyme aright,
So do three and me,
I'll set the town alight
Ere there are two.

Two little whores, shivering with fright,
Seek a cosy doorway in the middle of the night.
Jack's knife flashes, then there's but one,
And the last one's the ripest for Jack's idea of fun."

'It may not be verse in the accepted sense, but this is certainly not the composition of an illiterate. Jack would sometimes misspell words deliberately, then forget later on and write a word correctly. It was the same with his punctuation. He wrote "Jewes" with an extra *e* when he scrawled his message in chalk on the wall, and which the police so stupidly washed off. But he also spelt the word correctly in some letters.

'I was asked by the police to photograph the message on the wall before it was washed off, but Sir Charles Warren was so insistent that the message must not be preserved in any form that he ordered the police to destroy the prints I sent them. But the micro-photograph which I took definitely established that the writing was the same as that in some of the letters.'

Handwriting experts existed in the 'eighties, but they were notoriously unreliable and many judicial warnings were given to this effect. In three prominent trials after this date—those of Edalji, Adolf Beck and Archer Shee—wrongful convictions were made on the strength of the evidence of handwriting experts. Those were the exceptions; in nine cases out of ten the police were loath to accept the testimony of any such 'experts', even when this meant foregoing a prosecution.

The Times crime reporter had this to say about the handwriting: 'The language is full of Americanisms; the writing is clear and plain and disguised in part . . . it is that of a person accustomed to write in a round hand like that employed by clerks in offices.'

Mr. Forbes Winslow referred to a letter as late as July 1889, purporting to come from the Ripper, but he doesn't make it clear whether this tallied with the original correspondence or not. This letter warned the police that there would be another killing that month. It was followed by the murder of Alice McKenzie in Castle Alley, Whitechapel, that month.

'The first definite clue that came to me was on 30 August 1889,' said Mr. Forbes Winslow. 'A woman, with whom I was in communication, came to me and said that a man had spoken to her in Worship Street, Finsbury, who wanted her to go down a court with him. She refused, but followed the man until he went into a house in Finsbury.

'On the morning after 17 July [*the date of McKenzie's murder*] she saw him washing blood off his hands in the yard of the house referred to. When the house was searched the man was gone.'

The ubiquitous Mr. Winslow must have been one of the most fanatical amateur detectives who ever lived. He also learned of a 'gentlemanly looking man' who engaged a large bed-sitting-room in a lodging house, where he kept nine suits, as many hats and three pairs of rubbers, one of which he always wore when he went out at night. He invariably kept late hours.

On the night of 7 August 1888—the night of Martha Turner's death—he arrived back at the lodging house at 4 a.m., 'looking very rough'. The lodging-house-keeper was sitting up late and asked the man what had happened. The latter's story was that his watch had been stolen and that he had reported the matter at the police station. This subsequently proved to be untrue.

Mr. Winslow's interest was aroused because the man seemed to answer in every detail his own mental portrait of the killer. He was religious and a woman-hater. At 8 a.m. each day he attended service at St. Paul's Cathedral, while he spent many hours in his room laboriously writing lengthy tracts on religious matters. So it is not surprising when one learns that Mr. Winslow triumphantly took possession of a pair of the man's rubber shoes, which were 'covered with dried human blood' and that he confronted the police with his evidence.

The police were not impressed and they refused to cooperate with Mr. Winslow in his somewhat melodramatic scheme to arrest the suspect on the steps of St. Paul's Cathedral. 'I was severely criticised for informing the *New York Herald* of my clues,' said Winslow. 'But there were no more murders after the news of my researches had been published.'

The findings of this amateur sleuth are not particularly illuminating, and, negligent as the police may have been in some instances, they were not as stupid or as indifferent as this pansophistic medical specialist averred. He was a man obsessed with a theory, and the truth is that he was only looking for someone who fitted in with that theory. He soon became the target for crackpot letter-writers other than the Ripper, some of whom led him sadly astray.

Mr. Winslow makes the assertion that the Ripper letters were 'written by someone not accustomed to using a pen', which contradicts the view previously given. If this were so, and if, as he insisted, the killer were an intelligent and educated man, why did he pay so much attention to them? Years afterwards a letter from Melbourne convinced him that Jack the Ripper had been in Australia and had then left for South Africa. Once again he was convinced he had tracked down the killer, and once again the police were equally convinced that he had been fooled.

The Forbes Winslow theory was that the killer suffered from a form of epilepsy and that his murders were unpremeditated and probably committed when his mind was so unbalanced that he didn't know what he was doing. Thus, argued the specialist, he returned home sublimely unconscious of what he had done. This assertion doesn't fit in with Winslow's previous statement about 'shrewdness, caution and intelligence, yet alert to the consequence of being captured'. True, the Mitre Square murder, as far as the choice of a victim was concerned, must have been unpremeditated, but each crime was so diabolically and cunningly planned that the deed itself must have been premeditated. Nor would most modern psychologists agree with Winslow's reasoning. Inspector Walter Dew, the man who caught Crippen, and who also took part in the hunt for the Ripper, rejected Winslow's theory on the grounds that as the killer always had a weapon with him, his murders must obviously have been premeditated.

Also epileptics who indulge in murder are more likely to strangle their victims than to cut their throats.

Interesting is Major Smith's account of a letter he received four days after the Mitre Square murder. 'It was sent to me unstamped at my office, and I had to pay twopence for it. The writer was complimentary to me and anxious to see me, as he had a lot to tell about the murders.'

The writer said he was on ticket-of-leave and he hadn't reported to the police. For this reason he did not propose to call at the police station as this could only result in his being detained. If Major Smith would write to him and make an appointment for a secret meeting, he would oblige. He gave an address in Hoxton and added: 'The man you want is not in London. He's in Manchester. What you think is his writing isn't.'

Major Smith wrote, making an appointment to see the man at 10 p.m. 'in one of the quietest squares in the West End. I assured him I would be alone. I told him to stand under the lamp at the north-west end of the gardens.'

Punctually the man arrived. He was 'five feet three in height, stoutly built, black-bearded, ugly and forbidding'.

'Have you come to meet anyone, my man?' inquired Major Smith.

'No, I haven't.'

'Well, I have.'

There was an awkward pause. The man retreated backwards a few steps and then stood silently facing Major Smith for some five minutes. Then he turned abruptly and walked away.

'After the meeting I had a note from my friend,' wrote Major Smith.* ' "Now that I know I can trust you, I'll be at Old Jewry as soon as I can." '

* *From Constable to Commissioner.*

But there was no further news.

Undoubtedly the correspondence of maniacs, practical jokers, people with a grudge against their neighbours and would-be amateur detectives wasted a good deal of the police's time. Maybe, too, it befogged men's judgement and so irritated the authorities that they rejected all such 'evidence' as futile. But the comments of Dr. Dutton seem worthy of further attention. There was certainly one letter-writer, the most prolific of them all, whose handiwork called for more than a perfunctory glance. Major Smith obviously took this view, but he was one of the few who did.

The vital fact which emerges from all this is that only in the original Jack's letters was there information which only the killer could have obtained. It might be argued that it was a mere coincidence that the writer forecast the murders of 9 November 1888, and 17 July 1889. It could equally be claimed that when he said he would 'be at work on the 1st and 2nd inst. in Minories at twelve midnight' he prophesied wrongly as the murders were committed at least a day earlier. Yet his second murder on this night was carried out very close to the Minories and he would hardly be likely to give the police the exact time and place of his intended crimes, nor in fact would it be possible for him to do so. But his indication that he would clip off the ears of one victim and his undoubted attempt to do so, coupled with an apology for failure, are surely more than coincidence. When one sets these facts alongside his revelation that Elizabeth Stride cried out and the incident of the kidney, one can scarcely fall back on the excuse of coincidence any longer.

From this correspondence emerges a picture, if not of the man, at least of the mask. How much of the man is allowed to peep out of the mask one cannot be sure. The mask is that of a crude and moronic joker. The man himself was able to write in a variety of styles, though the outlook was always the same —a hatred of whores and a Puck-like delight in making the flesh creep. There can be no doubt at all that he read his newspapers avidly, that he followed every story published about the investigation of the crimes and was aware (for example, his jibe at Gladstone) of the most scurrilous gossip of the day. It has since been established that Gladstone's hours of relaxation—if one can call them that—were spent in prowling the streets in an attempt to rescue and reform whores. But the most remarkable feature of the correspondence and verse, with very few exceptions, is its irrepressible sense of fun. Jack revels in every aspect of the murders, not gloatingly, not pansexually, but in sheer glee and impishness. It is this very impudence which is the most effective disguise of all.

An analysis of the handwriting in the Ripper correspondence was made in an article in *The Criminologist* of August 1968 by Mr. C. M. MacLeod, a graphologist.

Mr. MacLeod argues that it is entirely possible to discern from handwriting the writer's attitudes towards sex and sexual violence. He went on to say that two specimens of the Ripper's handwriting revealed 'a propensity to cruelly perverted sexuality to a degree that even the most casual amateur graphologist could hardly mistake'.

Divining that there were two distinct letter-writers, Mr. MacLeod said that if there was only one real Jack the Ripper he would cast his vote for the writer of the letters to Mr. Lusk: 'he shows tremendous drive in the vicious forward thrust of his overall writing and great cunning in his covering-up of strokes; that is, the re-tracing of one stroke of a letter over another, rendering it illegible while appearing to clarify . . . I would say that this writer was capable of conceiving any atrocity and of carrying it out in an organised way'.

A Fleet Street journalist would hardly be likely to resist giving an impression of greater realism if he had composed the letters. Also he would not have employed occasional Americanisms; if he had wished to suggest the writer was an American he would have filled every letter and verse with such phrases. Jack only occasionally used American phrases such as 'quit ripping', 'boss', 'buckled' and 'codding' and then mostly in his longer epistles. When Americanisms occur they have the appearance of being accidental and not deliberate. It is important to note that they were not Americanisms already adopted in this country, but phrases only heard the other side of the Atlantic.

Twice Jack the Ripper wrote the number 7 with a horizontal stroke across the downward stroke and the number 1 with a downward flourish from the top of the figure to the left in the continental style. As on other occasions he wrote both figures in the normal English style this may have been another attempt at disguising his handwriting. But the fact remains that he was conversant with a continental style of writing, which would be unusual for anyone in this country other than a foreigner, or at least a well-educated Englishman who had travelled on the continent and was in the habit of receiving letters from France and elsewhere.

If Jack the letter-writer was Jack the killer, then he must have had an iron nerve and astonishing confidence in his ability to avoid capture. Dr. Dutton opined that he was not a skilled forger, that had he been one there would have been fewer variations in the writing. 'Possibly he wanted the police to think that not all his letters were written by the same person. If so, he certainly succeeded in foxing some of them.'

The references in the letters to the Minories and to such an obscure alley as Henage Court suggest the writer had an intimate knowledge of the East End. That he travelled seems certain, for Dr. Dutton not only confirms that the Liverpool letters were in his hand, but mentions 'a communication from Glasgow which stated:

' "Think I'll quit using my nice sharp knife. Too good for whores. Have come here to buy a Scotch dirk. Ha! Ha! That will tickle up their ovaries." '

And the doctor adds: 'The only mention in the press of a specific organ being removed from the Ripper's victims concerned the kidneys. Though the ovaries were on one occasion cut out of the body, the press merely referred to the removal of "a certain organ".'

Mr. Leonard Matters, who investigated the subject of the handwriting in the first letter and postcard, has this to say: 'The calligraphy [of the letter] was excellent. It is the sort of letter that might have been written by a young man after careful tuition at a night school. But it is not the writing of a man of middle age. . . . The postcard may or may not have been written by the same person, though the probability is that it was. This is by no means apparent, however. There is a striking degeneration in the quality of the penmanship.

'I should say at the first glance that two different hands had written the two documents. If this is correct, then obviously the second writer must have known precisely what was said in the first communication: otherwise he could not have followed up the argument.'

8

Inspector Abberline makes a discovery

Sir Charles Warren's fear of a wave of anti-semitic riots, supposedly his reason for ordering the removal of Jack the Ripper's chalked message on the wall, could not have been based on first-hand knowledge of the East End.

The probability is that the Commissioner of the Metropolitan Police had never visited this area before the Sunday of the two murders. Had he done so he would have observed that the vast Jewish population of Whitechapel, Stepney and neighbouring parishes was, by and large, as honest, industrious and co-operative as any of the other communities and that anti-semitism had never been a serious problem here.

It is true that the Jews were often envied because they worked harder and earned more than the average Cockney. But the English of the East End, though they affected to despise all foreigners (and they regarded Jews as such), were far too apathetic and tolerant to carry this dislike to the point of violent antagonism. They realised philosophically that a lot of the work they themselves were not prepared to do was willingly undertaken by the Jews, this being especially true of civic duties. A jury in Whitechapel had been known to consist entirely of Cohens, and, as we have seen, leaders of the Jewish community and the more prosperous of their shop-keepers had actually taken a lead in forming vigilance committees.

The press contained vague hints of anti-semitism which suggested the situation was tense. But in none of the newspapers were there any factual accounts of anti-semitic demonstrations and certainly no suggestion of riots. What anti-semitism there was during the Ripper murders was not inspired in the East End. It was prevalent in some sections of the Metropolitan Police and notably among some of the senior officers. But its most foolish and ill-timed manifestation occurred in the columns of *The Times* shortly before the murders in Berner Street and Mitre Square. The Vienna correspondent of this newspaper referred to a Jew named Ritter who, some years earlier, had murdered and mutilated a woman near Cracow. During his trial he was said to have tried to justify his actions by contending that the Talmud actually dictated such a course of action to any Jew who had had intercourse with a Christian woman.

This case was linked and compared with the East End murders and the implication made by *The Times* was clear: was some Jewish fanatic invoking a religious decree as an excuse for mutilating Christian women? Not unnaturally this suggestion soon filtered from the breakfast tables of Society to the servants' quarters and from there to taproom and tavern. But, though grossly exaggerated when passed from mouth to mouth, it failed to provoke any serious outburst of anti-semitism even in Whitechapel. It drew from the Chief Rabbi an indignant protest that there were absolutely no grounds for the statement that the Talmud countenanced such bestial practices.

Sir Robert Anderson showed marked prejudices against the Jews and was convinced that the 'Ripper' belonged to this community. Probably because of this, Sir Charles Warren, who detested Anderson, took the opposite view and it would appear that his determination to check any anti-semitism was one of his relatively few virtues. But, being a bungler by nature, he set about this in quite the wrong manner. For, when the news reached the East Enders that he had ordered the message to be washed off the wall, people began to say: 'The police are covering up for the Jews.'

There was even a suggestion in the press that the messages had been written by a Jew because in some dialects and in some countries the word 'Jews' was spelt 'Juwes'. There was considerable argument as to whether the writing was Juwes or Jewes. These arguments were largely irrelevant as nowhere, so far as can be ascertained, is there such spelling of this word.

It could, however, logically be argued that there were two distinct interpretations of the phrase. Either this was ungrammatical English, the meaning of which was that the Jews were not to be blamed for the crimes, or the writer was employing the double negative (always used in Russian, for example), and meant that the Jews were not blamed without good reason.

If it were a question of searching for a race or sect who practised mutilation of the human body after death, the obvious choice would have been among lower-class Malays and Lascars, of whom there were many in the East End. Such mutilation of a bestial nature, notably disembowelling, was a practice among these people in parts of Asia. It was a sign of the murderer's contempt for his victim.

Major Smith publicly ridiculed Sir Robert Anderson's statement that the Ripper was a Polish Jew, though Major Arthur Griffiths, a crime-writer of the period, supported Anderson's theory. He mentioned 'a Polish Jew, a known lunatic, who was at large in the district of Whitechapel at the time of the murder, and who, having developed homicidal tendencies, was afterwards confined to an asylum. This man was said to resemble the murderer by the one person who got a glimpse of him—the police constable in Mitre Court.'*

This statement is not strictly accurate, and neither Anderson nor Griffiths advanced any reasons for his assertions which were hotly disputed by other police officers working on the case. Griffiths, at a later date, largely contradicted his story by suggesting the Ripper was one of two other suspects.

Anderson, however, was unshakable in his convictions. In a preface to H. L. Adam's *The Police Encyclopaedia*, he wrote: 'Despite the lucubrations of many an amateur Sherlock Holmes, there was no doubt whatever as to the identity of the criminal [the Ripper], and if our London detectives possessed the powers and might have recourse to the methods

* *Mysteries of Police and Crime*, Vol. I, by Major Arthur Griffiths.

of foreign police forces, he would have been brought to justice.'

Meanwhile Inspector Abberline had theories of his own. 'The trouble is,' he told a colleague, 'that if anyone talks of a foreigner, most people in the East End think of a Jew. And you can be damned sure when it comes to an identity parade, it's the Jew people pick out and that's why we always get the wrong man.'

'Well, what does that prove?' asked his colleague.

'It proves we are wasting our time putting up Jews in identity parades. Look at the number of wrong arrests we've made. It isn't that the average East Ender hates the Jews, but he regards them as more foreign than Chinese or even Poles.'

Abberline's theory was that the killer was a foreigner, but he did not think he was a Jew. Murder by throat-cutting followed by mutilation was not, according to statistics, either a typically Jewish or a typically British crime. Sexual maniacs of the type of the Ripper were then more to be found on the continent of Europe or in Asia than in Britain.

So Abberline decided to check up on non-Jewish foreigners. He studied the statistics of the Metropolitan Police and consulted police officers who had knowledge of foreign criminals. A few thought the killer might be a Chinese, a Malay or a Lascar, but the majority took the view that it was unlikely that a person of any of these nationalities could escape detection for so long. Also there was the indisputable fact that not a single description of suspects, or of people seen with the victims about the time of the murders, tallied with that of a Chinese, a Malay or a Lascar.

And here again Dr. Thomas Dutton enters the story. The doctor had travelled widely after qualifying at Durham and Edinburgh universities. He had been ship's surgeon aboard the s.s. *Elysia* and, being interested in criminology, had studied foreign criminals. Dutton and Abberline were friends and the latter sought the doctor's advice. Dutton's suggestion was that if Abberline was looking for a foreigner, he should look for one who might pass for an Englishman. 'I would keep a special watch on Poles and Russians. They could pass for Englishmen at a pinch. They are fundamentally barbarous, treat women with scant respect and tend to have brutal natures, sexually speaking.'

Dutton added another point: 'You will find a larger number of Poles and Russians with a smattering of surgery and a knowledge of anatomy than in almost any other race. It's quite astonishing, in fact. I had to perform an operation once aboard the *Elysia* and I'd injured my right hand. 'Pon my soul if I didn't find a Russian seaman who had studied as a surgeon's assistant and was able to help me out.'

The doctor also ruled out Lascars and Malays on the grounds that they would not possess the anatomical knowledge which the Ripper had shown.

Abberline was perplexed by the diversity of medical opinions on the Ripper cases. More often than not the surgeons who examined the bodies were at variance with one another. Dr. Bagster Phillips, for example, thought that the method of killing Stride was 'markedly different' from that employed when Annie Chapman was murdered. Of course, this may have been due to the fact that Stride called out and that the killer was disturbed before he could complete his task; certainly there was no mutilation of Stride's body. Dr. Blackwell, on the other hand, formed the opinion that Stride was pulled backwards by her silk scarf and thought the man who slew her also killed Eddowes and the other victims of the Ripper.

There was considerable conflict of opinion and a certain amount of professional jealousy between the City Police surgeon, Dr. F. G. Brown, Dr. Sequeira, the divisional police surgeon, and Dr. William Saunders.

Dr. Brown stated that when Eddowes was found the intestines were 'drawn out to a large extent and placed over the right shoulder', or, as one writer more fancifully put it, 'part of the entrails were twined in a festoon round her neck'. In fact, however, this description was quite accurate: the arrangement of the mutilated parts of the corpse was such, according to Dr. Brown, that 'they made a pattern. It was obviously done by design. The liver was sliced through, a piece of the intestines was quite detached from the body and placed between the left arm and the body. The way in which the mutilation had been effected showed that the perpetrator of the crime had some anatomical knowledge.'

Drs. Sequeira and Saunders disagreed. They insisted not only that there was no design by the killer on any particular organ, but that no great anatomical skill was shown. Two against one may seem convincing evidence, but Dr. Brown refused to be shaken in his insistence that 'anyone carrying out this deed would need a good deal of knowledge as to the position of the organs in the abdominal cavity'. As to any suggestion of the degree of skill revealed, surely the point to be borne in mind was that this was carried out at great speed in a surprisingly short time and in the darkest corner of the square. Another important factor in assessing the reliability of Dr. Brown's evidence is that he made a sketch of the body exactly as it was found in the square and with detailed notes on the sketch.

The Coroner seemed impressed by Dr. Brown's arguments. 'But what about the removal of the kidney?' he asked at the inquest. 'Would this require surgical skill?'

'It would take a great deal of skill and of knowledge as to the position of the kidney to remove it. The kidney could easily be overlooked, for it is covered by a membrane,' replied Dr. Brown.

'Can you as a professional man assign any reason for the removal of certain organs of the body?'

'I cannot think of any.'

Dr. Brown's other telling point was that the killer made sure of silencing his victim by first severing the vocal chords: this, in his opinion, called for anatomical and surgical knowledge.

Professor Francis E. Camps wrote an interesting little monogram on the Ripper cases, based on findings in the archives of the London Hospital, in *The Criminologist* of February 1968. As pathologist and Professor of Forensic Medicine at London University, he was admirably qualified to make professional observations. He referred to the fact that the murders 'were associated with far less spillage of blood than might have been expected. This is in direct contradiction with the fact that they were all stated to have died without calling out. The probable explanation may lie in a comment in a contemporary number of the *Lancet* that it was strange that their faces were congested under the circumstances, which suggests that the absence of a cry was due to strangulation being the real cause of death, a common practice of sexual murderers.' There was, of course, one murder when a cry was heard and this was the one in which the killer failed to finish his work to his own satisfaction.

Abberline decided to accept Dr. Brown's theory rather than that of Drs. Sequeira and Saunders. He made up his mind to limit his search to a foreigner with surgical knowledge and anatomical skill. This line of investigation had been strengthened by the information he had obtained from a German who had left a foreigners' club close to Mitre Square shortly before the murder occurred. He had seen Catherine Eddowes with a man whom he described as 'young, about middle height, with a waxed, pointed moustache, dressed in something like navy serge and with a deerstalker's cap, with a peak both fore and aft'. The German was sure this man was not British: 'he didn't have the bearing of a Briton, nor of a German, nor a Frenchman, but he was certainly a foreigner'.

Abberline made calls at the various clubs for foreigners in the East End, hoping to find someone answering to this description. He did not find his man, but he learned a great deal, especially about Poles and Russians. Many years previously the British people had evinced a strong sympathy for Polish refugees from tyranny in their own country. So much so that, Henry Mayhew tells us, 'to be a Pole, and in distress, was almost a sufficient introduction and there were few English families who did not entertain as friend or visitor one of these unfortunate and suffering patriots. So excellent an opportunity for that class of foreign swindlers which haunt roulette tables . . . the "destitute Pole", with false military documents and stories of miraculous escapes from Russian prisons, became a feature of the underworld.'

But in recent years more Russians than Poles had been

flocking into the East End. They had been disregarded by the police—foolishly, as it transpired—and allowed to form clubs of their own in Whitechapel, Houndsditch, Stepney and other centres, where they established compact political organisations. Anarchism, that political theory which propounds that any form of government is bad, had found its chief propagandist in Proudhon, and his ideas had been enthusiastically adopted by such Russian thinkers as Bakunin and Kropotkin. Since then theoretical anarchism had been superseded, in Russia at any rate, by the doctrine of 'propaganda by deed', on the principle that the more dastardly the deed the more effective the propaganda. From about 1883 onwards most European countries had passed severe repressive measures against Anarchists, but Britain had taken no action, with the result that London's East End became the safest refuge they could find.

No one has yet solved the problem of the exact links between anarchy as a political philosophy and unbridled crime. Lombrose went so far as to write his history of Anarchists with the sub-heading *A Study in Criminal Psychology and Sociology*. But, though many of the Anarchists were criminals and often criminal lunatics, there is a good deal of evidence that the Czarist secret police manufactured many of the indictments against them.

Detective-Sergeant B. Leeson, in his book *Lost London*, spoke of 'Nihilists and Anarchists overrunning the East End of London. There is no doubt that Russian *agents provocateur* were already at work, sowing the seeds of the revolutionary movement which those forefathers of Bolshevism hoped would permeate the Metropolis and thence spread all over the world.'

This is a slight over-simplification of what was a much subtler and more complex movement which had its origins in men who would have detested Leninist or Stalinist communism. But in the 'eighties there were at least seven such revolutionary clubs in East London. One named the Jubilee, and founded under this innocuous title in 1887, was the centre of the Anarchists; it also had a West End headquarters known more romantically as the Bohemian Club.

To all these centres Abberline tried to gain admission, but he failed and no attempt was made by the C.I.D. to place a Russian-speaking agent in them. But he found another method of keeping watch on a list of suspects he had drawn up: several of the Poles and Russians were employed as assistants in barbers' shops, so the inspector decided to visit some of these establishments.

One day he called at a hairdresser's shop in Whitechapel High Street. He was reading a newspaper while waiting his turn to be shaved when he heard someone call 'Ludwig'.

This name made Abberline start. For Ludwig had been the name of the German who had been wrongly arrested on the suspicion that he was Jack the Ripper. Cautiously, over the top of his paper, Abberline looked at the man addressed. He was astonished at the likeness between the foreign-looking barber's assistant and the man they had let go.

The detective-inspector returned to Scotland Yard to check up on Ludwig. But he was disappointed. Despite the likeness, the hairdresser's assistant was not the same man. Nevertheless, thought Abberline, I'll have another look at this chap. He returned to Whitechapel High Street only to find that his man had disappeared.

'We called him Ludwig,' said the barber, 'but his name's Schloski, or something like that. I don't know where he's gone. He was a strange chap.'

'What nationality would he be?'

'A Pole, I think.'

It was some weeks before Abberline tracked down Schloski, who had taken another job in a barber's shop in West Green Road, Tottenham. There again he was known as Schloski, which was probably the nearest an Englishman could get to the correct pronunciation of his real name—Klosowski.

Severin Antoniovich Klosowski had been born on 14 December 1865 in Nargornak, a village in the district of Kolo, Poland. On a passport issued on 24 November 1886 he had been described as 'height medium, hair dark, eyes blue, birthmarks none'. But more interesting was the information about his occupation—*feldscher* in the Russian Army.

Abberline rushed round to see his friend, Dr. Dutton. 'Tell me, Doctor,' he inquired, 'what is a *feldscher* and what would he be doing in the Russian Army?'

'A *feldscher* is an assistant to a doctor in Poland and Russia. There is nothing quite to be compared to the post in this country. How can I put it? He's a cross between an apothecary and a junior surgeon, with a smattering of knowledge of both medicine and surgery. Usually a very useful chap for an assistant. Wish we had something like it over here. Of course, there's the danger that they may fake a few certificates and become a quack.'

'But what would a *feldscher* be doing in a hairdressing establishment?'

'Well, if it was a barber's, he could be the barber's assistant. On the continent, and especially in Poland and Russia, a barber's shop is rather different from what you get over here. In fact, the barber is the poor man's doctor. Once upon a time barbers did a spot of minor doctoring in this country. The red and white barber's pole is a relic of those days, and it is really not a hairdresser's sign, but an indication that bleeding and cupping are carried out on the premises.

'In Russia barbers often employ what they call barber's surgeons, and that is just what a *feldscher* often is. If you've found a Polish or Russian *feldscher* working in a hairdresser's here, the probability is that he naturally migrated to the only type of business he knows. But he must find shaving rather dull after bleeding.'

Nobody knew much about Klosowski. There wasn't even any record of when he had arrived in this country, though it would appear to be some time between 1887 and 1888.* Abberline discovered a hairdresser's traveller named Wolff Levisohn, who had known Klosowski in Poland and had seen him in Warsaw in 1887. The next occasion he saw him was in the hairdresser's in Whitechapel High Street in the summer

* Ex-Superintendent A. F. Neil in *Forty Years of Man-Hunting* states that Klosowski came to Britain in June 1887, and that he lived at 54, Cranbrook Street, Green Street, London, E.

of 1888. 'He had not been long in England then,' said Levisohn.

Unfortunately for Abberline he had no evidence against Klosowski and was therefore only able to give a limited amount of time to checking up on him. He knew it would be useless to discuss the matter with his seniors who were now ultra-cautious in their approach to the case as they had been precipitate and rash in the panic arrests made earlier on. Each day seemed to bring some new incident to make the police look foolish: late in October Alfred Napier Blanchard, a canvasser of Handsworth, Birmingham, was charged, on his own confession, with being the Whitechapel killer. Inevitably he proved to be another victim of alcoholic delusions.

But Abberline was impressed by the fact that Klosowski closely resembled some of the descriptions of a man seen with the Ripper's victims shortly before they were murdered. He was a repulsive, brutish-looking character, about five feet six inches in height, possessing great strength. Sometimes he affected a short moustache, curled at the ends, at others he sported a beard which heightened his ferocity of appearance.

Had such a man roamed the West End instead of the mean streets of Whitechapel and Stepney, mused Abberline, he would surely have been picked up by the police. 'Any prostitute who consorted with such a villainous-looking person must be in a desperate plight,' he told Dr. Dutton. 'He would scare the daylights out of a West End whore.'

But, as Dr. Dutton pointed out, the victims of the Ripper were the dregs of prostitution, far from young, mostly inveterate drunkards and in every case so hard up as not to have the price of a bed for the night. 'In any event,' added the doctor, 'ugliness often has a peculiar attraction for a certain type of woman.'

And Klosowski apparently had little difficulty in making himself agreeable to women who were far from being prostitutes and in being accepted by them on terms of affection. He was reputed to be more than just a lady-killer, but a notorious night-prowler and an insatiable lecher. But he changed his address and place of work so frequently that it was far from easy to keep track of him.

Abberline planned to have him shadowed and a police officer went down to the shop in West Green Road, Tottenham, with the object of following him home. But he was a day too late: Klosowski had left this place of employment the day before. It was several days later that it was learned he had acquired a shop for himself in High Road, Tottenham.

There was, however, one great objection to Abberline's theory that Klosowski might be the Ripper. The Pole did not appear to be a man who made casual liaisons with women, but one intent on setting up home with them and combining the services of a housekeeper and cook with those of a mistress. True, he rang the changes with his women, but the tactics were always the same. At one time he was living with two women in the same room, one an Englishwoman, the other a Pole who claimed him as her husband and insisted on sharing his *ménage*. It seemed probable that she was blackmailing Klosowski. Remarkably enough this *ménage à trois* in one room worked extremely well. There were no complaints of rows between them, both women appeared equally devoted to Klosowski and, surprisingly, were friendly to each other.*

Had there been in 1888 the advantages of radio communications, teleprinters and Interpol, Scotland Yard might have been persuaded to take a keener interest in the Pole. It was not until many years later that all the facts of his early life came to light. He had been registered at birth as a Roman Catholic, and, in his youth, had been given an exemplary character. Apprenticed to a surgeon named Moshko Rappaport in Zorlen, he had obtained numerous certificates for proficiency and had taken a degree as a junior surgeon. 'Of diligent and exemplary conduct, Severin Klosowski has studied with zeal the science of surgery, (*signed*) Moshko Rappaport, senior surgeon', read one certificate.

For a time he worked as a hospital assistant and later as a 'barber's surgeon'. He became 'assistant surgeon' in a hos-

* This fact allayed suspicion—so much so that they never checked on the identity of the Polish woman.

pital at Prague before leaving for Warsaw and enlisting in the Russian Army. Eighteen months later he sailed for Britain, and, as was the custom with all Poles emigrating to the United Kingdom, he made straight for Whitechapel.

The main puzzle about Klosowki's earlier life was that in the two years prior to his arrival in London his activities were veiled in mystery. Of these two years all was rumour and nothing was fact. Klosowski was said to have married in Poland and to have joined the Russian Army to escape from his wife. But there was no trace of any marriage certificate. Again it was rumoured he had got into serious trouble with hospital authorities at Prague, that the Polish police were looking for him and, finally, that he had joined the Czarist secret police.

Abberline made discreet inquiries among the Polish and Russian communities in the East End to try to learn whether Klosowski had any contacts with anarchist clubs. But the Pole appeared to be only a rare visitor at a club in Whitechapel, and, as far as could be ascertained, had no political affiliations. Either no one would talk about him, or nothing was known about him by his fellow countrymen.

Even the hairdresser's traveller, Levisohn, who had known Klosowski in Warsaw, could tell Abberline very little. 'He wasn't a friend of mine, but he was much humbler in those days,' said Levisohn. 'Though I always said he was a boy with ambitions. Oh, bless you, yes! He was the budding genius, he was, in his own opinions. And now he wants to have nothing to do with people like me. Why he's more British than the British now—all la-di-da, high hat and umbrella.'

Perhaps Levisohn guessed that Abberline was looking for the Ripper. For he made an odd remark one day:

'I think you are wasting your time bothering about Severin. He isn't the sort who'd get on the wrong side of the police, y'know. Far too clever for that. He's out for the high life and to get himself a business. A public, that's what he's after. And you don't get a public unless you're in the police's good books, do you?'

'And who said the police had anything against him?' asked Abberline sharply.

'Ah, Inspector, I knows you can't let the likes of me into your trade secrets. But with all these murders about, it wouldn't be natural if you didn't think this fellow Klosowski was a likely suspect. But he looks fiercer than he is. Now if I was you, I'd look further afield than the East End. You don't think the killer would hang around these parts. Not him. I'd take a look across the river—Southwark, Walworth, Camberwell and Brixton.'

'And why?'

Levisohn gave the inspector a broad wink. 'Because if he's a foreigner, and they say he is, then that's where a foreigner would make for. Across the river he is safe from his own countrymen, who might give him away. Not so many foreigners across the river, you know. But I know one who might be the very chap you're looking for. Don't know his name, but he lives somewhere in Walworth, supposed to be a doctor. I wouldn't know whether he is, or he isn't. But he's a Russian and very handy with the knife, he is.'

'What do you mean?'

'Well, one or two barber's shops I know does quite a business with him. A little doctoring on the side, you might call it. Cuts out warts and moles and generally tidies yer face up. Wouldn't fancy having him mess me around, but he is clever and no mistake.'

'Nothing very wrong in that, providing he has been properly registered.'

'Ah, but that's just it. He isn't registered. Being a foreigner, I don't suppose they'd recognise him. Not over here anyhow.'

'But why do you suspect him?'

'Well, it so happens that on the night of the Berner Street murder I happened to see him in Commercial Road shortly before midnight. Funny, I thought, him being over in the East End at this time of night. I was going to speak to him, but he turned away and went down a side street as soon as he saw me.'

Inspector Abberline wondered whether Levisohn had invented this story on the spur of the moment to distract attention from Klosowski. Levisohn's story was just a little too vague, he thought. And he decided to intensify his efforts to find out more about the Pole.

Never in the history of crime can there have been so many suspects as in the Ripper murders. This is not surprising when one considers that the criminal scum of the whole country were concentrated in the vicinity and that it would have been an impossible task for the police to have shadowed every suspect.

The Ripper was as elusive as the Scarlet Pimpernel. Of all the senior officers in the police none was more persistent in following up every clue than Major Smith. Yet he, too, was baffled. 'There is no man living who knows as much of these murders as I do,' he wrote long afterwards. 'And before going further I must admit that, though within five minutes of the perpetrator one night and with a very fair description of him besides, he completely beat me and every police officer in London.

'I have no more idea now where he lived than I had twenty years ago. After the second crime I sent word to Sir Charles Warren that I had discovered a man very likely to be the man wanted.

'He had been a medical student; he had been in a lunatic asylum; he spent all his time with women of a loose character whom he bilked by giving them polished farthings instead of sovereigns, two of these farthings having been found in the pocket of the murdered woman.'

[Two new farthings were found laid out by the murderer at the feet of Annie Chapman, found dead in Hanbury Street. It was suggested at the time that the killer had lured her into the backyard by pretending that the farthings were two sovereigns.]

'Sir Charles Warren failed to find him. I thought he was likely to be in Rupert Street, Haymarket. I sent up two men and there he was. But, polished farthings and all, he proved an alibi without a shadow of doubt.'

9

Grand Guignol in Miller's Court

Slowly autumn gave way to winter. As the crinkled yellow leaves mouldered in the gutters of the squares, grey, sooty fog-enveloped London, seeping up from the river and laying a cinereal pall over the city.

Fog, now almost unknown in the smokeless zones of modern London, was the annual killer of the aged and the bronchial in the 'eighties. But in that October and November of 1888 fog added a grotesque fantasy to the nightmare of the East End. Those who had to venture out at night groped their way through narrow streets in the fog, fearing every step they heard behind them. It was as though Nature in her most malignant mood had decided to provide her own smokescreen for the Ripper. For it was the dreaded, unknown killer that people thought most about and often a scream brought police running —only to find that somebody had been scared of his own shadow.

An increasing number of police had been drafted down to the East End and throughout October they visited every lodging house in the area, taking down statements and interviewing the inmates. But little new was learned, and by the time November had arrived apathy and a desire to stay indoors away from the fog had damped down the early enthusiasm of the members of the vigilance committees.

Catherine Eddowes' daughter was located. She was Ann Phillips, living at an address in Southwark, but she could help the police hardly at all. Her origins were obscure and she was vague about them herself. She believed that a man named Thomas Conway was her father, but couldn't say for cer-

Attempted murder by Jack the Ripper. From a drawing published in *The Illustrated Police News*, 1889

Sir Melville Macnaghten

POLICE NOTICE.

TO THE OCCUPIER.

On the mornings of Friday, 31st August, Saturday 8th, and Sunday, 30th September, 1888, Women were murdered in or near Whitechapel, supposed by some one residing in the immediate neighbourhood. Should you know of any person to whom suspicion is attached, you are earnestly requested to communicate at once with the nearest Police Station.

Metropolitan Police Office,
30th September, 1888.

The first notice circularised to householders in the East End during the hunt for the Ripper

A group of Spitalfields prostitutes outside a doss-house in Flower and Dean Street

'Clay Pipe Alice.'
Drawing from *The Illustrated Police News*

'Clay Pipe Alice.'
A sketch drawn after her murder

29 Hanbury Street. The yard where the murder was committed

Bucks Row, scene of one of the Ripper murders

Kitchen of a typical Spitalfields doss-house

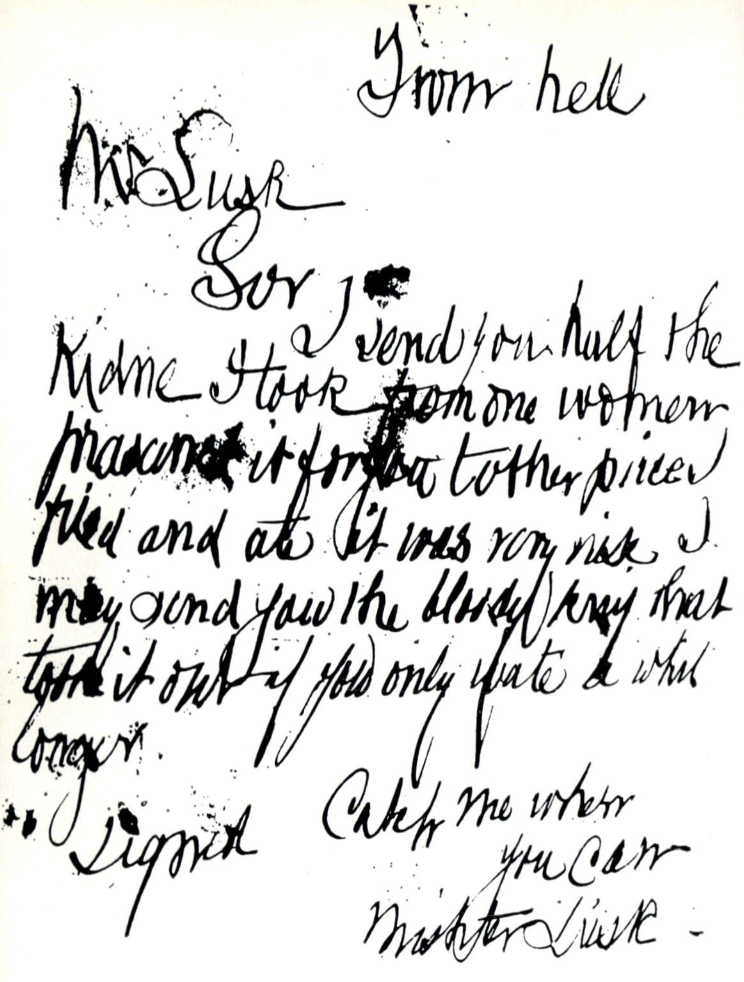

From hell

Mr Lusk

Sor

I send you half the

Kidne I took from one women

prasarved it for you tother piece

I fried and ate it was very nise I

may send you the bloody knif that

took it out if you only wate a whil

longer

signed Catch me when

you Can

Mishter Lusk

The Ripper letter sent to George Lusk after the murder of Catherine Eddowes tain whether he had married her mother. All she knew was that Conway left her mother because Catherine Eddowes drank so heavily. She had seen her mother occasionally in the past few years, mostly when the latter called on her to beg for the odd shilling.

Eventually Thomas Conway reported to the police. Apparently in order to escape from the attention of Eddowes he had been living under the name of Quinn. But it was soon clear that he had nothing to do with Eddowes' death. The mystery of Elizabeth Stride's identity was never satisfactorily cleared up. Mrs. Malcolm's sister turned up and indignantly declared that it was she, and not Elizabeth Stride, who had been married to the wine and spirit merchant of Bath. But Mrs. Malcolm stuck to her story and declined to withdraw her statements. Meanwhile the police found in the books of the Poplar and Stepney Sick Asylum a record of the death of John Thomas William Stride, a carpenter, and a police constable, Walter Stride, testified that this was his uncle who had married Elizabeth Gostsdotter in 1872. There was some suggestion at the time that P.C. Stride might have been the policeman who was the father of one of Stride's children.

Letter-writers to the newspapers continued to offer advice as to how the killer should be caught. Others, like the Rev. William Rogers, of the Rectory, Bishopsgate, offered solutions to the sociological problems of the East End. To *The Times* this clergyman put forward a suggestion which would be considered highly irregular even today, but which in Victorian times must have seemed absolute heresy. He wanted to have prostitutes registered and licensed. 'I offer two suggestions. The first is that all those women who ply the meretricious trade should be registered and, if need be, licensed. I know the cry that will be raised against this, but, I ask, are the interests of society to be sacrificed for a blatant prudery? Secondly, I suggest house-to-house visitation. . . .'

Mr. Rogers' idea was that by registering these women some check could be kept on them and, through the medium of official visitors, some attempt at redemption and reform might be made. 'I would undertake this task myself,' he added somewhat whimsically, 'but, being what I am, slanderers would render me useless for the task I set myself.'

Questions about the murders and the activities of the police were asked in the House of Commons. Sir Charles Warren was under constant attack by members of the Opposition. Even Queen Victoria took a lively and not altogether impracticable interest in the Ripper crimes, as is shown in a letter she wrote to the Home Secretary:

'The Queen fears that the detective department is not so efficient as it might be. No doubt the recent murders in Whitechapel were committed in circumstances which made detection very difficult; still, the Queen thinks that, in the small area where these horrible crimes have been perpetrated, a great number of detectives might be employed and that every possible suggestion might be carefully examined, and, if practicable, followed.

'Have the cattle boats and passenger boats been examined?

'Has any investigation been made as to the number of single men occupying rooms to themselves?

'The murderer's clothes must be saturated with blood and kept somewhere.

'Is there sufficient surveillance at night?

'These are some of the questions that occur to the Queen on reading the accounts of these horrible crimes.'

Which shows that the ageing Queen, so often misrepresented as shutting herself away from the facts of life, was fully cognisant of what was going on and that she had read about the murders in the greatest detail. Some of the points she makes are elementary enough, but the suggestion about a check on the cattle freighters was shrewd. These ships came up the Thames from continental ports usually on Thursdays or Fridays and left on Sundays and Mondays once a month. The Ripper murders generally occurred at monthly intervals always between a Thursday night and a Monday morning. Usually each boat carried at least one butcher who had more than a smattering of knowledge about anatomy.

Two hundred yards from Hanbury Street, where Annie Chapman had been murdered, was Dorset Street in the parish of Spitalfields. Nearly all the buildings in this street were common lodging houses, one of which had accommodation for 300 men and was fully occupied every night. No. 27, Dorset Street, was a chandler's shop, rented by a Mr. John M'Carthy, who also had the house next door, No. 26, which he let out in single rooms to tenants of the poorest class.

Not all the rooms, however, could be entered from Dorset Street. One room—No. 13—had previously been the back parlour of 26, Dorset Street, but a partition had been built to cut it off from the rest of the house so that its sole entrance was by way of Miller's Court, a dark and squalid passage at the side of Dorset Street. There were six other houses in the court.

The occupant of Room 13 was a gay, attractive, fresh-complexioned girl of twenty-five, known sometimes as Mary Anne, more often as Mary Jane and, occasionally, more pretentiously as Marie Jeannette Kelly. Beauty and gaiety were rare enough qualities in this part of London where disease, poverty and appalling living conditions militated against them. In consequence the youthful attractiveness of Mary Kelly, her natural vivacity and wit, made her not only a well-known character, but something of a phenomenon.

But having said this in her favour, and while admitting that her good looks and pert bearing raised her above the level of the average street-walker, Mary was no different from and no better than the typical prostitute. For that was what she was. And like the rest of her class she drank heavily when she had the money.

In the early part of 1888 she had arrived in Dorset Street with a labourer whom she referred to as 'my husband, Joseph Kelly'. In fact this was a polite fiction, as she had met him in the streets only the previous night. They had lost no time in deciding to live together and rented Room No. 13 on the ground floor overlooking Miller's Court for four shillings and sixpence a week. Not a high rent, but too high for both of them, it would seem, for they were often in arrears with their weekly payments to M'Carthy. It was a poorly furnished room

—just an old iron bedstead, two rickety tables and a single chair, with some tatty and torn muslin for curtains.

Perhaps the reason for their frequent financial troubles was that Mary drank a lot. Or it may have been that Joseph was sometimes out of work. To do him justice, he worked as often as he could get odd jobs as a porter at Spitalfields Market and made no attempt to exploit his attractive mistress. As long as they lived together Mary Kelly kept off the streets. Such at least was the testimony of the neighbours who agreed that, on the whole, this couple got along together fairly well.

At times, however, especially when Mary Kelly had been the worse for drink, there were quarrels. At the end of October 1888 there had been one particularly violent row which ended in blows being exchanged and a window smashed.

The reason for this quarrel was that Mary had brought in a whore from the streets to share their room and Joseph had taken the strongest objection to this. So much so that he had decided there and then to end this liaison and to leave No. 13. He went off to live in Buller's lodging house in Bishopsgate Street.

Possibly there was more to it than this. Though Joseph would not admit it, the probability is that he had discovered his mistress had been secretly whoring again. At any rate, her habitual association with whores had alienated his affections.

Joseph's real surname was Barnett. He had no illusions about Kelly's past. He knew that she had been a prostitute as, during the months they had lived together, she had told him all about her past. She was Irish and a Catholic, born in Limerick, and Kelly was her maiden name. When she was quite young her family had moved to Carmarthenshire, where her father was employed at an ironworks.

At the age of sixteen she had married a collier named Davies who was killed in a mine explosion two years later. Mary then went to Cardiff where she appears to have adopted whoring as a profession. When she was twenty-one she made up her mind to exploit her talents in London. She had heard stories of the glamorous adventures of *filles de joie* in the West End and the gay night life of Haymarket and Piccadilly was an irresistible attraction for her.

If her own story was to be believed, she met with some success. For a while she lived in a high-class bordello in the West End, where her clients were dashing young blades and champagne her chief beverage. Here she met a good-looking young man with some pretensions to culture; he rescued her from the bordello and took her off to Paris as his mistress. It is a romantic story and it may be true. When drunk, Mary Kelly would sometimes say a few words in French and she insisted on Joseph calling her 'Marie Jeannette'. She often described her life in Paris and other parts of France, her visits to the Folies at the Moulin Rouge. But, according to Joseph, she 'didn't like life with the Froggies and came back to dear old London'.

If, however, this story was true, it is difficult to see how so young and pretty a girl could have fallen so low in the space of two years. Maybe her protector grew bored and jilted her. But, if so, it would not seem so very difficult for her to have taken advantage of her experience by finding some other gallant with money and good education. There was a gap in her story somewhere and Joseph could not discover what happened between her departure from France and her next liaison with a man named Morganstone with whom she lived in Ratcliff Highway.

If Mary Kelly really had been in Paris then the only possible explanation for her swift fall into prostitution in the East End can be drink. For short periods she lived with different men, but nearly always parted from them as a result of a drunken tiff. In between these liaisons she became a streetwalker, but her aim, generally speaking, seems to have been to find a man who would provide a room for her. Before she met Barnett she had been living with a stone-mason named Joseph Fleming in Bethnal Green.

Few other people in Spitalfields knew anything about her. M'Carthy had heard that she walked the streets of Aldgate and that occasionally she used to visit someone near the Elephant and Castle. Her education, he said, was far superior to that of the average East End woman.

As soon as Joseph Barnett left her, Mary Kelly took to the streets again. Maria Harvey, the whore she had brought back to No. 13, stayed with her on Monday and Tuesday and was in the room on Thursday afternoon when Barnett called in. They all parted quite amicably about 7.30 p.m. and that was the last time that Barnett saw her.

Later that night Kelly was seen by several people in Commercial Street: she was slightly the worse for drink. At 11.45 p.m. Mary Ann Cox, a widow who lived in the last house in Miller's Court, saw Kelly with a 'short, stout man, shabbily dressed and wearing a billycock hat.

'Mary Kelly was very tipsy. I said good night to her, and she replied: "Good night. I'm going to sing." '

Mrs. Cox went to her room for about a quarter of an hour. When she came out she heard Kelly singing 'Only a violet I plucked for my mother's grave'. There was a light in Kelly's room—she was sure of that. But when she returned to Miller's Court about ten minutes past three the light was out and all was quiet. About five minutes—or it might have been fifteen minutes—after six o'clock she heard a man leave the court, but she took no notice and thought it might be a patrolling policeman.

But did Kelly go out again between 12.30 a.m. and three o'clock? If George Hutchinson's story is to be accepted, she did. Otherwise Mrs. Cox's story of the events of that night are inaccurate. Hutchinson was another labourer who found work none too easy to obtain. And on this night he had no money and nowhere to sleep. The lodging house where he usually stayed was closed.

About two o'clock on the Friday morning on 9 October Hutchinson came out of Whitechapel Road into Commercial Street where he noticed a man standing on the corner. He did not pay much attention at the time for, as he approached Flower and Dean Street, he caught sight of Mary Kelly whom he knew quite well.

He had always liked the girl and more than once toyed with

the idea of 'teaming up with her. But what was the use? I hadn't got the brass for the likes of her.'

And it was 'brass' that Kelly wanted that night. She made the first approach. Sidling up to Hutchinson and taking hold of his arm, she asked: 'Can you lend me sixpence?'

Whether she genuinely wanted to borrow so small a sum, or whether this was her method of soliciting, Hutchinson couldn't be sure. In any case it made no difference, for he had to admit he could not manage to lend even this meagre sum.

'Well,' said Kelly, smiling, 'if you can't manage it, I must go and look for some money elsewhere.'

She smiled again, quite good-naturedly, and walked off in the direction of Thrawl Street, which was about 300 yards from Dorset Street. Hutchinson looked back and saw that she was talking to the man on the corner. The man stepped forward, put his hand on Kelly's shoulder, said something to her, at which they both laughed. Then the pair of them walked slowly along in Hutchinson's direction.

Hutchinson didn't quite know why he should stand still and watch the couple. In the back of his mind was a certain curiosity about the type of man Kelly was speaking to, and, to be honest, a little jealousy. George Hutchinson pondered on his misfortune. Here was a charming girl who had actually asked him for sixpence. Six miserable pennies! For that paltry sum no doubt he could have solved his accommodation problem for the night and enjoyed her caresses as well. It was galling to think of what he had missed.

George was somewhat of an optimist. Perhaps nothing would come of this and the man would go away. Then, as it was getting late, maybe Kelly would take pity on him when she knew he had nowhere to sleep.

But when the couple came closer George had a shock and he knew at once that Mary Kelly would be unlikely to let her prey go. 'My suspicions were instantly aroused,' he said later, 'at seeing so well dressed a man in this part of London. I felt there was something queer about it.'

A burning hated of this apparently well-to-do philanderer welled up inside Hutchinson. With greedy, hungry eyes he watched the pair as they ambled slowly towards him. They walked at so leisurely a pace that he couldn't fail to notice every detail about the man's appearance.

Something about Mary Kelly's new-found companion seemed familiar to Hutchinson. He felt sure he had seen him before, prowling about the neighbourhood. Come to think of it, he was very like a chap he had noticed in Petticoat Lane the previous Sunday morning. But he couldn't be absolutely certain of this.

The man's soft felt hat was drawn down over his eyes. He was not tall—about 5 feet 6 inches in height—of a dark complexion, with dark eyes and bushy eyebrows. Hutchinson particularly noted his thick moustache which was curled up at the ends. He looks like a foreigner, thought Hutchinson, not only about the face, but in his dress, too.

His age was difficult to judge because the clothes he was wearing made him look older than he probably was. Perhaps he was about thirty-five, certainly not more than that; it could be that he was much younger. If only I could see beneath that hat of his, I could tell much better, pondered Hutchinson. The man was enveloped in a long, dark coat, trimmed with astrakhan; he wore a white collar with a black tie, secured by a horseshoe tie-pin, and over his buttoned boots were spats.

'I could swear to the man anywhere. I should certainly recognise him again. His coat was open and I saw he had a huge gold watch-chain which had a big seal with a red stone hanging from it.

'In his left hand he carried a small parcel—a thin parcel about eight inches long. It was covered with dark American cloth and he held it by a piece of string. He carried a pair of brown kid gloves in his right hand.'

For a few seconds the man glanced at Hutchinson and seemed annoyed that he was being watched. He tightened his lips and frowned; then he turned his head away and walked down the street with Kelly. The girl isn't drunk, thought Hutchinson, but she's a bit spreeish, and it's no time of night to be out with a strange man in these parts. Still, he supposed she knew how to look after herself, and anyhow it was no business of his. All the same, as he had nothing else to do and nowhere to go, he might as well follow them and see where they went.

At the corner of Miller's Court Kelly and the stranger stopped and chatted for about three minutes. Kelly said: 'I have lost my handkerchief.' The man pulled a red handkerchief out of his pocket and gave it to her. Though he was standing some little distance away, Hutchinson was quite sure it was a red handkerchief. There was enough light to notice the colour. Then they disappeared into the court together.

He didn't think they had seen him following them; they never looked in his direction, though most of the time he was quite close behind them. But he did not follow them into the court and couldn't say whether they went into Kelly's room. He assumed they must have done as he waited for about three quarters of an hour to see whether they came out. But all was silent and Hutchinson decided that the stranger was spending the night with Kelly.

As he left Dorset Street the church clock nearby struck three times. Dejected and weary, he continued his aimless tramp round the East End streets until dawn came. Then, utterly exhausted, he crept into an alleyway and fell asleep on a pile of sacks.

M'Carthy was busy with his books in his shop at ten o'clock on Friday morning. Looking through his ledger, he noted that Mary Kelly was thirty-five shillings in arrears with her rent. Pursing his lips and whistling, he ringed the amount due with a red pencil.

'Bowyer!' he called.

His assistant, wiping his hands on his apron, rushed into the tiny room which M'Carthy used for an office.

'Yessir.'

'Look, John, the Kelly woman in No. 13 is owing several weeks' rent. We've had promise after promise that it will be paid next week. Always the same phrase—*next week*. But next week comes and goes and still there's no sign of any money. It wasn't so bad when that fellow Joseph was there. When he was in work they paid up regular like. But now he's gone I'm not so sure we can afford to keep Mrs. or Miss Kelly whoever she is. If we don't watch out, one of these nights she's going to do a moonlight flit. Go round to No. 13 and see if you can get some of the money right now. Tell her it's the last chance.'

'I'll do my best, sir, but she's a tricky customer.'

It was about 10.45 when Bowyer went round the corner into Miller's Court and knocked on the door. There was no reply. Bowyer listened, then knocked again, this time loudly and impatiently. Still there was silence.

I bet she's a good idea who it is, thought Bowyer. She's hiding. Well, I'll show the saucy bitch she can't escape me so easily.

Angrily he tried the door handle, rattling it vigorously only to find that the door was locked. Peeping through the keyhole, he noticed that the key was missing. This seemed distinctly odd for Bowyer knew from past experience that Kelly usually left the key on the inside of the door.

The left-hand side of Room No. 13 faced Miller's Court; the window looked out on the court. Bowyer saw that a pane of glass had been broken—probably the one that was smashed in Kelly's final quarrel with Joseph Barnett. There was an aperture just large enough to put his hand through. Carefully edging his arm through the crack and avoiding the jagged edges of glass, he caught hold of the flimsy muslin curtain and drew it aside.

An involuntary cry of horror escaped from his mouth as he quickly withdrew his hand, cutting it against the glass. He had only drawn the curtain back a few inches, but what he had seen was like a grotesque tableau in a Grand Guignol thriller.

Lying on the bed was an obscene parody of a woman. But for the fact that she obviously had a trunk, arms and legs, Bowyer might have been forgiven for mistaking her for the carcass of a butchered beast. She was completely naked and covered in blood. Her throat was cut from ear to ear right down to the spinal column. The ears and nose had been severed from her head, the stomach and abdomen ripped open. Her clothes lay in a neat pile at the foot of the bed.

Bowyer's eyes wandered round the room. On a table placed beside the bed was the final and most awful horror. There, symmetrically arranged, were what appeared at first to be piles of flesh. Then, slowly, it dawned on Bowyer what had happened. The maniacal killer had cut off the woman's breasts and set them on the table. Alongside them were her heart and kidneys. Other parts of her body were hanging on picture frame nails.

Not until he reached the shop at No. 27, Dorset Street, did Bowyer stop running. Then, white-faced and retching, he collapsed across M'Carthy's table. He managed to stutter out a few incoherent phrases.

'Jack the Ripper . . . No. 13 . . . fetch the police.'

10

Sir Charles Warren resigns

M'Carthy could make little sense of what Bowyer was saying, so he went round to look for himself. He returned from Miller's Court with more alacrity than Bowyer.

'It's more like the work of a devil than of a man. You'd better go for the police at once,' he told his assistant.

So Bowyer went to Commercial Street police station and saw Superintendent Arnold, who returned with him to Miller's Court. Even the hardened superintendent was shocked by what confronted him.

'No one must enter this room, not even the police, until Scotland Yard has been notified,' said Arnold. 'Those are my orders. This is terrible. It's far and away the worst murder this madman has committed yet.'

Sergeant Thicke was detailed to keep a watch on the court and to make sure that no one left the other houses in it before Detective-Inspector Abberline arrived. Meanwhile Superintendent Arnold dispatched a telegram to Sir Charles Warren, telling him what had happened.

Needless to say, as with most things that concerned Warren, confusion reigned as soon as he received the telegram. He wasted time by having a long discussion with Abberline; he gave two orders to Anderson, then countermanded them. Finally he demanded that bloodhounds be sent down to Whitechapel at once.

An hour later it was discovered that the bloodhounds were no longer in the police's possession: they had been restored to their owner. This caused a further delay in investigations as the Commercial Street police had been told on no account to enter the room until the bloodhounds had been able to pick up the scent.

It was a bad day for Sir Charles Warren. His strained relations with the Home Office had been further aggravated by an article which had appeared under his own name in *Murray's Magazine*. Mr. Matthews, the Home Secretary, was furious, for the article dealt with a subject which no servant of the police force should write about without permission—the management and discipline of the Metropolitan Police. To make matters worse, it was an exceedingly controversial article. Warren had neither asked for nor had he been given permission for the article to be published.

Matthews had drawn Warren's attention to this breach of the rules, and Warren had replied only the day before, tendering his resignation.

Whether this resignation would have been accepted but for the new crime committed by the Ripper is problematical. Matthews was a very weak administrator and he had twice before declined to accept similar offers of resignation by Warren, despite the intense provocation to which the latter subjected him. The Ripper's latest atrocity, however, decided even Matthews. But it was not until 12 November that the Home Secretary announced the Commissioner's resignation to the House of Commons, where it was greeted by unruly cheers from the Opposition. There can rarely have been a more unpopular police chief.

Eventually Room No. 13 was broken open and four doctors carried out an examination of the body. They were Bagster Phillips, Gordon Brown and Dr. Duke of Spitalfields, and Dr. Duke of Westminster. It took them six and a half hours to complete their work. Every particle of flesh and every organ removed from the body were finally accounted for and assembled. No part of the body was missing, but the surgeons were agreed that in savagery this crime was undoubtedly the worst the Ripper had yet perpetrated, presumably because, being indoors, he was able to carry out his mutilations without interruption.

Large crowds gathered to watch the corpse being taken to

Shoreditch Mortuary. The terror and emotion among the masses, which had begun to subside towards the end of October, now approached hysteria. The police were kept exceedingly busy coping with false alarms on the next two nights. Three men suspected of being Jack the Ripper were surrounded by hostile crowds and had to be rescued by constables on patrol duty. One of the men was a policeman in plain clothes; he was about to be strung up on a lamp-post when two of his colleagues came along and recognised him. But for their timely intervention there would have been another murder that night.

It became dangerous even to glance at a woman in the streets of the East End after dark. One quite innocent and respectable man happened to stare into the face of a passing woman and she immediately shrieked out 'Jack the Ripper!' Again the police had to save someone from lynching.

A popular fallacy of the day was that, when anyone died, the reflection of the person he or she last looked upon was retained photographically and indelibly on the retinae. No one had ever tested this theory and Sir Charles Warren's last inspiration was to order a photographer to take a close-up picture of the dead woman's eyes. This was carried out and, as far as is known, was the first recorded instance of disproving this fable. Yet the superstition lived on for many years, even until the 'twenties of the present century when a man shot a policeman in each eye in the belief that he was removing incriminating evidence.

Much criticism had been voiced concerning the appalling conditions of improvised mortuaries in the East End of London, and it may have been for this reason that Kelly's body was taken to Shoreditch Mortuary instead of to the local workhouse morgue, which had been so severely condemned by doctors at earlier inquests on Ripper victims. But there may also have been another reason for this. The police had been annoyed by the manner in which Mr. Wynne Baxter had conducted some of the inquests, especially that on Annie Chapman. So, too, had the doctors: they had strongly resented being forced to make public all the gruesome details of their findings.

By removing the body to Shoreditch, the police had technically placed the responsibility for an inquest in the hands of Dr. Roderick McDonald, the Shoreditch Coroner. There were some grounds for suspecting that this was done deliberately to thwart Mr. Wynne Baxter, in whose territory the murder was committed. Possibly Mr. Baxter sensed as much; at least he protested vehemently that the police had no right to remove the body from his district. For a while there was considerable argument as to who was to conduct the inquest.

It was Mr. McDonald, however, who won this argument, and his method of conducting the inquiry lent some substance to allegations that the whole business was prearranged with the police. The Coroner told the jury he was only going to take preliminary evidence on the first day and that the inquest would be adjourned.

When Dr. Bagster Phillips came to give his evidence the Coroner again stressed that he only proposed to hear part of it that day. No one, therefore, took much notice when the Coroner failed to put obvious questions to witnesses. It was assumed that these would be asked at a later hearing. Then, after listening to Dr. Phillips' evidence for a few minutes the Coroner interrupted to give the jury a broad hint. 'I do not know whether the jury have heard sufficient to be able to draw their own conclusions as to how this unfortunate woman met her death, but . . .'

The foreman of the jury, doubtless correctly interpreting the wishes of his colleagues to be spared the more horrible details of the post mortem, indicated that they had heard enough. The usual verdict of 'murder by a person or persons unknown' was recorded.

Thus, in what was perhaps the most important of all the Ripper crimes—important in the sense that it provided more clues than all the others put together—there was no adequate cross-examination of witnesses. The police's excuse was that further revelations at an open inquest might assist the killer: this plea is hardly valid in view of the fact that much information that did not come out at the inquest was published in the press. The main point is that it would have been very useful to expose some of the witnesses to rigid cross-examination. There are occasions in which inquests can help the police: this was surely one of them.

Detective-Inspector Abberline thought so. His task was to try to find which witnesses were telling the truth. Someone, he felt sure, was lying, and cross-examination at an inquest would possibly have revealed this.

For the police's task was rendered more difficult by the fact that two women claimed to have seen Mary Kelly *after 8 a.m. on Friday morning*.

'If that is true,' said Abberline, 'then we are back where we started. We are as far from solving the crime as ever we were. And I can't help wishing I could prove that both these women were lying.'

'It would be more charitable to say they could have been mistaken, sir, wouldn't it?' asked Sergeant Thicke.

'Charitable maybe, but it wouldn't be likely. I say they are either lying, or what they say is true. There's too much detail for it to be just a mistake, too much sticking to their story. Women, Thicke, are the queerest creatures, and, like fish, you never know what they're going to do or say. If they take it into their heads to make up a story, they'll do so. Right up to the very moment when they come to believe what they've only invented.'

One woman had been in Dorset Street between 8 a.m. and 9 a.m. Friday and she swore she had seen Kelly walking towards Commercial Street. But her evidence was vague. Far more important was the testimony of Mrs. Caroline Maxwell, the wife of a lodging-house-keeper at 14, Dorset Street.

'I had known Mary Kelly for about four months,' said Mrs. Maxwell. 'But I had only spoken to her about twice. On Friday morning, between eight o'clock and half past I saw Kelly at the corner of Miller's Court. I am quite certain it was her.'

'Why are you so certain?' asked Abberline.

'Well, you couldn't miss her. She was different like from these other girls.'

'Why are you so sure about the time?'

'Oh, I'm certain about that because my husband leaves off work at eight o'clock. Besides I couldn't help but notice Kelly because it was unusual seeing her at that time of day.

' "You're out and up with the cockerels properly this morning, aren't you, ducks?" I said to her. "Come and have a drop of rum," I said.

'But no, she wouldn't have no rum, or nothing. Said she'd just had a pint of ale and it had made her proper sick. She looked ill, too, poor soul.

'Well, I left her then and went about my business. Then about an hour later I saw her outside the Britannia public house talking to a man. He wasn't a tall man, but I didn't notice him particular like. Mary Kelly was wearing a dark skirt, a velvet bodice and a shawl.'

Abberline cross-questioned Mrs. Maxwell again and again, but he failed to break her story or to catch her out.

'Don't you think, Mrs. Maxwell, that it is just possible that the woman you saw may not have been Kelly?'

'Ho! Ho! Going to call me a liar, are you? If that ain't the police all over. Well, I'm quite sure, see. I'd know Mary Kelly anywhere.'

'Now, look here, Mrs. Maxwell, it's no use you arguing with me. If you do, you might get into trouble. All right, you think you saw Mary Kelly . . .'

'I'm dam' sure I did.'

'All right, all right. But how came you to see her when at that very hour she was lying dead in her room?'

'What do you mean?' asked Mrs. Maxwell suspiciously.

'Well, the doctor who examined her body says she had been dead five or six hours when he saw her.'

'And how can a doctor tell for sure? You tell me that.'

'Well, they can, Mrs. Maxwell. You've got to accept what the experts say. Now let's go over your story again. You didn't see Mary Kelly come out of her room, did you?'

'No. She was on the corner of Miller's Court.'

'Now about what she was wearing. Had you seen her in those clothes before? Would you, or rather did you, recognise her by the clothes?'

'Well, I can't rightly say that I had or I hadn't seen her in those clothes before. But that macaroon shawl she was wearing I had seen.'

'*Maroon* coloured shawl?'

'Yes, that's right.'

'Did she seem to recognise you?'

'Of course she did.'

It was hopeless. Abberline decided that either the woman was lying, or it was a case of mistaken identity and she was just being obstinate in refusing to admit she was wrong. The latter seemed the likeliest answer. On the other hand, why should she lie? Women did sometimes lie in order to draw attention to themselves: perhaps Mrs. Maxwell was vain enough to want to be a key witness in the case and so she invented the story. Or was there another explanation: could it be that Mrs. Maxwell saw a woman who looked like Kelly—possibly even wearing Kelly's clothes—that she wasn't sure whether it was Kelly and spoke to her, and that *the woman pretended to be Mary Kelly*?

'Good God!' muttered Abberline under his breath as he pondered the implications of this. He dashed off to Westbourne Villas, Bayswater, to see his friend, Dr. Dutton.

'Well, Abberline, are we any nearer to solving the mystery?' asked the doctor.

'If anything, Doctor, we are further than ever from the truth. But I'd like to ask your advice about a new theory of mine.'

'Fire away, Inspector,' replied the doctor, filling his pipe.

'Well, sir, do you think it could be a case not of Jack the Ripper, but Jill the Ripper?'

'Good God, man, what a preposterous idea! You don't seriously think . . .?'

'No, but there's something odd in the evidence. The doctors all say that Kelly must have been dead five or six hours before she was discovered. Yet there are two women who swear they saw Kelly alive between eight and nine o'clock that morning. What's more I can't even make them admit they might have been mistaken. And I'm blessed if I can sort out that puzzle. At least there is one possibility. Suppose another woman was wearing Kelly's clothes and supposing, when spoken to, she pretended to be Kelly.'

'You mean that the murderer was a woman, that she put on some clothes of Kelly's and . . .'

'Exactly. Could a woman have done this awful job? I know it sounds mad, but then the murderer is mad anyhow. And, if he's a man, why haven't we caught him before now? But if it's a woman, well, there's the answer. Nobody would suspect a woman. And you see the terrible implications there, sir. If it is a woman, well, unless we get wise to the fact, she's going on ripping up other women without getting caught.'

'Well, it's just possible, Abberline, though I must admit that I find it a little hard to believe. If you had asked me before this last murder, I would have said it could well have been a woman, but I doubt very much whether a woman could have done this last murder. If it is a woman, however, you shouldn't have far to look for her.'

'Why?'

'The only woman who could have done it, I should say, is a midwife. She might have just enough knowledge of anatomy and surgical skill to carry out these diabolical crimes. But I doubt it, I very much doubt it. My money is still on a foreign doctor.'

The theory that the Ripper was a woman was developed at considerable length by William Stewart in his book *Jack the Ripper: A New Theory*. He argues that only a woman could have escaped the cordon of police that was thrown round the East End after the first few murders. If a woman was the killer, the victims would be taken by surprise and have no time to cry out. Again, argued the author, a midwife would have sufficient knowledge to be able to carry out these crimes. She would not be as skilled as a surgeon, and William Stewart plays up the testimony of those surgeons who argued that no great anatomical skill was displayed by the killer. But, as had already been pointed out, a murderer operating in the open, in the dark and in great haste, not to mention the possibility of interruptions on occasions, could hardly be expected to display 'great skill'.

What is much more to the point is that the majority opinion of the doctors stressed that the crimes revealed 'considerable knowledge of anotomy'. And in the case of Mary Kelly, as Dr. Dutton stressed, there could surely be no room for doubt that, working without fear of interruption, the killer showed marked skill in dissecting the body.

Abberline thought at first that it was possible that the murderer's clothes were so soaked in blood after the orgiastic killing in Miller's Court that she—if it were a 'she'—burnt these clothes and put on Kelly's before making her escape. But neither of the two women was prepared to swear that she had seen Kelly wearing these clothes before. The other possibility was that the clothes the murderer wore were those belonging to Maria Harvey, the whore who had stayed with Kelly on the Monday and Tuesday nights. Harvey told the police that she had left 'several articles in Mary's care, some sheets, an overcoat and a bonnet'. The only article left in the room after the murder was the overcoat.

Abberline went over the evidence again. First, there were no signs of a struggle in Room 13. That had been a feature of all the crimes, but in this case it almost certainly suggested that Mary Kelly had brought the killer back to her room, not that she had had a surprise nocturnal visitor. Again there was no trace of any weapon.

Unless the killer had committed the murder in the dark he ran a grave risk of being discovered. The muslin curtains provided no real protection and anyone passing by could have put a hand through the hole in the window and flicked them aside. What was more, several people had passed in and out of the court that night.

But could the killer perform all these barbarities in darkness? Abberline thought this was unlikely, but possible. Even so, the Ripper must have drawn aside the muslin curtains to obtain some light, and, in doing this, he ran the risk of someone peeping through at him, or the chance that a policeman, noticing the broken window, might flash his lantern through the crack.

There must have been some sort of light in the room after the killer had entered: there was ample evidence of this from witnesses. That light was probably provided by a partly burnt candle found in No. 13. It would be safer to have a light with the curtains drawn than not to have had one and to have pulled them back. Also, if any of Kelly's friends, such as Maria Harvey, had seen a light on, they would be more likely to knock or call out, whereas if they thought she were asleep they might go to the window and pull back the curtains.

But there remained the puzzle of the remains of a fire in the grate. There was still some warmth in the grate, so the fire must have been kept in until a very late hour. Certainly Kelly hadn't the means to purchase coal or wood, and it was unthinkable that she would try to keep herself warm by burning clothes. And in the grate were the charred remains of a woman's felt hat, some other clothes and a piece or burnt velvet. It had been an exceptionally fierce fire for these were the only recognisable fragments and the rim, handle and spout of a kettle had been burnt away. The clothes might have been Kelly's, or they might have been Harvey's: Harvey wasn't sure, but she thought the hat might have been hers. Mary Kelly's clothes were in a neat pile by the bed, so it was possible that they were someone else's clothes.

If so, whose clothes? The murderer's? Was the killer a woman, perhaps a midwife who practised abortions, something that was fairly common in the East End? Or was the killer a man masquerading in woman's clothes? If the latter were true, then why should he burn these clothes? The assumption would be that they were so blood-stained that it would be too risky to wear them again.

This seemed to be the only answer to the puzzle of the fire. And yet when he (or she) committed the other murders, there was no means of making a fire to burn blood-stained clothes. 'The murderer's clothes must be saturated with blood,' Queen Victoria had observed. But Abberline doubted this. The killer was too careful to fall into such an error. What other purpose could there be for the fire?

It was possible that the Ripper had made a fire in order to see what he was doing. But why take the trouble to make a fire when a candle was available? And the candle, according to Harvey, had been barely half consumed since Wednesday night. True, a fire might enable the killer to work with less risk of detection than if he had relied on candlelight; but against this was the fact that a fire, especially a fire stinking of burnt clothes, might attract attention. Someone in the court could have sniffed the acrid smell of burnt clothes and imagined the house was on fire. If an alarm had been given, it would have been extremely awkward for the murderer.

No, argued Abberline, look at it whatever way you like, the fire must have been lit for the purpose of destroying something. The burnt kettle seemed to support this theory. The burnt clothes were not those of a man; therefore, either the killer was a woman, or . . .

Or he was a man who had bought these clothes for Kelly and feared they could be traced to the shop that sold them to him.

At first the police thought that the murderer had taken the key away with him, as there was no trace of it anywhere. But Joseph Barnett, who was a most helpful witness, said the key had been lost sometime before and that they pushed back the bolt through the broken window when they wanted to get in.

Elizabeth Prater, who occupied a room immediately above that of Kelly, said that between 3.30 and 4 a.m. on the Friday she heard a cry of 'Oh, murder!' It came from somewhere quite near, but she didn't take any notice as such a cry was often heard round and about Dorset Street.

It may seem odd that in the middle of the night and at a period when the Ripper was known to be roaming around that a woman could accept such a cry as something commonplace and with complete equanimity. But similar evidence—indeed positive confirmation—was supplied by Sarah Lewis, a laundress, of Great Pearl Street, Spitalfields. The nocturnal perambulations of East Enders in these days were often inexplicable. But Sarah Lewis for some reason or other went to Miller's Court at 2.30 a.m. to call on a Mrs. Keyler.

As she entered Miller's Court she noticed a man standing by himself at the door of Room 13. He was 'stout, but not very tall, and wore a wideawake hat'.

Sarah Lewis chatted with Mrs. Keyler and decided to stay the night. About half past three she heard a woman cry out 'Murder!'

'But I didn't take much notice,' she added.

And yet, thought Abberline morosely, a dozen other women would run to the police saying they had seen Jack the Ripper with far less evidence than this to go on. Women and fish, he ruminated, you never knew how they'd react!

Abberline checked up on the midwives in the district, but he had no luck in that line of inquiry. All had alibis. Two, it was true, had been out at the time the murder was committed, but, as one told the inspector: 'Bless your life, our work takes us out at all hours. Children often choose the middle of the night to be born.'

It was the fact that the presence of midwives in the street late at night would arouse no suspicion that William Stewart used as his argument that it was Jill the Ripper. Further, said Stewart, blood-stains on their aprons would not be unnatural. This argument is a little hard to follow.

A chronological picture of events on the night of Mary Kelly's murder had emerged, though it left many questions unanswered. Mary Ann Cox had seen Kelly with a man at Miller's Court at 11.45 p.m. She heard someone leave the Court shortly after 6 a.m. George Hutchinson saw Kelly with a man shortly after 2 a.m. Sarah Lewis saw a man alone outside No. 13 at 2.30 a.m. From their respective descriptions it would seem that the man seen by Mrs. Cox was not the well-dressed stranger Hutchinson encountered.

Now there was no evidence that the 'shabbily dressed man wearing a billycock hat', whom Mrs. Cox saw with Kelly, ever entered No. 13. Most probably he was penniless and of no use to Kelly. Also it was unlikely that Kelly would have been singing about a violet picked for her mother's grave with a prospective client in the room. It would have scarcely been a harlot's theme song.

The probability was that Kelly said goodbye to this man before she went indoors. She was tipsy, but not sleepily drunk and she did not go to bed. She had said she 'felt like a song' and people who are tipsy often sing the most maudlin and dismal ditties. Her need for money was urgent: she owed several weeks' rent to M'Carthy and Friday was rent day. So she went out on the streets again. Then, if Hutchinson's evidence was to be believed, she took the well-dressed stranger to her room. It was 2 a.m. when Hutchinson first saw Kelly: it would be about 2.15 or 2.20 when the pair disappeared into Miller's Court.

But at 2.30 Sarah Lewis noticed a man *standing alone* outside Number 13. This must have been the man Hutchinson had seen; Sarah's description of him was vague, but as far as it went it tallied with that of Hutchinson.

What was the man doing alone? Possibly he had observed Hutchinson following him and Kelly and had come out of the court to see whether the labourer was still lurking around. He wanted to make sure the house was no longer being watched. Gradually the sequence of events was revealing itself. Hutchinson left Dorset Street at three o'clock. It was not until 3.30 that the cry of 'Murder' had been heard. Possibly the killer looked out of the door on a number of occasions to see whether Hutchinson had gone. Then, when he was satisfied that the inquisitive labourer had departed, he slit Mary Kelly's throat.

The doctors' examination of the corpse had been delayed because of the futile wait for the bloodhounds. The dissection of a body made it much more difficult to assess accurately the actual time of death, but the doctors estimated that the woman had been dead at least five or six hours before the body was found. This would mean that Kelly had been killed not later than 5.45 p.m., but more likely before five o'clock.

Yet the doctors admitted that the mutilation of the body and the removal of the organs must have occupied the killer for two to two and a half hours. Therefore the probability was that the murder was done about 3.30 (when the cry was heard by Elizabeth Prater and Mrs. Cox) and that between 5.30 and 6 a.m. the fiend completed his operations and left shortly afterwards. It was just after six o'clock that Mrs. Cox heard someone leave the court.

So far the reconstruction of events is logical if one accepts the evidence as reliable. But two unsolved problems remained: the evidence of the women who claimed to have seen Kelly after 8 a.m. and the puzzle of the fire.

It was almost certain that Kelly, who was so hard up, had no coal or wood with which to make a fire. What did the killer use to start it? For it seemed highly unlikely that the fire was lit before Kelly was killed. Then there was the enigma of the burnt-out kettle. The kettle must have been put on the fire for a purpose and then forgotten. It could be that the Ripper was alarmed about Hutchinson lurking about outside and that, to bide the time until he was absolutely sure nobody was about, the killer of Kelly said he could do with a cup of tea. Maybe he and Kelly found a few odd sticks and some newspaper and made a fire for this purpose.

But if the kettle was boiled and they had made the tea, why would the Ripper want to put it back on the fire again?

Sergeant Thicke pointed out to Abberline that the key of the door was lost so that the door could not have been locked. Yet Bowyer could not get in, so the door must have been bolted. 'Now, if it was bolted from the inside,' said Thicke, 'how did the killer leave the room?'

'He could have got out of the window,' replied Abberline, 'but somehow I don't think he did. It's more likely that he went out through the door, then put his hand through the broken window and slipped the bolt back.'

Meanwhile Sir Charles Warren's last act—two days after he resigned, but two days before this was officially announced—was to issue the following notice, unparalleled in the history of the Metropolitan Police:

'MURDER—PARDON. Whereas on November 8 or 9 in Miller's Court, Dorset Street, Spitalfields, Mary Jane Kelly was murdered by some person or persons unknown, the Secretary of State will advise the grant of Her Majesty's pardon to any accomplice not being a person who contrived or actually committed the murder who shall give such information and evidence as shall lead to the discovery and conviction of the person or persons who committed the murder.

(Signed) Charles Warren,
Commissioner of Police of the Metropolis'

Punch had the last word on the end of Sir Charles Warren's regime when it published a nursery rhyme entitled 'Who Killed Cock Warren?':

'Who chased Cock Warren?
"I," said the Home Sparrow,
"With my views cramped and narrow,
I chased Cock Warren." '

II

Clay Pipe Alice and Carroty Nell

Opinions still differ, not only in police circles, but among medical men, as to the exact number of murders which can be attributed to Jack the Ripper. It is not possible to answer this question with any degree of certainty.

I have examined some fourteen cases of murder between January 1887, and February 1891, and some of these so obviously have no link whatsoever with the Ripper crimes that I have omitted them in this book.

Forbes Winslow, who claimed that there were eight Ripper victims in all, insisted that the first murder was that of an unknown woman 'near Osborne and Wentworth Streets, Whitechapel in Christmas Week, 1887'. There is, however, little justification for this theory.

Sir Melville Macnaghten did not think that either Emma Smith or Martha Turner was a victim of the Ripper, but listed Nichols, Chapman, Eddowes, Stride and Kelly as 'positively being killed by the same man'.

Chief Constable Wensley in *Detective Days* wrote that 'officially there were only five, perhaps six murders attributed to Jack the Ripper'.

William Stewart, who made considerable researches into the subject in the early 'thirties, says: 'There was not the slightest evidence that Jack the Ripper killed Elizabeth Stride. It was merely a coincidence that Stride was killed within an hour of Eddowes.' And he puts the total of Ripper crimes at only four: 'whoever killed Mary Nichols, Annie Chapman, Catherine Eddowes and Mary Kelly had nothing whatsoever to do with the murders of Emma Smith, Martha Turner and Elizabeth Stride.'

So much for views on murders committed up to November 1888. But were there later atrocities perpetrated by the same savage killer? Sir Robert Anderson denied the possibility of this. 'However the fact may be explained, it is a fact that no other murder occurred in the Jack the Ripper series. The last and most horrible was on 9 November 1888. I assume that the murder of Alice McKenzie on 17 July 1889 was by another hand—an ordinary murder and not the work of a sexual maniac. The Poplar case of December, 1889, was a death from natural causes.'

After the death of Mary Kelly the East End was free from similar crimes for seven months. Kelly was buried in the Roman Catholic cemetery at Leytonstone after a service at Shoreditch Church. The coffin bore the inscription 'Marie Jeannette Kelly', thus preserving in death the fiction she had maintained in life. A Shoreditch clerk, Mr. Henry Wilson, offered to pay the cost of the interment, though there was no indication that he knew Kelly or was any relative of hers. Some of the funeral expenses, however, were met by a fund spontaneously raised by the East Enders themselves.

On the night of 21 November 1888 a murderous attack was made on a prostitute named Annie Farmer at a lodging house in George Street, Whitechapel. The man with whom she was spending the night attempted to cut her throat, panicked when she screamed and ran out of the building before he could be caught. But the police were sure that this affair had no connection with the murders, a conclusion which can be safely accepted.

The next real scare was what became known as 'The Thames Mystery' in June 1889. Portions of a human female body were found at various places on the foreshores on the Thames throughout this month. A thigh was discovered near the Albert Bridge, a piece of pelvis was found at Horsleydown and other fragments of flesh and bone were located in Battersea Park, Fulham and Limehouse. One of the last portions of the body to be retrieved was wrapped in a piece of white cloth such as is used by medical students engaged in a certain type of work. The head was never found, but a scar on the wrist of the victim enabled the remains to be identified as those of Elizabeth Jackson, a whore from a common lodging house in Turks Row, Chelsea.

Yet, despite certain similarities with the Whitechapel murders, it is almost certain that The Thames Mystery could not be attributed to the Ripper. But in the early hours of Wednesday, 17 July, of that year, the sickeningly familiar technique of the unknown killer was repeated. At 12.50 a.m. Police Constable Andrews was patrolling in Castle Alley, Whitechapel, when he came across the body of a woman lying in the shadow of a doorway. Her throat was cut and there were severe gashes across her abdomen.

Castle Alley was a narrow thoroughfare, about 180 yards in length, composed principally of workshops along one side and sheltered by a high wall on the other. Throughout the day and night the alley was blocked by tradesmen's carts, wagons and barrows. It was entered by means of an even darker passage which was not more than a yard in width.

Being so secluded and dark and with so narrow and—at night—sinister an entrance, Castle Alley lent itself to crime and so many people had been attacked and robbed there in the past that even hardened prostitutes hesitated to use it.

Police Constable Andrews had patrolled the alley regularly every quarter of an hour while on his beat. At 12.15 a.m. he had actually stopped to have his supper at the very spot where, twenty-five minutes later, he came across the body.

Mr. Monro, who was now Commissioner of the Metropolitan Police, was convinced at first that this was another Ripper crime. He was supported in this belief by the fact that only two weeks before a letter, signed Jack the Ripper, stated that it was the writer's intention 'to resume operations in July'. Presumably this was the letter to which Forbes Winslow referred.

The only clue which the police had to work on was a clay pipe found underneath the body. This enabled them to identify the victim as Alice McKenzie, of Gun Street, Spitalfields. She was known as 'Clay Pipe Annie' on account of her habit of smoking a clay pipe in bed, which was confirmed by the man with whom she had been living for the previous six years, John McCormack.

He testified that McKenzie was 'highly respectable', that she had come to London from Peterborough and was a charwoman to a Jewish family in Whitechapel. But the police told a different story; several of them said they had seen her soliciting men in Gun Street, Dorset Street and Brick Lane. She also had the reputation of being an habitual drunkard.

Thus, the type of victim, the neighbourhood of the crime, the thoroughness with which it was carried out and the ability of the killer to slip through a police cordon—two other police were on duty at each end of Castle Alley—suggested that the Ripper was at work again. There was even a bright, bronze farthing underneath the body.

But Dr. Bagster Phillips' post mortem did not seem to confirm this. The cuts on the lower part of the body, he said, were 'superficial' and seemed to be caused by the 'finger and thumb nails of a hand'. The throat was cut with 'a shortish blade' (in the other crimes a long blade had been used) and the injuries to the abdomen and throat 'were not similar to those in other East End murder cases'.

'There was no particular skill about this crime except that it showed sufficient knowledge of how to deprive someone of life speedily,' was the doctor's somewhat odd summing up of the affair.

Mr. Wynne Baxter, the Coroner, who seems to have had a genius for rambling on with irrelevancies in his summing up at inquests, made this comment:

'I hope at least these cases will open the eyes of those who are charitable to the necessity of doing their duty by trying to elevate the lower classes.'

An icy east wind lashed through the alleys of Whitechapel on the night of 13 February 1891. It whistled and moaned as it cut through the labyrinth of narrow passages and dark courts between Commercial Road and Leman Street, those dingy retreats where the women of the streets lured sailors, sometimes to seduce them, more often to rob them.

But on this night the wind had forced most of them to seek shelter, if they had the wherewithal. The alleys were practically deserted. Rubbing his hands and occasionally blowing on them, Police Constable Leeson cursed the fate that had given him such a drab, cheerless beat on a night like this—the neighbourhood of the Mint.

He had tramped the streets and alleys for twenty minutes without seeing a soul. If only something would happen, he thought, something to take his mind off this devilish cold. If only there were someone to talk to . . .

Peeep! Peeep! Peeeeep!

Leeson listened. In the wind he couldn't be sure, but he could swear it was the sound of a police whistle. He stopped, turned his ear to windward.

Peep! Peep!

There was no mistaking it now. It was a police whistle. Leeson needed no further prompting; he was only too glad to run and keep warm. He dashed off in what he thought was the direction of the call.

Round the corner was Swallow Gardens, a railway arch running from Royal Mint Street to Chambers Street, Whitechapel. There may have been gardens in this vicinity a century before, but certainly nothing at that time justified so rustic a name. It was a squalid, tumbledown district of mean houses.

In Chambers Street, Leeson found a colleague, P.C. Thompson, of 'H' Division. They had served together as recruits on the drill ground, so they were old friends. Thompson, like Leeson, still rather an inexperienced policeman, was standing, white and shocked, in the company of two night watchmen who had been patrolling the area.

'What's up?' asked Leeson.

Thompson didn't speak. He pointed to mid-way under the railway arch where a woman lay with a deep gash right across her throat. She was breathing very faintly still, but the wound in her throat made speech impossible. It was obvious she would not live many minutes.

'It's a Jack the Ripper job,' said Thompson.

Leeson bent and looked at the body. It was that of a young and rather pretty woman, about twenty-five to thirty years of age, with a shawl wrapped tightly round her. Her clothing was disarranged and there was no doubt that she had been brutally attacked; not only were there injuries to her throat, but mutilations of the lower part of her body.

'Well, at least we know who she is,' was Leeson's emphatic comment. 'She's Carroty Nell. Can't say off hand where she lives, but I've seen her touting for men round Tower Hill.'

In the gutter, close to her body, was what appeared to be a brand new crêpe hat. Yet, pinned to her shawl, crushed under her body was an old black hat. It would seem that she had only recently bought the crêpe hat and had pinned the old one to her dress after making the purchase.

P.C. Thompson had found the body while working his beat. It was his first murder case. Poor Thompson, he was to have a very brief career in the police force. Within a short time of this incident he was stabbed to death in a coffee-house brawl by a man named Abraham.

'I just can't understand it,' said Thompson. 'You can see that she's still alive. The job can only have been done seconds, or a minute at most, before I got here.'

'Well, she's dead now,' replied one of the night watchmen. 'We couldn't have done a thing even if a doctor had been on the spot.'

'Did you hear any noise?' asked Leeson.

'No, nothing at all. It was deadly still and there had been a lull in the wind, so I'd have heard any cry all right.'

Other police rapidly converged on the scene in response to the whistles. Swiftly they deployed in all directions in an effort to cut off the killer's retreat. A police inspector directed operations and planned to throw a cordon round the whole area.

Thompson was wearing rubber heels on his boots. He was quite sure no one could have heard him coming—'not within twenty yards at least,' he said. But he had neither seen nor heard anyone about.

The railway arch under which the body was found ran under the Great Eastern Railway goods yard and extended for about fifty yards into Royal Mint Street, coming out just opposite the Royal Mint Refinery. Here a policeman had been on duty all night, always within earshot of the place where the murder was committed. But, like Thompson and Leeson, he had heard nothing and seen no one.

Hundreds of police and civilians took part in the hunt for the killer, despite the weather. That same night every house in the district was searched. The police felt sure that, as nobody had been found, the killer must have taken refuge in one of the houses, or in some warehouse.

But the most thorough search revealed nothing. A cordon of police was thrown round the docks and no boats were allowed to leave until every member of the crews had been interviewed and been able to give a satisfactory account of his movements that night.

The woman was identified as Frances Coles, who had been living in a lodging house in Thrawl Street. There was ample evidence that prostitution was her sole means of support. She had been seen two hours before midnight in company with a 'short, wild-looking sailor, who seemed silent and morose', according to a statement from a witness taken by the police.

At daybreak the police called at several shops in the Spitalfields area to try to trace where the new hat which Coles had been wearing was bought. In this quest they were fortunate for not only was the shop located, but they obtained useful information about the purchase. The shopkeeper recalled that Coles had bought the hat the previous afternoon for one shilling and elevenpence halfpenny.

'I remember the sale because the woman first of all wanted to buy the hat by paying sixpence down and the rest of the money in two weekly instalments. I said "No", so she went outside, very disappointed. But I couldn't take a risk with the likes of her. Maybe I'd never have seen her again.

'While she was in the shop I noticed a man hanging around outside. I couldn't see him properly, as he kept his head turned away, but he was middle-aged, thick-set and fairly well dressed.

'Well, she went outside and I saw her talking to this chap. Then back she comes with the one and elevenpence halfpenny and says she'd found a friend who was willing to lend her the cash.

'After she'd bought the hat, she said her old bonnet might come in useful later, so she pinned it on her dress under her shawl. When she left the shop she joined the man some little distance down the street.'

Further inquiries elicited that Coles had been in the habit of taking men to a lodging house in White's Row, and that the previous night a man answering to the description of the person seen by the shopkeeper had called and asked for her. His hand was bleeding profusely and he explained that he had been attacked by some hooligans who had knocked him down and stolen all his money. He stayed half an hour with Frances and was heard to leave the house at 1 a.m. Half an hour later Coles left the house and she never returned afterwards.

But at 3 a.m.—shortly after the time of the murder—the man went back to White's Row. The lodging-house-keeper said he 'had a beard, cut pointed, and wore a peaked cap. He appeared agitated and was covered with blood.'

'What's happened to you this time?' asked the lodging-house-keeper.

'I've been attacked and robbed in Ratcliffe Highway,' was the reply.

'But how could you be robbed if you'd lost all your money already?'

'Well, not exactly robbed. They thought I'd got the spondulicks and that's why they beat me up. Then they found their mistake, so they gave me another walloping and left me in the gutter.'

The bearded man wanted a room for the rest of the night. But the lodging-house-keeper demurred. He was not altogether satisfied with the man's story and advised him to go to hospital for treatment.

The police called round at the London Hospital. Sure enough a man with a pointed beard had called there, complaining of an injury to his ribs, but the only injury the duty doctor could find was a severe cut over his eye. This had bled so profusely that the man's clothing was saturated with blood. After treatment he was allowed to go. The doctor surmised that he was a seafaring man.

News spread that at last the police were hot on the trail of the Ripper. There was more excitement in the East End than at any time since the murder of Mary Kelly. Large crowds gathered in front of Leman Street police station to await an arrest.

A London evening newspaper gave this description of the scene in Spitalfields:

'The night following the murder groups of roughs and even young boys and girls gathered near the scene of the crime. Many matches were spent by brutalised larrakins in examining the police mark—a cross on the wall—showing where the body had been found by the constable.

'The matchburners and creatures around them laughed, joked and swore as they searched the spot for traces of the victim's blood. A loud-thumping piano-organ was dragged to the spot and struck up a tune. The roughs and girls danced, the former bawling improvised choruses about Jack.'

Meanwhile a watch was kept at the docks for the bearded man's return to his ship. Police Constable Bryan recognised someone answering to his description outside the dock gates. He followed him to a public house, sent a message to Leman Street police station and shortly afterwards two detectives arrived to detain the stranger.

Admittedly the man's appearance was against him. He looked rather wild and ferocious, like an animal at bay. But he made no attempt to escape, nor did he seem to have heard about Coles' death. Indeed the story he told was straightforward and truthful—so truthful that he appeared deliberately to incriminate himself. He gave his name as James

Thomas Sadler, and it was soon discovered that this information was correct and that he was ship's fireman aboard the S.S. *Fez* in St. Katherine's Dock.

Without any further delay, or even any attempt to sift the evidence and cross-examine him, the police took Sadler to Leman Street police station and charged him with the wilful murder of Frances Coles. However incriminating the evidence was against him it cannot be said that he was treated fairly either by the police or the public. It was at once assumed that he had done the murder; the police behaved as though he were already convicted and, when he was taken to the cells, the crowd tried to lynch him.

After making his first appearance in the police court, Sadler was asked by the magistrate whether he wished to question any of the witnesses.

'There are several things I wish to say, but I am hungry and cold,' he replied. 'I have had nothing to eat since tea-time last night and I have been shifted from one cold cell to another. I am too hungry to speak.'

Public opinion was inflamed by many stories printed in the newspapers. These were highly prejudicial to the prisoner. His wife was found to be living in Kent, and she told an interviewer that her husband, who had left her and their five children, 'had fits of fury and would smash up the furniture when we lived together'. This story, headlined 'Prisoner's Wife: Amazing Tale', led to questions being asked in the House of Commons. The Home Secretary expressed regret that 'newspapers should seek to gratify public curiosity by publishing statements not made upon oath'.

Sadler protested his innocence from the first. Not hesitantly, or shiftily, but with indignation and conviction so that even the police began to see that the evidence against him was far from conclusive. Sadler did not deny that he had met Frances Coles. He even admitted buying her the hat, but he stoutly denied seeing her again after leaving her lodgings at 12.40 a.m.

No effort was made to give him legal aid. At last, in despair, and being ignorant of how to protect his own interests, Sadler wrote a letter from Holloway Prison to the secretary of the Stokers' Union, of which he was a member. This pathetic and ill-spelt letter complained bitterly of his ill-treatment at the hands of the police:

'What a godsend my case will be to the police if they can only conduct me, innocent as I am, to the bitter end—the scaffold! The whole detective system of Scotland Yard will be whitewashed in the sight of the world. The knife business is false.'

The 'knife business' was a reference to an entirely false statement published in one newspaper that Sadler's seaman's chest contained 'a dangerous weapon that very well might have been used to commit many murders'.

undertook his defence. Wilson probed every allegation that

Sadler's letter was passed on to Mr. Harry Wilson, who had been made against Sadler and was soon able to prove that most of them were unfounded. 'I studied minutely every detail of all the previous Ripper cases,' said Wilson, 'and I came to the conclusion that the murder of Frances Coles could not be included in this grisly category. I felt that if this case could be detached from the Ripper crimes it might be possible for police and public to view it more dispassionately.

'I went over the whole locality and compiled a mass of gruesome evidence bearing out this theory. An examination of the dates of previous crimes showed that on these occasions Sadler was on the high seas. The Ripper had always chosen an isolated alley or similar place which he knew was not often frequented by other people at night time. But the place where Coles was found was a notorious and regular resort of women of ill fame and was frequented by many people at all hours of the day and night.

'I found that the "startling stories" concerning Sadler's fits of temper and "wild staring eyes" were moonshine. Three sea captains made affidavits that Sadler was a peaceable and well-conducted man.'

It was the most improbable part of Sadler's story which saved him in the end. It proved to be the major flaw in the police's case. For it was established beyond any doubt that he had been twice attacked that night.

Nevertheless the police were most reluctant to admit defeat. Police court proceedings were drawn out by remands from week to week in the hope that some new piece of incriminating evidence would finally clinch the issue. Sadler should never have been arrested: there was insufficient evidence to justify the charge and eventually the police were forced to agree that they could not go on with the case. Mr. (later Sir) Charles Matthews informed the magistrate that he had been in consultation with the Attorney General and it had been decided that no more evidence could be offered. Sadler was immediately discharged.

Despite this the mob outside the police court was in a vindictive mood. Sadler was bundled into a cab which for some distance was pursued by a crowd of fist-shaking, cursing citizens.

A few nights later Mr. Harry Wilson was walking down Bow Street from his office when suddenly he was confronted by a short, thick-set man, dressed in black, with a hat well down over his eyes.

'The noiseless feet and his uncanny appearance started me,' Wilson confided later to a close friend.* 'How could I fail to see he clutched a big black bag.

' "Who are you?" I asked.

' "I am Jack," whispered the unknown, and added with a light laugh: "Perhaps there will soon be some more work for you to do, Mr. Wilson."

'A moment later I found myself alone.'

No murder—in Britain, at least—within a period of twenty years after the death of Frances Coles can be compared, even remotely, with the Ripper crimes. A most careful check has been made from available records in this country and it seems reasonable to draw a line after the murder in Swallow Gardens in February 1891.

* This story is cited from reminiscences of Harry Wilson which appeared in an article entitled ' "*Jack the Ripper*": Harry Wilson, Famous Bow Street Defence of Sadler' in the *Sunday News*, of 15 May 1927.

Once again the killer was not brought to justice.

In this book I have aimed to give in some detail all possible cases of murder which *might* be attributed to the Ripper. I must stress the word *might*. There is insufficient evidence to link the deaths of Martha Turner, Mary Nichols, Annie Chapman, Catherine Eddowes, Elizabeth Stride, Mary Kelly, Alice McKenzie and Frances Coles positively with one and the same killer. All one can say is that it is just possible that one man slew all eight. Modern forensic science would undoubtedly have enabled experts to decide positively which were the work of one and the same man.

Only Forbes Winslow was so bold as to assert that there were eight Ripper victims and, as we have seen, in his list he omits Frances Coles and includes an unknown woman murdered in Whitechapel in 1887 on far scantier evidence than that in the case of Coles.

On the other hand the figure of four murders, suggested by William Stewart, seems much too cautious, especially as the majority police opinion puts the total at five or six.

My own submission is that, taking into account police and medical evidence, the technique employed and the fact that similar weapons were used in each instance, Turner, Chapman, Nichols, Stride, Eddowes and Kelly were killed by the same person. I attribute the lack of systematic mutilations in the cases of Turner and Stride to the fact that on each occasion the killer was disturbed.

The medical evidence regarding Alice McKenzie seems to rule her out and, apart from this, there is the doctor's view that this crime was committed with a short-bladed knife. It seems unlikely that the Ripper would change his weapon.

It is against Frances Coles' name that the most important query lies. Doctors disagreed again in this case. Some said the technique of throat cutting and mutilation was similar to that in earlier crimes; others said there was no comparison. But it must be borne in mind that Coles was still breathing when P.C. Thompson found her. She must have been murdered less than half a minute before Thompson arrived on the scene, so the probability is that the killer was disturbed before he could carry out further mutilations. If the Ripper was the killer of Coles, then this, as will be seen later, rules out at least one if not more of the major suspects in the Whitechapel murders.

Whether the Ripper murdered other prostitutes elsewhere in the world either before or after the Whitechapel crimes is a question which must be examined later. From Tunis, Paris, the United States and St. Petersburg came reports of similar killings between the years 1886 and 1894. But on careful investigation some of these reports can be rejected, while others were totally unfounded. On 15 January 1889 a newspaper report from Tunis hinted that the Ripper had been tracked down in that city. The French police, in rounding up a gang of bandits and assassins, came across a Briton named Alfred Gray, who answered the Scotland Yard descriptions of the man wanted in connection with the East End murders. But he was cleared of suspicion.

For a long time after the death of Mary Kelly there was a belief in some quarters that the murderer was an American. The chief of the New York police paid a visit to Scotland Yard and is said to have reported a similar series of killings in Texas and Jersey City. The investigation of some of these cases and a nation-wide check on Americans residing in this country gave Detective-Inspector Abberline and his colleagues almost as much work to do between 1889 and 1892 as that involved by all the Ripper cases of 1888.

This last fact is of the utmost importance in assessing some of the statements which will be recorded in the next chapter.

12

The case of the drowned barrister

It was a remarkable coincidence that during August 1888 the Lyceum Theatre was let to an American actor, Richard Mansfield, who opened a season of plays at this home of melodrama with *Dr. Jekyl and Mr. Hyde*, based on the book by Robert Louis Stevenson.

This may or may not have given rise to the view, developed in the first place by amateur criminologists and later adopted by the police, that the Ripper was a mad medico masquerading as a member of the working classes. But doctors became prime suspects, as Dr. D. G. Halstead testifies in his memoirs, *Doctor in the Nineties*: 'Naturally those of us at the London Hospital were in the limelight. The East End was alive with plain-clothes men. They were lurking in every alleyway, ready to pounce, and this more than anything gave us a sinister feeling. . . . On more than one occasion I became aware that I was being shadowed by the plain-clothes men. . . . I must be the only man living to have been suspected of being Jack the Ripper.'

At this stage of the story it is useful to pause and take stock. The evidence so far given is so conflicting, often so contradictory, that the reader may be forgiven for assuming that the identity of the Ripper must for ever remain a mystery.

As an antidote to such pessimism it will be helpful to examine some of the theories held by the police and other experts at the time, and, equally important, to analyse some of those expounded in more recent years by criminologists and writers who have had the benefit of information denied to their predecessors. By doing so it is possible to eliminate some of the dead wood of the wilder theories, to sweep away the swirling leaves of illusions and to see whether in the clearing we make there is any marked unanimity of opinion.

This will at least remove many misconceptions and enable the reader—and, one hopes, the author, too—to concentrate on essentials in this quest for the most remarkable mass-murderer of the past century.

Yet before doing this I am tempted by a criticism of Colin Wilson, himself an interested student of the Ripper crimes, to mention briefly some of the wilder theories. In his review of the first edition of my book Colin Wilson mentioned that there were 'a few stones' which I had left unturned. For example Mr. Wilson, having obtained his information from the magazine *Tit-Bits*, quoted the fact that General Booth of the Salvation Army had a secretary who had dreams about the murders before they were committed and who, after the killing of Carroty Nell, disappeared, leaving General Booth convinced the man was the Ripper.

As Mr. Wilson made this point, I will add a few more of the wilder theories. It was said that the Ripper was an illegitimate son of British royalty, a legend which arose out of a suspicion that in the end the police seemed anxious to hush up the whole affair. Pat Pitman, who collaborated with Colin Wilson in an *Encyclopaedia of Murder*, has even mentioned the idea that Jack was George Gissing, the novelist—while even so benevolent a character as Dr. Barnardo has been named on the grounds that he was devoted to waifs and strays and that most of the unwanted children in his district were the offspring of prostitutes.

Yet another suggestion made is that Walter Sickert, the painter, was Jack the Ripper. This is completely wide of the mark, but it does lead one to an interesting sidelight on the case. The reason for Sickert being suspected is that he was believed to have made sketches and paintings of the Ripper crimes. I have not been able to establish whether or not this is true, but the idea may have mistakenly arisen from the fact that one of his paintings, *The Camden Town Murder*, depicted a nude woman on a bed in a dingy bedroom. But there is no doubt that Sickert was personally interested in the Ripper crimes as is shown in *A Free House: Being the Writings of Walter Richard Sickert*, edited by Osbert Sitwell.

Referring to 'the intrinsic and abiding horror of that extraordinary series of crimes', Sitwell writes that Sickert was interested in them 'because he thought he knew the identity of the murderer. . . . Some years after the murders he had taken a room in a London suburb. An old couple looked after the house and when he had been there some months the woman, with whom he used often to talk, asked him one day, as she was dusting the room, if he knew who had occupied it before him. When he said "No", she had waited a moment and then replied, "Jack the Ripper?" . . . .

'Her story was that his predecessor had been a veterinary student. After he had been a month or two in London, this delicate-looking young man—he was consumptive—took to occasionally staying out all night. His landlord and landlady would hear him come in about six in the morning and then walk about in his room for an hour or two, until the first edition of the morning paper was on sale, when he would creep lightly downstairs and run to the corner to buy one. Quietly he would return and go to bed. But an hour later, when the old man called him, he would notice, by the traces in the fireplace, that his lodger had burnt the suit he had been wearing the previous evening. For the rest of the day the millions of people in London would be discussing the terrible new murder, plainly belonging to the same series, that had been committed in the small hours. Only the student seemed never to mention them: but then he knew no one and talked to no one, though he did not seem lonely . . . the old couple did not know what to make of it: daily his health grew worse and it seemed improbable that this gentle, ailing, silent youth should be responsible for such crimes. They could hardly credit their own senses and then, before they could make up their minds whether to warn the police or not, the lodger's health had suddenly grown much worse and his mother, a widow who was devoted to him, had come to fetch him back to Bournemouth where she lived. . . . From that moment the murders stopped.

. . . He died three months later.'

Osbert Sitwell added that in discussing this matter with his brother while he was actually engaged in writing this account of Sickert, the latter reminded him that the painter 'had told us that when his landlady had confided to him that morning the name of Jack the Ripper, Sickert had scribbled it down in pencil on the margin of a French edition of Casanova's *Memoirs* which he happened to be reading at the time and that, subsequently, he had given the book away—we thought he had said to Sir William Rothenstein. Sickert had added: 'And there it will be now if you want to know the name.' Accordingly I wrote to Lady Rothenstein, but neither she nor Sir William remembered the book. On my consulting Mrs. Sickert, she maintained that he had given the volume to Sir William's brother, Mr. Albert Rutherston. And this proved to have been the case. My friend Mr. Rutherston informed me that he had only recently lost the book during the bombing of London and that there had been several pencil notes entered in the margin, in Sickert's handwriting. . . .'

I have quoted the above in some detail because it will be worth while following up this slender clue later on.

Even as recently as February 1959 *Reynolds News* pubished an interview with a retired blacksmith of Worthing, Mr. George Henry Edwards, who believed that his late cousin Frank was Jack the Ripper. The report stated that Mr. Edwards recalled 'a night in 1888 when a woman was murdered in Whitechapel . . . A few hours later Cousin Frank—an accountant, then between thirty and forty—arrived from his South London home at the Edwards house in Northgate, Chichester, Sussex.

'Frank was wearing a bowler hat, gold-rim spectacles, a black moustache and a brown cardigan with red spots. He carried an attaché case. In it were a razor and a blood-stained collar.'

One would have thought that the blood-stained collar explained the purpose of the razor: that a careless shaver had cut himself.

But the report went on to say that 'a report of the murder

in the evening paper said a policeman had seen a man with a bowler hat, gold-rim spectacles, a black moustache and an attaché case walking away from the scene'. Mr. Edwards recalled that his cousin was always saying that he hated women. When asked why he did not reveal his suspicion before this date, he replied: 'I kept my mouth shut. Otherwise I might have been done in too.'

Then again on 15 February 1960 the *New York World Telegram and Sun* revealed that a Mrs. Elizabeth Ross, of 115 Ocean Avenue, Brooklyn, believed that a friend of her father's was Jack the Ripper. Mrs. Ross's father was Griffith S. Salway, an official of the English Speaking Union, who died in 1952. Until his death he believed that he was the only man in the world who knew the identity of the East End killer. The tale, as Mrs. Ross recalled it, was as follows:

'Mr. Salway was twenty-two and working as a secretary in a brokerage firm in Gresham House in London. There he made the acquaintance of a South American called Alonzo Maduro—a stocky man with coal-black hair and unusually large hands.

'Maduro, who dressed like a fashion plate, said he had discovered gold in America and was in England to float a stock issue. Young Salway was flattered when the stranger befriended him and invited him to frequent dinners at expensive restaurants.

'It was the night of Easter Sunday, 1888—the night before the first Ripper murder [in fact, this was the date of the killing of Emma Smith which is not regarded as being in the category of Ripper crimes] that Salway ran into Maduro in a slum quarter of the city. This time he was wearing, not his band-box attire, but a black cape to the ankles and a black slouch hat. In his hand was a little black bag.

'From that time on the stranger kept more to himself and one woman of the streets after another was viciously mutilated. On the morning after the seventh Ripper murder the South American came to the brokerage house and it was obvious to Salway that his friend was upset:

' "Go to my room at once," he said, "and put my things

into a trunk and send it to this hotel. I will be waiting for it. Please . . . My life is in danger."

'Mr. Salway agreed and as he was packing the box he noticed it had a false bottom. Curiosity prompted him to investigate and he found: a long black cape that would reach to a man's ankles, a black slouch hat and a brown-paper package. Inside that was an oilskin bundle which contained several glittering surgical instruments.

'He never told the police about his find because they were constantly besieged by crackpots and he did not want to be ridiculed. There was never another Jack the Ripper murder and the stranger was never seen again.'

Sir Melville Macnaghten's views on the Ripper crimes are specially interesting if only because on one occasion he stated that he had 'documentary proof of the identity of the criminal'. This raises the reasonable query as to where this documentary proof is to be found. In the first edition of my book I quoted a statement given to me by a reliable source that Sir Melville admitted not only having had the 'documentary proof', but that he had 'burnt the papers'. This seemed an amazing admission from a senior police officer: it is even more incredible that it has never been officially refuted or confirmed.

After the first edition of my book was published the Dowager Lady Aberconway, daughter of Sir Melville, expressed her doubts as to the truth of this statement. She had good reason to do so because her father left behind his personal notes on the Ripper cases which I have been permitted to read. Her view was that her father may have been so pestered by friends at his club about the identity of the Ripper that he tried to put them off the scent by jokingly pretending to have destroyed the papers.

But I am reliably informed by police authorities today that any such 'documentary proof' is no longer in existence and that all that remains is a relatively short memorandum of Sir Melville's opinions, based, presumably, on evidence he had studied. The official view is that someone destroyed the evidence.

In his book *Days of My Years* Sir Melville wrote: 'Although, as I shall endeavour to show in this chapter, the Whitechapel murderer, in all probability, put an end to himself soon after the Dorset Street affair in November, 1888, certain facts, pointing to this conclusion, were not in possession of the police till some years after I became a detective officer.

'The fury of the murderer,' Sir Melville stated in this same book, 'increased on every occasion. The man was a sexual maniac, but such madness takes Protean forms . . . lust for blood and hatred of women—not infrequently the maniac possesses a diseased body and this was probably so in Jack's case.

'I incline to the belief that the individual who held up London in terror resided with his own people; that he absented himself from home at certain times and that he committed suicide on or about the 10th of November 1888.'

Sexual madness certainly takes varied forms, but it is an error to assume that it is often linked with bodily disease. Ignorance of psychiatry and venereal diseases in this period caused some to believe that the killer was in the tertiary stages of syphilis. But it is, of course, ridiculous to suggest that such a man could also be a subtle and efficient killer. A man in the tertiary stages of syphilis might become suddenly violent and kill someone, but by the time he had reached such an advanced stage of the disease—bones, muscles and brain tissues infected—he would certainly be so completely insane as to be unable to repeat the attack without detection.

Sir Melville's statement about the suicide theory is supported from other quarters. Major Arthur Griffiths, who, as already mentioned, first supported the theory that the killer was a lunatic Polish Jew, finally, 'after careful consideration', narrowed down his suspects to three men. 'The second possible criminal was a Russian doctor, also insane, who had been in the habit of carrying about surgical knives and instruments in his pockets; his antecedents were of the very worst and at the time of the Whitechapel murders he was hiding, or, at least, his whereabouts were never exactly known.

'The third person was of the same type, but the suspicion in his case was the stronger and there was every reason to believe that his own friends entertained grave doubts about him. He also was a doctor in the prime of life, was believed to be insane, or on the borderland of insanity, and he disappeared immediately after the last murder, that in Miller's Court on the 9th of November 1888.

'On the last day of that year, seven weeks later, his body was found floating in the Thames and was said to have been in the water a month. The theory in this case was that after his last exploit, which was the most fiendish of all, his brain gave way and he became furiously insane and committed suicide.

'It is at least a strong presumption that Jack the Ripper died or was put under restraint after the Miller's Court affair, which ended this series of crimes. It would be interesting to note whether in this third case the man was left-handed or ambidextrous, both suggestions having been advanced by medical experts after viewing the victims.'*

Griffiths' assertions lack any supporting evidence and they are mainly interesting only in that they coincide to some extent with what Macnaghten said. Macnaghten had access to police files whereas one assumes that Griffiths did not. But Griffiths, the amateur criminologist, was the first writer to publish such a theory—thirteen years before Macnaghten went on record in print.

Yet Griffiths is obviously unsure of himself in that he named three possible suspects. The case he made out for the third suspect is unimpressive. If this doctor were known, his body could have been identified even though it had been in the water a month. Griffiths does not say that it was identified: he merely implies that it was. Then he makes the curiously contradictory statement that 'Jack the Ripper died or was put under restraint after the Miller's Court affair'. He can't have it both ways. Was the doctor found drowned, or was he put in an asylum?

In *The Story of Scotland Yard*, by Sir Basil Thomson, published in 1935, the former Assistant Commissioner of the Metropolitan Police wrote of the Ripper murders that 'the belief of the C.I.D. officers at the time was that they were the

* *Mysteries of Police and Crime*, by Major A. Griffiths.

work of an insane Russian doctor and that the man escaped arrest by committing suicide at the end of 1888'.

This, coming from a distinguished police chief, seems categorical enough. Sir Basil, however, rather spoiled the effect of his statement by adding that 'the only clue was the fact that the man who ripped women up with what must have been a surgical knife had probably been at some time a medical student'. If this were the only clue, how in heaven's name could the C.I.D. be sure of the killer's identity?

Then again, Sir Basil commented: 'Though there was one other murder of the same kind at the beginning of 1889, it was considered that this was one of the imitative crimes so often committed after a series of crimes has deeply impressed the public mind.'

But there is no trace in newspapers of the period of any such crime 'at the beginning of 1889'. Perhaps Sir Basil was thinking of the Coles murder of February 1891. If so, this suggests he was relying on his memory rather than on factual records.

Thus two police chiefs and one criminologist have gone on record as declaring that Jack the Ripper committed suicide at the end of 1888. Needless to say countless writers since have repeated this theory and some have even suggested it disposes of the mystery.

Yet, in fact, it only confuses the issue. For the simple test for the theory is to find out what doctor was found drowned in the Thames on the last day of December 1888. And as soon as this test is applied the theory is destroyed. For in none of the leading morning or evening newspapers of the day is there any report of such an incident at any time between 9 November 1888 and the end of January 1889. Nor do the obituary columns of the newspapers, nor those of the Medical Directory for 1889 and 1890, provide any clues. In the London area only one doctor's death was recorded for the last day of December 1888—that of George Anderson, Medical Inspector-General of the Army, from natural causes.

It is unbelievable that, if any doctor had committed suicide, or had been found drowned, the news would not have been published somewhere. If the police suspected that the dead doctor were the Ripper, then it is even more remarkable that the story never found its way into print. For, contrary to the current belief that in Victorian times the press was more easily silenced, the reverse is true: the crime reporters of the 'eighties gave a much more detailed account of criminal investigation than the by-lined specialists of today.

The answer, according to Tom Cullen in his book, *Autumn of Terror*, is that Jack the Ripper was not a doctor, as has been alleged by some police chiefs, but a barrister! True, Mr. Cullen admits that Sir Melville Macnaghten describes this man in his notes as 'M. J. Druitt, a doctor of about forty-one years of age and of fairly good family, who disappeared at the time of the Miller's Court murder, and whose body was found floating in the Thames on 3rd December, i.e. seven weeks after the said murder'.

But Mr. Cullen goes on to show how contemporary newspaper reports make it quite clear that the Montagu John Druitt whose body was recovered from the Thames on 31 December 1888 was 'a barrister-at-law . . . recently an assistant at a school in Blackheath'.

The facts are as follows: on the last day of 1888 the body of 'a well-dressed man' was discovered in the Thames near Chiswick by a waterman named Winslow. From papers found on his body it was clear that he had friends at Bournemouth. The *County of Middlesex Independent* of 2 January 1889 stated that he was 'a man of about forty years', an estimate close to that made by Sir Melville Macnaghten, adding that he had been in the water about a month. But the *Independent* of 5 January, reporting the inquest, stated that he was 'thirty-one years of age' and that the pockets of the deceased were found to contain stones.

The fullest report of the inquest appeared in the *Southern Guardian* of 5 January 1889:

'An inquiry was on Wednesday held by Dr. Diplock, at Chiswick, respecting the death of Montagu John Druitt, thirty-one years of age, who was found drowned in the

Thames. The deceased was identified by his brother, a solicitor residing at Bournemouth, who stated that the deceased was a barrister-at-law, but had recently been an assistant at a school in Blackheath. The deceased had left a letter, addressed to Mr. Valentine, of the school, in which he alluded to suicide. Evidence having been given as to discovering deceased in the Thames—upon his body were found a cheque for fifty pounds and sixteen pounds in gold—the Jury returned a verdict of "Suicide whilst of unsound mind".

'The deceased gentleman was well known and much respected in this neighbourhood. He was a barrister of bright talent, he had a promising future before him, and his untimely end is deeply deplored. The funeral took place in Wimborne cemetery on Thursday afternoon.'

I propose to examine in some detail Sir Melville Macnaghten's full notes on the Jack the Ripper crimes later on. But at this stage it is necessary to see on what other grounds Tom Cullen bases his case for Montagu John Druitt being the Ripper. 'The key to the mystery probably lies in Macnaghten's statement,' writes Cullen: ' "From private information I have little doubt but that his own family suspected this man of being the Whitechapel murderer." ' But beyond that statement Mr. Cullen offers no evidence at all, only surmise. The text of the letter left behind for Mr. Valentine is not produced, nor is any evidence given as to the state of Druitt's mind, nor any mention whatsoever that he had ever been seen in the vicinity of the crimes.

'At some time between 3 December, when he was last seen alive, and 31 December, when his body was taken from the Thames, Montagu John Druitt's family must have reported his disappearance to the police,' writes Cullen. 'In reporting him missing, did one of the Druitts seize the occasion to confide to the police the family's private fears concerning Montagu John?'

Naming Jack the Ripper became almost a parlour game in the years between 1888 and 1900. Many criminologists are apt to be romantics and there was a great temptation to identify the Ripper with some other villain executed for other offences round about this period.

'On the twenty-first of May,
Frederick Deeming passed away;
On the scaffold he did say—
"Ta-ra-da-boom-di-ay!"
"Ta-ra-da-boom-di-ay!"
This is a happy day,
An East End holiday,
The Ripper's gone away.'

Such doggerel led to the statement in the press that 'Scotland Yard is convinced that the Ripper was Frederick Deeming, who was caught in Australia for the murder of his wife in Britain'.

It is a preposterous suggestion for which there is not the slightest foundation or any police evidence to back it up. Deeming murdered several women and cemented their bodies under kitchen or scullery floors before he went off to Australia, where he was convicted of a similar offence. In one of his statements Deeming openly declared he murdered these women because they 'spread a vile infection'. This would seem to be the slender basis for linking him with the Ripper. Deeming was hanged at Swanston Jail, Melbourne, in 1893.

Oddly enough, the same motive for killing—revenge for the contraction of venereal disease—was attributed to Dr. Thomas Neill Cream, yet another murderer who was said to be the Ripper. Cream poisoned prostitutes for no other apparent reason than to gratify some sadistic quirk. Sir Melville Macnaghten declared: 'It has been widely published that on the scaffold Neill Cream exclaimed: "I am Jack the —— just as the bolt was drawn. But during the whole period covered by the East End murders Neill Cream was in prison in U.S.A.'

H. M. Wallbrook also mentioned this theory,* saying that

* *Murders and Murder Trials,* by H. M. Wallbrook.

Billington, the executioner, was a witness of this incident and swore positively that he heard Cream utter these words. But, even if this were true, the explanation is obvious: Cream was a notorious exhibitionist. It was his incurable exhibitionism, his delight in drawing attention to himself that brought him to the gallows.

Cream was in prison in the United States from 1882 to June, 1891, which clearly leaves him out of the reckoning. But two points about the Cream case are of interest to the student of the Ripper crimes. When he came to London in October, 1891 Cream was, despite his criminal record, able to pass himself off as a 'Dr. Neill' in Lambeth. Before he was caught by the police he carried on a surreptitious practice—mainly in abortions—and poisoned four prostitutes. The significance of this is that there was no adequate supervision of migrant doctors in this country at the time. Foreigners with criminal records, quacks with inadequate qualifications could and did practise in Britain, even though this meant taking rooms in the back streets of the slums. Thus a foreign doctor, who was not registered here, or an unqualified Briton, might well have been the 'Dr. Jekyll' to whom the various police chiefs referred. This factor has not been ignored in research into the theory of the mad doctor who drowned himself in the Thames. Because of this possibility details of *all* Thames suicides during the period have been reviewed and the conclusion is still the same. There was no suicide which could be linked with the murders.

The second point of interest about Cream was that the great criminal advocate, Edward Marshall Hall, once defended him (without knowing it at the time) at the Old Bailey. Some years before Cream was convicted, Marshall Hall was briefed by Mr. Harry Wilson to defend a man for bigamy. When he walked into court he was aghast to find a bevy of young women who claimed to have been married to the prisoner.

The case seemed hopeless even to so skilled an advocate as Marshall Hall and he advised his client to plead guilty.

'Nothing of the kind,' replied the prisoner. 'This is a case of mistaken identity. Communicate with the jail at Sydney, Australia, and you will find that I was there at the time that I am supposed to have committed these offences.'

A cable was sent to Sydney, giving the name and a full description of the prisoner and, to the amazement of all concerned, except the prisoner, a reply came back immediately confirming his statement.

The prisoner was released and Marshall Hall, wrote his biographer, Edward Marjoribanks, 'left the court, musing on the narrow escape of an innocent man. He was astonished later when he recognised Cream in court. The mystery was never explained, but Marshall Hall's theory was that Neill Cream had a double in the underworld and they went by the same name and used each other's terms of imprisonment as alibis for each other.'

What baffled criminologists most was the lack of motive for the Ripper crimes. Sexual sadism in various forms is more common, even in civilised communities, than people care to admit. When it takes the form of murder and mutilation it is usually accompanied by an exhibitionism which ultimately gives the culprit away. But the sexual crimes perpetrated by the Ripper were extraordinary in the almost unique combination of seemingly uncontrollable bestiality, a detached, clinical attitude to sex and a disciplined, systematic mind allied to a relentless purposefulness. This is the paradox which is hardest to probe. Mr. Wallbrook spoke of the 'joy in mutilation of the sexual degenerate', the careful arrangement of the removed organs, 'the entrails twined in a festoon round the dead woman's neck'. Yet all these crimes were concentrated on one relatively small area—not much more than a square mile—where, after the first two murders, police patrols were trebled. The killer selected an area where, as murder succeeded murder, the risk of arrest increased. This certainly is not true to type, at any rate in the case of the average sadistic killer, though it was to some extent true of Neill Cream and Neville Heath.

Not only did the Ripper concentrate on victims in the same area, but of the same class, of the same drab profession and, invariably, drunkards. Now such a maniac might well possess, as the Ripper correspondence puts it, 'a down on whores'. But he would hardly be likely to concentrate on whores in one district, or even of one class—the lowest. If he thought he had a 'divinely appointed mission', as suggested by Forbes Winslow, then he would wish to kill whores everywhere, in the West End as well as the East, in Westminster just as much as in Whitechapel, at Spithead as well as Spitalfields.

The suggestion made by Mr. Wynne Baxter, the Coroner, that the killer's desire 'was to possess the missing abdominal organ' could only have been true in the cases of Annie Chapman and Catherine Eddowes. When the murderer had the maximum opportunities for removing and taking away with him any organ he wished—the Miller's Court murder—he made no attempt to do so.

As for the theory that there was 'a market for that missing organ', this is little more than fantasy. Yet, because the killer chose his victims from the dregs of society, this was advanced as a powerful factor in favour of this argument. One wonders whether the Coroner himself was hoaxed as the mysterious hunter after female organs was never traced.

Mr. Leonard Matters decided that the probable motive was that the Ripper was looking for one particular woman—Mary Kelly—and that, having found her, he ceased his killings. His opinion was that the murderer was a West End doctor, whose son had died of venereal disease contracted from Mary Kelly, and that the father vowed to find the woman and kill her.

Why, then, did he kill other women first? Mr. Matters' reply to this is that the doctor knew that Kelly was somewhere in the East End, that he associated with whores in an effort to find out her address, and that once these whores knew he was looking for Kelly they became potential witnesses against him. So he slew to silence them for ever. Perhaps his earlier inquiries sent him in search of the wrong Kelly, for Eddowes had used this name as one of her aliases.

Mr. Matters did not name this doctor, but merely gave him the pseudonym of 'Dr. Stanley'.* The origin of his reconstruction of the case is as follows: 'I had spent some years

* *The Mystery of Jack the Ripper,* by L. W. Matters.

in Buenos Aires as editor of an English newspaper published in the Argentine capital and had found the confession of Dr. Stanley printed in Spanish in one of the local journals. While I cannot vouch for the genuineness of the story of Dr. Stanley, I still think it is very probable that he went abroad after the murders.'

A report in an Argentinian journal told how some years previously a British doctor on his death bed in a Buenos Aires hospital had confessed to a former colleague that he was Jack the Ripper. But neither the identity of this doctor nor that of his colleague was revealed. Nor do obituary lists or records of deaths in Buenos Aires support the statement.

There was, it is true, no positive cure for syphilis in the 'eighties, but there was treatment for the disease. One would assume that a doctor's son, who was also a medical student, would be able to receive such treatment. Syphilis is a slow killer even when there is no treatment and it is unthinkable that this young man could have died from it within five years, assuming that he could only have met Mary Kelly within this period.

Mr. Matters' proposition rests mainly on the flimsy evidence that Kelly served her apprenticeship in prostitution 'in a house in the West End under the tutelage of a "madam"' and that it was Dr. Stanley's son with whom she went to France. It would seem unwise to accept Joseph Barnett's version of Kelly's past. Barnett was a straightforward, honest witness, but he was only repeating what Kelly had told him. If Mr. Matters had conducted his researches further into Kelly's past he would have found there was no basis at all for the suggestion that she had been a highly successful West End whore who, contrary to custom, had broken loose from a London brothel to live a luxurious life in Paris.

Surely the obvious flaw in Barnett's story was the puzzle of how a girl of only twenty-five—and still good-looking—could have plunged from the dizzy pinnacle of a gay life as mistress of a rich young man in Paris to the depths of Whitechapel street-walking in a period of little more than three or four years. The progress of a harlot may be spectacularly swift when it is uphill, but on the downward path it is not as headlong as this at so early an age.

The answer is that Kelly's story was just as much romantic fantasy as the name of 'Marie Jeannette' which she gave herself. Kelly was a little above the average East End whore for two reasons only: first, her youth and attractiveness, secondly, that she only went street-walking when she lacked a man to keep her. Mr. Henry Wilson, who paid her funeral expenses, discovered that, after leaving Cardiff, she went, not to the West End of London, but to set up a tiny, drab shop in Commercial Road out of the paltry proceeds of compensation paid by the mineowners after her husband's death. And it was because these tycoons of the coalfields had kept her waiting eighteen months for this meagre sum that she had drifted into prostitution in Cardiff.

She was never in any West End bordello, high class or otherwise; she may have ventured to the bright lights of Piccadilly on a few occasions, but for the whole of the time she was in London she was domiciled in the East End. She had no business sense, no education, and she squandered her money in drink; not unnaturally her venture into shopkeeping ended in dismal failure. Afterwards she lived with three different men in the Whitechapel area until she met Barnett. But to give her legend the appearance of reality she borrowed the name of a French whore.

The final flaw in Mr. Matters' theory is, however, that Mary Kelly was definitely not suffering from syphilis. Dr. Bagster Phillips' findings—not given at the inquest—were that Kelly was 'in the early stages of pregnancy and that she was healthy and suffering from no other disease except alcoholism'.

Mr. Robin Odell in his own research into the Ripper crimes concentrated on the fact that, as he puts it, 'whilst a great deal of effort has been expended by various writers on trying to prove Jack the Ripper's identity, comparatively little has been written about the murderer's motive'.* It is a fair enough criticism, but the quest for the motive is beset with many complexities. For example Mr. Odell considered the possi-

* *Jack the Ripper in Fact and Fiction,* by Robin Odell.

bility that the Ripper was an epileptic killer, but had to admit that such a murderer invariably made no attempt at concealment or escape. Finally, Mr. Odell hazarded his own opinion that Jack the Ripper was a *shochet* or ritual Jewish slaughterman, and the nearest he could suggest as a motive for such a man being the killer was that 'a ritual slaughterman steeped in Old Testament law might have felt some religious justification for killing prostitutes. Talmudic law was harsh where harlotry was concerned and in certain instances whores could be punished by strangulation or stoning.'

It is an interesting theory. The *shochet*, trained in anatomical knowledge for the purpose of carrying out the orthodox Talmudic slaughter of animals for meat, would have had sufficient skill to carry out the murders perpetrated by the Ripper. Similarly the method of carving up the bodies bore a resemblance to that of the Jewish slaughterman—ensuring that the throat had been properly cut, opening the abdomen and examining the organs for defects. Also, as Mr. Odell says, 'the *shochet*'s background and social standing among his own people, together with his education and official position, would have made him a cut above the ordinary East Ender'. In short, he would have been able to walk around in the East End without attracting suspicion to himself because he looked respectable.

So much for theory. The truth was that by the time the Ripper had committed the third and fourth of his crimes most people were beginning to look for a respectably dressed man of some social standing. Respectability was no longer a safeguard for the killer. And from the very beginning the police and others had not only considered the theory of a slaughterman being responsible, but had carried out a thorough examination of abbatoirs and a check-up on all known slaughtermen. They questioned and even arrested slaughterers, including a *shochet*, but all to no purpose. One and all were cleared of suspicion.

13

Dr. Jekyll or 'Mrs.' Hyde?

The most ingenious solution put forward is that of Mr. William Stewart, to which reference was made in Chapter 10—that the killer was a woman.

This opinion deserves detailed consideration because Mr. Stewart argued his case logically and presented it convincingly. And, indeed, the theory is much more plausible than that of Mr. Matters. Who could carry out such murders and avoid suspicion more easily than a woman? And, even if a policeman detected her beside a recently murdered prostitute, who, in such circumstances, would be more likely to remain unsuspected than a midwife? She could say that she had been summoned to attend an *accouchement* in the early hours of the morning, that she had come across the woman and had examined her to see whether she could render assistance. A midwife, known to the street-walkers, could take her victims by surprise, which would explain the fact that there were no cries for help. A midwife would also have some knowledge of anatomy.

Midwives in the East End were known to practise abortion and this, Mr. Stewart suggested, provided a possible motive. A midwife whose activities in abortion resulted in death might have been betrayed to the police by a street-walker and, after a jail sentence, become embittered against whores generally. But this is not a particularly convincing motive for a mass-murderer. Also, while it is true that many female killers have been guilty of mutilating their victims, such mutilation is invariably frenzied, senseless, hysterical destructiveness. And the Ripper's technique was very different: it was systematic, orderly in a bizarre way and, in the case of Kelly's death, was far too skilfully performed to be the work of a midwife.

Yet it is on the case of Kelly that Mr. Stewart largely based his arguments in favour of a murderess rather than a murderer. He seized on the fact of the fire in the grate in the Miller's Court room. This, he argued, could only have been to destroy something: 'the remains of the bonnet and piece of charred velvet were from articles which had never been in the possession of the murdered woman, though some of her clothing was missing'.*

Thus a new picture of the Miller's Court crime was built up. The midwife, under some pretext (perhaps Kelly's pregnancy), calls on Kelly in the middle of the night. She kills her, mutilates her and then, finding her own clothes soaked in blood, takes them off and burns them in the fire which she has lit. Then, putting on Kelly's clothes, she makes her escape through the window.

But Kelly had only been pregnant for about three months, so she would be unlikely to summon a midwife, still less to be expecting a call from one. And Mr. Stewart omits three vital pieces of evidence from his deductions. In the first place Kelly's clothes were lying in a neat pile beside her bed after she was found dead. There was no indication that any of her clothes were missing: she was much too poor to have a wardrobe. Maria Harvey, who had been staying with Kelly, was 'almost certain Mary hadn't any other clothes'. And though her testimony on this very point is of the utmost importance, Mr. Stewart made no reference in his book to Maria Harvey.

For Maria said she had left 'some sheets, an overcoat and a bonnet' in Kelly's care. The only article recovered afterwards was the overcoat; in the grate was the charred wire rim of the bonnet. So it is almost certain that the murderer, whoever he (or she) was, did not leave the room wearing either Kelly's or Harvey's clothes. If she wanted to borrow any clothes, one would have thought that Harvey's overcoat was the obvious article to choose at that time of the year.

Had the police suspected a midwife, it should not have been

* *Jack the Ripper: A New Theory,* by William Stewart.

difficult for them to question registered midwives in the area and to have checked on their movements. But the weakness of the Jill the Ripper solution is that there is no evidence of any woman having been seen alone with any one of the victims shortly before they were found dead. There is, however, overwhelming evidence of a male of a certain fairly definite description having been seen with at least four of them within half an hour or less of the actual murder. And in the case of Kelly a number of people testified to seeing her with a man shortly before her death.

Oddly, Stewart failed to make the most of the one point which could effectively bolster his arguments—the fact that two women swore they saw Mary Kelly after 8 a.m. on the morning of her death. For, if the killer was wearing Kelly's clothes, she could have been mistaken for the dead woman. This was the line Abberline first followed up; Mr. Stewart did not pursue this intriguing poser.

He did, however, strongly attack the testimony of Hutchinson, alleging that the labourer 'overdid' his detailed description of the man with the 'American cloth parcel'. This description, argued Stewart, was merely a hotchpotch of every previous description of the Ripper suspects published by the police, with a few details added. It was too good to be true.

Certainly Hutchinson displayed in his evidence a wealth of detail that might have done credit to Sherlock Holmes himself. It is feasible that he might, through some perverted desire for notoriety, have invented the mysterious stranger and merely embellished the published descriptions of wanted men.

This thought occurred to Abberline. But it also occurred to him that Hutchinson himself was taking a grave risk of being implicated in the murder. Hutchinson had nothing to gain, but a great deal to lose by making this statement voluntarily. He had not slept anywhere on the night of the murder; he had, on his own admission, been in the vicinity of Miller's Court at the hour of the crime. Could he confirm his statement? Could he provide an alibi?

Abberline cross-examined Hutchinson relentlessly. He re-read his statement and, by a system of snap questions, sought to see whether Hutchinson would slip up on details. But Hutchinson persisted in giving the same answers. If he had invented the description, he had certainly learned it by heart. So Abberline tried another tack: he suggested that he might wish to detain the labourer. But even with this threat hanging over him Hutchinson did not behave like a man who had invented a mysterious stranger. He still insisted he had noticed every detail about the man—right down to the red handkerchief.

'How could you see a red handkerchief in that light and so far away?' asked Abberline.

'He flourished the handkerchief in front of her. It caught the rays of the lamp. He waved it about like one of them bull fighters and made her laugh.'

'If you care to admit you made up this tale, I'll accept your word and let you go.'

But Hutchinson refused to do so. Fortunately for him two other people had seen him talking to a woman who looked like Kelly and they both agreed that 'when she left him, she went off with another man'. Unlike Hutchinson, however, they could not recall what the man looked like.

It transpired afterwards that Hutchinson had once had a job as a night-watchman, which was not only one reason for his inability to sleep at nights, but for his talent for memorising exactly what people looked like.

The theory of Jill the Ripper was revived in 1955 in an article in the *Evening News* by Richard Herd. This told the story of an old lag who, eighteen years previously, while in the prison hospital at Parkhurst, had been informed by a fellow convict that the latter's wife was the Ripper.

'For obvious reasons,' wrote Mr. Herd, 'the identities of both the penman and his friend, the old lag, must be withheld. The penman is spending his last few years of his life in a bungalow near the sea. I have checked his prison record . . . it goes back to 1896 and includes three terms of seven years for forgery, hence his nickname.'

The story has an authentic ring all right—the ring of a typical old lag's tale. But this time Jill the Ripper is not a midwife, but a nurse. She married a steward from a ship who secured a job as a porter in the hospital where she was working in the East End. One night the porter was seduced by a street-walker. His wife, having learned about this, thereupon selected one of the carving knives given to her as a wedding present by the hospital and slaughtered whores until she found the woman who had led her husband astray. Needless to say this turned out to be Mary Kelly.

And the husband? He discovered a pair of his sailor's trousers, drenched in blood, lying in the sink one night. And his wife confessed that she had dressed up in these clothes over her nurse's uniform to lure prostututes to perdition.*

I find this yarn less credible than the theory presented by Mr. Stewart.

So much for the diversity of 'solutions' offered by amateur criminologists. Once again one must turn to the views of the experts, or at least to those policemen who actually assisted in the investigations.

Police Constable Leeson, who found the corpse of Frances Coles, later became Detective-Sergeant Leeson of Scotland Yard. 'I am afraid I cannot throw any light on the problem of the Ripper's identity,' he wrote in *Lost London*. 'But one thing I do know, *and that is that amongst the police who were most concerned in the case there was a general feeling that a certain doctor, known to me, could have thrown quite a lot of light on the subject. This particular doctor was never far away when the crimes were committed and it is certain that the injuries inflicted on the victims could only have been done by one skilled in the use of the knife*.'

From the statements of positive opinion given in this and the preceding chapters a quite definite pattern emerges. This pattern to a large extent compensates for the contradictions, evasions and purely imaginative reconstructions of the theorists. Out of the experts, six of them senior police officers, one—Sir Henry Smith—has no semblance of a solution to

* 'The Secret of Ex-Convict SYF 45', *Evening News*, 8 September 1955.

offer. This is disappointing for Sir Henry was the most enterprising and imaginative of all the police chiefs at the time. But it is not surprising as Sir Henry, being only in charge of the City of London Police, was denied access to information which the Metropolitan Police had, and this may be the answer to his cautiousness. Yet even he believed that the killer was a doctor, a view shared by nine of these ten experts. The sole dissentient was William Stewart.

Here it is perhaps worth while pointing out that a distinguished doctor and writer supports this opinion. Dr. Harold Dearden expressed the view that the Ripper was 'some doctor or medical student'.*

Three of the nine claimed that the doctor committed suicide by drowning himself in the Thames, though one of three had reservations on this subject. Again it should be noted that it was the amateur criminologist who made the reservations, the two senior police officers who were so positive.

Five of the nine, if we include Chief Inspector Abberline (and his views will be developed later on), allege that the doctor was a Russian or a Pole.

This is not by any means conclusive, but it provides a far sounder basis for further investigation than any of the other theories. Dr. Thomas Dutton added his own opinion: 'after the Kelly murder I felt that there was no longer any doubt that the killer was a man with a rudimentary knowledge of surgery. I am quite certain that the police thought likewise. But I was prepared to go further than this and to state quite emphatically *that the surgeon was a foreigner.*

'I am quite prepared to admit that by English standards the technique of the Ripper was not in the same class as that of a highly proficient English surgeon. But that is not the point at issue and it is quite erroneous to argue that because of this the killer could not be a surgeon.

'It was only between the years of 1877 and 1887 that modern surgery as taught and practised by Joseph Lister enabled doctors to operate with deliberation and confidence. From 1880 onwards a majority of British surgeons were able

* *Great Unsolved Crimes.*

to operate accurately, without hurry, and to dissect carefully. But on the continent, and especially in Central Europe and beyond, the old methods prevailed. The barber-surgeon was still the people's doctor in such places as Poland, Russia and the Balkans. He had little, if any, knowledge of anaesthetics, and so, for him, the great desideratum was speed, and almost everything was sacrificed to that. Speed was the substitute for skill. An amputation or a lithotomy was a question of a few seconds' work.

'And, without doubt, the Ripper was a fast operator, much faster than the average British surgeon could possibly have been.'

On the strength of this formidable array of expert opinion, and weighing carefully the disagreeements between the doctors who performed the post mortems, the search would seem to be narrowed down to a doctor and a foreigner. A doctor might be resident in this country, but neither practising nor registered here. Indeed, the fact that he was a doctor, holding degrees in another state, might not be known to the police.

There remains the puzzle of the doctor who was supposed to have committed suicide in the Thames. If the police were so sure of their facts, why did the Ripper inquiries continue for so many years? As was pointed out in an earlier chapter the investigations were conducted as late as 1892. And both Leeson and Thompson, members of the force, thought they had stumbled across another Ripper crime in February 1891.

After the Kelly murder the police were more bewildered than at any other stage of their investigations. There was panic at Scotland Yard; Warren had resigned and the Home Secretary followed him into the wilderness shortly afterwards. The Government was harried on all sides and Queen Victoria was once again writing a tart note to the Home Office.

Throughout the rest of November the police were expecting further Ripper crimes. Towards the end of the year some information reached Scotland Yard which caused C.I.D. officers to believe that they might have found the killer. Whatever this information was it could not have amounted to very much for the quest for the killer went on. But when three months had passed without a further murder the police began to reduce the number of patrols in the East End. There were protests against this and, to placate public opinion, the police by obscure methods seem to have put out the story that the Ripper either (a) had been put in an asylum, or (b) had died. This story was never published for the simple reason that there was nothing to substantiate it. Naturally, it would have been very awkward for the police if it had been published. When they were asked to comment, they declined to make a statement. Silence was taken for tacit admission of the truth of the story—that the Ripper had drowned himself.

'I was given this information in confidence about March, 1889,' said Mr. Albert Backert, a prominent member of the Whitechapel Vigilance Committee, referring to the Thames suicide rumour. 'I had complained to the police that there seemed to be too much complacency in the force simply because there had been no further murders for some months.

'I was then asked if I would agree to be sworn to secrecy on the understanding I was given certain information. Foolishly, I agreed. It was then suggested to me that the Vigilance Committee and its patrols might be disbanded as the police were quite certain that the Ripper was dead.

'I protested that, as I had been sworn to secrecy, I really ought to be given more information than this. "It isn't necessary for you to know any more," I was told. "The man in question is dead. He was fished out of the Thames two months ago and it would only cause pain to relatives if we said any more than that."

'I again protested that I had been sworn to secrecy all for nothing, that I was really no wiser than before. "If there are no more murders, I shall respect this confidence, but if there are any more I shall consider I am absolved from my pledge of secrecy."

'The police then got very tough. They told me a pledge was a solemn matter, that anyone who put out stories that the Ripper was still alive might be proceeded against for causing a public mischief. However, they agreed that if there were any other murders which the police were satisfied could be Ripper murders, that was another matter.

'I never believed the yarn, though I kept my pledge until after the McKenzie murder in 1891. Maybe some police officers kidded themselves this was the truth, though I have my doubts about that. Detective-Inspector Abberline told me years later that he was quite certain that the story was untrue and that the Ripper remained alive and uncaught.'

The testimony of Backert is seized on by Tom Cullen in support of his theory that the Ripper was the barrister found dead in the Thames on the last day of the year, 1888. He also quotes in his book a statement by a grandson of General Sir Charles Warren, Mr. Watkin W. Williams: 'I cannot recall that my grandrather ever stated in writing his personal views on the identity of Jack the Ripper. . . . My impression is that he believed the murderer to be a sex maniac who committed suicide after the Miller's Court murder—possibly the young doctor whose body was found in the Thames on December 31st, 1888.' Tom Cullen also cites Sir John Moylan, police historian and one-time Assistant Under-Secretary at the Home Office, as stating that 'the murderer, it is now certain, escaped justice by committing suicide at the end of 1888'.

On the other hand another ex-Commissioner of Police, Sir Harold Scott, made a much more accurate and apt comment in his *Concise Encyclopaedia of Crime and Criminals.* Sir Harold did not fall into the error of earlier police chiefs by referring to a doctor, but mentioned that the identity of Sir Melville Macnaghten's suspect was established at Somerset House as that of a barrister. Sir Harold then pointed out that such a person would hardly have fitted the bill, if only on account of his lack of medical knowledge.

There are, therefore, these important questions to be answered:

Who started the story that it was a doctor who committed suicide at the end of 1888?

Why did Sir Melville Macnaghten describe Montagu John Druitt as a 'doctor' when in fact he was a barrister?

Why were some at least of the senior police officers

apparently convinced they had solved the question of the Ripper's identity?

The first reference to the Ripper having committed suicide at the end of 1888 came from the police themselves, if we accept the testimony of Albert Backert. This still leaves the first question partly unanswered as we do not know their motives for putting out this story. For the same reason it does not answer the third question. But there seems a strong probability that a partial answer to each of these questions is that the police were convinced by the end of January or early February 1889 that the Ripper was either dead or that he had escaped from the country. They wanted the Ripper scare to be exorcised and to achieve this they told Backert the suicide story.

There can be no doubt, however, that Sir Melville Macnaghten was the man mainly responsible for suggesting that it was a doctor whose body was found in the Thames on 31 December 1888. In his memoirs Sir Melville wrote that the two great disappointments of his life were that he never played cricket for Eton against Harrow and that 'I became a detective officer six months after Jack the Ripper committed suicide and never had a go at that fascinating individual'.

Undoubtedly Sir Melville's notes on the crimes led to other police chiefs, who did not check the facts as carefully as did Sir Harold Scott, perpetuating the story of the doctor's suicide. As Tom Cullen points out, 'Major Arthur Griffiths copied the notes almost verbatim, merely omitting the names of the three individuals whom the police strongly suspected.'

Thus the degree of certainty with which later police chiefs pointed to a doctor as being the Ripper means that they accepted Sir Melville's views unquestioningly.

I think that a number of senior police chiefs were convinced after the Mary Kelly murder that the killer was a doctor because they were certain that nobody else could have displayed such skill in removing organs from the body.

One cannot be certain that Sir Melville even made his notes in 1894 after consulting official records, for he did not become Assistant Police Commissioner in charge of the C.I.D. until 1903. His notes are minimal and lacking in detail: they could even have been compiled from memory after having had conversations with men engaged on the case. It is hard to believe he made a mistake in writing 'doctor' instead of barrister. Certainly this fact suggests he did not consult official records when making his notes. Is there a clue in his boast that he 'never kept a diary, nor even possessed a notebook'? For not only did he describe Druitt as a doctor, but he said he was forty-one years old when in fact he was only thirty-one. Was Sir Melville's memory defective on this occasion? In his memoirs published in 1914 he puts the facts rather differently: 'Although the Whitechapel murderer, in all probability, put an end to himself soon after the Dorset Street affair in November 1888, certain facts pointing to this conclusion were not in the possession of the police till some years after I became a detective officer.' Yet if we accept Backert's testimony the suicide story was being put forward in confidence by the police in March 1889.

Bad memory may be one explanation, indeed it would seem to be the likeliest, yet to mistake a barrister for a doctor in such circumstances seems improbable. But when one comes to examine the other poser as to whether someone, not necessarily Sir Melville, destroyed any official records, it is hard to ascertain the truth. Lady Aberconway denies that her father actually destroyed any documentary proof concerning the Ripper's identity. But against this must be set the statement by Hargrave L. Adam that Sir Melville told him he had 'documentary proof' of the Ripper's identity, but that he had burnt the papers. There is also the fact that according to my own inquiries the only documentation on the identity question today in police archives in London comprises Sir Melville's brief notes.

Certainly some records on the Ripper case would appear to have been destroyed. It is clear, too, that at the same time that the police were anxious in the months following Mary Kelly's murder that the suicide story should be made public, there was a strong suggestion that they wanted to hush things up. This desire to hush things up could not have concerned Druitt because it was apparent at the inquest on Mary Kelly that the police did not want too inquisitive a coroner to investigate the case and at that time Druitt's body had not been found.

I have studied Sir Melville's notes in great detail and the fact remains that he is far from categoric about Montagu John Druitt. He gives an impression one moment of being absolutely sure and then later expresses doubts. For example he writes: 'A much more rational and workable theory . . . is that the Ripper's brain gave way altogether after his awful glut in Miller's Court, and that he then committed suicide, or, as a less likely alternative, was found to be hopelessly insane by his relatives, that they, suspecting the worst, had him confined in a lunatic asylum.'

This remarkable statement would seem to throw the greatest doubt on Tom Cullen's theory that Druitt could have been the Ripper. Druitt was undoubtedly found dead in the Thames; therefore he could not have been confined to a lunatic asylum. In other words Sir Melville himself had doubts about his original theory.

Of the three suspects named by Sir Melville he has this to say:

No. 1. Druitt: 'The body was said to have been in the water for a month or more—on it was found a season ticket between Blackheath and London. From private information I have little doubt but that his own family suspected this man of being the Whitechapel murderer.'

No. 2. Kosminski (possibly a misspelling for Karminski): 'A Polish Jew, who lived in the very heart of the district where the murders were committed. He had become insane owing to many years' indulgence in solitary vices. He had a great hatred of women with strong homicidal tendencies. He was (and I believe is) detained in a lunatic asylum about March, 1889. This man in appearance strongly resembled the individual seen by the City P.C. near Mitre Square.'

No. 3. Michael Ostrog: 'A mad Russian doctor and a convict and unquestionably a homicidal maniac. This man was said to have been habitually cruel to women and for a long time was known to have carried about with him surgical knives and other instruments; his antecedents were of the very worst and his whereabouts at the time of the Whitechapel murders could never be satisfactorily accounted for. He is still alive.'

We have already noted the errors regarding Druitt's age and his profession and it would seem that Macnaghten compiled the notes in a hurry from memory. The spelling of the name of the Polish Jew, for example: it almost certainly should have read 'Karminski', and the Russian Ostrog's first name would almost certainly have been spelt Mikhail, not Michael.

Leaving aside Sir Melville's preference, however, if one examines each suspect's brief dossier carefully, who seems likeliest to be the Ripper? Not, I submit, Druitt. There is nothing in the notes to link him directly with the crimes. On the other hand 'Kosminski' lived in the district and resembled the individual seen by 'the City P.C. near Mitre Square', while Ostrog had all the qualifications for being the Ripper as well as being unable to account for his movements (presumably in the area where the crimes were committed) at the times of the murders. Both 'Kosminski' and Ostrog make likelier suspects than Druitt.

However, at the moment it is with Druitt alone that we are concerned. What other evidence is there to support Sir Melville's claim to name him as chief suspect? No other police chief has ever supported this thesis. Mr. Cullen, as we have seen, turns up no new evidence other than the fact that at the time of the Ripper crimes Druitt was still occupying his chambers in the Temple within walking distance of the City and East End, and that he *might* have been doing social welfare work at Toynbee Hall which would have made him acquainted with the East End of London. As to how Druitt could have acquired the knowledge to cut up bodies efficiently and to remove organs, Mr. Cullen's theory is that Druitt came from a family of doctors, including his father, grandfather and uncle.

'It is more than possible, indeed it is probable, that Druitt, as an interested spectator, sat in a surgical amphitheatre and watched his father practise his art,' writes Tom

Cullen. 'He would thus have gained some knowledge of surgery, even though that knowledge was rudimentary.'

It is true that the Temple was within walking distance of the scenes of the crimes. But if Druitt had been the killer, one would have expected him to make his way back there speedily after the second murder in one night—the one in Mitre Square. Instead the killer went in the opposite direction—to the north-east.

As to the theory that Druitt may have been working, or living at Toynbee Hall, this seems to be based on nothing more substantial than the fact that a contemporary of Druitt at New College, Oxford, Cyril Jackson, later chairman of the London County Council, was at Toynbee Hall in this period and that because of this Druitt may have joined him and developed a passion for social service which turned into a pathological hatred of prostitutes. But the present Warden of Toynbee Hall, Mr. Walter Birmingham, states that 'We have a full record of all residents at Toynbee Hall during the appropriate period [i.e. during the Ripper murders], but Mr. Druitt's name is not in it. So far as we know he was never resident here.'

Nor is there anything in the *Toynbee Record*, which was published monthly from 1888 onwards, to throw any light on the matter.

On the question of whether Druitt could have acquired the knowledge to cut up bodies and remove organs, I think it would be fairer to say that it was possible, but improbable. It would have been possible if young Druitt had ever intended to take up surgery as a career, but there is absolutely no evidence of this. Otherwise most medical men with whom I have discussed this point think it highly improbable that he 'sat in' on his father's operations, but, as they point out, he would not have gained any practical experience from this. In any case the Druitt family were not surgeons in the strict sense of the word, but general practitioners.

It is true that Druitt kept on his chambers in the Temple and that he travelled to and from there to Blackheath each day by train. But this was only during term time when he was teaching at the school at Blackheath. During the holidays he stayed with his relatives, occasionally at Wimborne in Dorsetshire, sometimes at Bournemouth. And on the occasions of the murders of both Mary Nichols and Annie Chapman, Montagu John Druitt was living in Bournemouth. This fact alone would seem to rule out any possibility of his being the Ripper.

How then to explain how the idea ever arose that Druitt could have been the Ripper? Curiously the trail leads back to Walter Sickert, for a London doctor who knew Sickert and whose father was at Oxford with Druitt gave me his own explanation of the Druitt mystery.

'Sickert must have told his story to various people and in consequence there are various second-hand and even third-hand versions of it. The story as told to me was much the same as the version given by Osbert Sitwell. Sickert was often uncertain about names and the name of the young veterinary student was something like Druitt. It may have been Drewett, or even Hewitt. Anyhow Sickert told me he had repeated the yarn to Sir Melville Macnaghten once at the Garrick Club and that Macnaghten was convinced it must have been Druitt because he had a widowed mother living at Bournemouth, the same as Druitt. Possibly Sir Melville developed his own theory in consequence of what Sickert told him. Knowing about Druitt through my father, I naturally cross-questioned Sickert, who was convinced that the young man who had had his rooms was either in his late teens or only just turned twenty, and that he was definitely not a barrister. My father was positive that there was no connection between Sickert's story and Druitt. He always told me that the story about Druitt being the Ripper arose through the barrister being blackmailed by someone who threatened to denounce him as Jack the Ripper to the school at which he worked. Whether this was a heartless hoax or a cruel method of extorting money from a man who was just recovering from a nervous breakdown was not clear. There was nothing seriously wrong with Druitt, but he suffered from insomnia and blackouts and these threats preyed on his mind and paved the way to a further breakdown. He may under severe stress have given a muddled account of the threats to his mother. My father, who was an experienced doctor, was quite convinced he could not have been the Ripper and that the gold found on his body was originally intended to pay off the blackmailer. He certainly confided in his mother about the whole affair and she presumably told the police when he was reported missing sometime during December 1888. Anyhow, my father was emphatic that Druitt was living at Bournemouth when the first two Ripper crimes were committed.'

And this seems finally to dispose of the case that Druitt had any connection with the crimes.

14

The barber from Warsaw

Detective-Inspector Abberline never completely lost touch with Severin Klosowski, the barber-surgeon from Warsaw, during the next few years. He had never forgotten how this strange character had come into the Ripper inquiries. But though this man's conduct was sometimes suspicious and Abberline was convinced he was a crook, he was wily enough to avoid trouble with the police.

The shop which Klosowski had acquired for himself in High Road, Tottenham, soon proved to be an unprofitable business and the Pole once again became a hairdresser's assistant. For several months he was employed by a hairdresser named Radin in Rushton Street, Shoreditch. Later he went to work in a shop in Church Lane, Leytonstone, where he received thirty shillings a week wages and was described as 'quiet, steady and industrious'.

But he never stayed in one place for long. By the middle of 1889 he was keeping a barber's shop in Cable Street. During this period he met a fellow Pole, a tailor named Stanislaus Baderski, who worked in Hoe Street, Walthamstow. They were members of a Polish club in St. John's Square, Clerkenwell. Baderski introduced Klosowski to his sister, Lucy, and in a remarkably short time the amorous Pole proposed to her.

There is a mystery about the actual date of their marriage. Even the records suggest there were two marriage ceremonies —one on August Bank Holiday, 1889, and another on 23 October, of the same year, in Union Street, Whitechapel. The probability is that the first of these weddings was a bogus affair, cunningly staged by Klosowski with forged certificates. But of the second marriage there is no doubt.

The pair lived together in Cable Street, then in lodgings at Commercial Street, Whitechapel, and afterwards in Greenfield Street. Abberline, however, always suspected that Klosowski had known Lucy Baderski in Poland long before and that they had cohabited together prior to their marriage, both facts which they had hidden from her brother.

In 1890 the Klosowskis disappeared suddenly and were next heard of in the United States where they settled down in Jersey City. In February 1891 Mrs. Klosowski returned to Britain alone. Apparently there had been a quarrel over some other woman. Two years later Severin left America and rejoined her in the East End of London. Years afterwards the police discovered in his diaries this cryptic note: 'Came from America in 1892. Independent. Deposits £100 when from America I had £1,000.'

The reconciliation of the Klosowskis was short-lived. Severin just disappeared one day and made no effort either to retain custody of their two children, or to contribute to their support. Abberline, who was once again on his track, felt sure that Klosowski was trying to give him the slip. It was some few years before he came across him again.

In the meantime the Pole made every effort to change his identity. He dressed more like an Englishman, became quite a dandy and when he went to live with a woman named Annie or Betsy Chapman, adopted her name.

This liaison was of brief duration. Betsy Chapman seems to have become suddenly frightened of Klosowski; at any rate she very wisely left him. And once again the Pole 'disappeared'—to turn up again at Hastings where he opened another barber's shop and 'married' a Mrs. Spink. Years afterwards a Mrs. Harriet Greenaway, of Braybrook Road, Hastings, recalled Chapman as a 'rather fierce-looking character who strutted about the town carrying a little black bag'.

During the next few years Chapman was always on the move. After the sudden death of Mrs. Spink he became a tavern-keeper and at each of his hostelries a common factor was the presence of an attractive barmaid. The Pole was never without a 'wife' and, despite his allegedly repulsive appearance, he seemed to have an irresistible attraction even for refined and educated women. Indeed the descriptions of him as being 'ferocious' and 'frightening' may well have been overdone because Mr. S. W. Turner, of Boxmoor, Hertfordshire, recently wrote to me to say that he knew Chapman when the latter had a public house near St. George's Church in the Borough High Street: 'I was a medical student at Guy's at the time and we students sometimes went into the Borough High Street for a drink in Chapman's pub. He was a pleasant enough character.'

But just as Chapman, as he was now known, had quite naturally entered into a *ménage à trois* in his early days in Whitechapel, so he could never resist carrying on with two women at the same time. His methods rarely varied; he would stage a bogus form of marriage with some woman, pass her off as his wife and then, after only a few weeks, introduce into his tavern some young girl whom he would promptly seduce.

He always did his best to cultivate the goodwill of the police. While licensee of the Prince of Wales public house in Bartholomew Square, off City Road, he actually joined the local Police Cycling Club, regularly attending their parties and convivial evenings and accompanying them on weekend excursions.

Possibly all this made him careless. Perhaps he felt too confident that he could never arouse the suspicion of the police. But when two other 'wives'—Bessie Taylor and Maud Marsh—like Mrs. Spink before them died suddenly and mysteriously after suffering violent pains and vomiting, suspicion was directed against him notwithstanding the fact that doctors' certificates had proclaimed their deaths to be due to natural causes.

This time people began to talk and inevitably the police heard the ugly rumours about George Chapman. All his bonhomie and goodwill towards the police availed him nothing. Abberline, now a chief inspector, soon recognised Chapman as Severin Klosowski. While Superintendent Neil and Inspector Godley completed their inquiries into the deaths of the three women, Abberline sought documentary proof that his quarry was in fact the barber's assistant from Warsaw. The bodies of the three women were secretly exhumed and, to their amazement, the police noted how remarkably well preserved they were. The post mortems not only conclusively showed that they had all been poisoned, but for the first time in the annals of criminal investigation a Home Office pathologist was able to demonstrate the peculiar power of antimony to preserve the human body after death. The use of antimony had been Chapman's biggest blunder.

An example of the Pole's amazing effrontery was the stone he erected over the grave of one of his victims. On this he had engraved the following verse:

'Farewell my friends, fond and dear,
Weep not for me one single tear,
For all that was and could be done,
You plainly see my time has come.'

It was only because of the speed with which the police acted that Klosowski did not disappear again. He had made all preparations for flight and when arrested by Inspector Godley had in his pockets a loaded revolver, notes on the departure times of ships, a single ticket to Antwerp and a large bundle of ten-pound Bank of England notes.

The trial opened in March 1903. Edward Carson appeared for the prosecution and there was very little doubt from the start which way the verdict would go. The impression Klosowski made on the jury could hardly have been worse. His defiance, arrogance, lack of feeling and brazen conduct alienated them at the outset. The judge, Mr. Justice Grantham, referred to 'his knowledge of poison and medicine which had enabled him to baffle the surgeons for five or six years'. In passing sentence of death after the jury had found the Pole guilty of the murder of Maud Marsh, Grantham, voicing the chauvinistic sentiments of the day, said: 'Severin Klosowski, for I decline to call you by the English name you have assumed, the only satisfactory feature in the case we have just completed is that I am able to address you as a foreigner and not as an Englishman.'

Up to the moment of his execution the Pole insisted that his true name was George Chapman, that he was an American citizen and not Severin Klosowski. To a Roman Catholic priest who saw him in prison he made the same statement. It was a futile pretence. The police had found in his safe papers in German and Russian which proved conclusively who he was. Among them was a certificate dated 5 December 1886, showing that he had been granted the degree of junior surgeon by the Medical Administration Department of the Ministry of the Interior in Warsaw.

Information from Poland suggested that Klosowski had married before he left that country and that the reason for his sudden disappearance from his native land was that he had beheaded his first wife. His passport, issued in Warsaw in 1886, was discovered; the photograph was indisputably that of Chapman and the description of him at the age of twenty-one read: 'Height, medium; hair of a dark shade; eyes, blue; nose and mouth medium; chin and face longish; birthmarks none.'

When Lucy Baderski confronted her husband in an identification parade she recognised him immediately.

'I do not know this woman,' was Klosowski's brusque comment.

'Ah, Severin,' replied Lucy deliberately and reproachfully, 'don't say that. You remember the time you nearly killed me in Jersey City.'

Mr. Montgomery Hyde, in his biography of Lord Carson, stated that 'Chief Inspector Abberline was convinced that Chapman and Jack the Ripper were identical. His theory was that when Chapman returned from America he came to the conclusion that the Ripper type of murder was too dangerous and he consequently turned to poisoning as a safer mode of killing.'

Both H. L. Adam and Montgomery Hyde testified that

when Inspector Godley arrested Chapman, Abberline said: 'You've got Jack the Ripper at last!'

Superintendent Neil wrote: 'Chapman (like the Ripper) was ambidextrous . . . the only description ever given by an eyewitness of the Ripper tallied exactly with Chapman, even to the height, deep-sunk eyes, sallow complexion and thick black moustache.'*

Mr. Montgomery Hyde, who had access to the Carson papers, declared that, 'while it is true that the mystery of the Ripper murders has never been officially solved, the grounds for supposing that this sadistic Pole was the author of them are very strong'.

Detective-Sergeant Leeson also referred to Klosowski as a suspect. 'About the period of the murders Chapman was living in Whitechapel, where he carried on a hairdresser's business under a sort of "dive" in a public house at the corner of George Yard.

'I have no data to assist me, but I remember there were a dozen murders attributed to Jack the Ripper during the years 1888–90 and so far as I can ascertain Chapman was in London for nearly the whole of that period. He left before the end of 1890 and went to America where it is believed he was responsible for several murders. As far as my information goes, he did not return to London in 1891, the year in which Frances Coles met her death.'

But what exactly were the grounds for believing that Klosowski was the Ripper? H. L. Adam summed them up in his book on the trial of George Chapman and succeeded in building up a powerful case against the Pole. He pointed out that the first Whitechapel murder was committed shortly after Klosowski arrived in Britain and that throughout 1888–90, the Polish barber was living either in Whitechapel, or at least within easy reach of the scenes of the various crimes. Also the description of the man seen with Mary Kelly was, he argued, 'a good description of Chapman'.

Americanisms were used in the letter and postcard purported to have been written by Jack the Ripper; Chapman

* *Forty Years of Man-Hunting,* by Superintendent A. F. Neil.

often posed as an American and used similar phrases in his conversation. When the 'last Ripper murder was committed in July 1889 Chapman was still in the vicinity'.

Adam, like Abberline, was impressed by the fact that Chapman had medical and surgical knowledge and had been trained as a surgeon. He could, therefore, be capable of the type of surgery practised by the East End killer.

Quoting Abberline's account of an interview with Klosowski's wife, Adam stated: 'He questioned Lucy Baderski about his [Klosowski's] nocturnal habits at the times of the murders. She said that he was often out until 3 or 4 a.m., but she could throw little light on these absences.'

Between 1891 and 1893 there were no Ripper murders in Britain, Adam asserted, but 'similar crimes occurred in Jersey City, U.S.A.'. At that time Klosowski and his wife were living in Jersey City, where the former had opened a barber's shop. 'In the beginning of 1892 the Ripper murders ceased in U.S.A. and Klosowski returned to London.'

If this circumstantial evidence is duly weighed, then there is at least a case for investigating thoroughly the question of whether Klosowski could have been the East End killer. Yet the more one examines this line of argument, the less impressive it appears and a closer examination of the theory, and particularly of Adam's statements, reveals positive weaknesses.

To take a small, but not insignificant point, first. Adam referred to the last Ripper murder as being in July 1889. It would have been wiser to have accepted the majority verdict that the last crime which experts were *certain* was done by the Ripper was the slaying of Mary Kelly in November 1888. For, why stop at the July 1889 killing of Clay Pipe Alice? If one includes this murder, then there is no logical reason why one should not also include that of Frances Coles in February 1891. The reason for this omission is obvious: Chapman was out of the country when the crime was committed.

Yet if Detective-Sergeant Leeson could point this out, so, in fairness, should Adam have given Klosowski the benefit of being 'not guilty' on this count. A small quibble, perhaps, but enough to show that Adam was hardly objective.

Then again, neither Adam nor Leeson are quite accurate in alleging that the description of the man seen with Mary Kelly tallied completely with that of Klosowski. The labourer Hutchinson said that this man 'was perhaps about thirty-five; it could have been that he was younger'.

In 1888 Klosowski was only twenty-three. Would so keen an observer as Hutchinson have made an error of twelve years in assessing the man's age? True, there were certain similarities, but not enough to prove the case. Klosowski did not possess anything like the funds in 1888 that he flaunted in the late 'nineties and early part of the twentieth century. Judging by his poor lodgings and low pay as a hairdresser's assistant, he would hardly be likely to be wearing 'a dark coat, trimmed with astrakhan . . . a horseshoe tie-pin, and over his buttoned boots spats'. Nor would he have a 'huge gold watch-chain'.

But the crucial test is surely to be found in an examination of the 'similar murders' occurring in the United States between 1890 and 1892. Adam, who pursues his theory in great detail, merely briefly mentions these crimes, yet obviously this part of his argument is the most important. What are the facts about these Ripper-type killings? All Leeson said was that 'it is believed' Chapman was responsible for several murders in America. But Adam is quite definite about the scenes of these crimes . . . 'in the locality of Jersey City'.

Despite a thorough search in United States criminal records and close questioning of leading crime historians in that country, I have been unable to discover one Ripper-type murder in the Jersey City area between the years 1890 and 1893.

Edmund Pearson, an authoritative American crime-writer, in an article in *Vanity Fair*, in September 1933, pointed out certain discrepancies in Adam's theory. Other U.S. crime-writers have taken much the same view. Pearson also made exhaustive investigations for these 'similar crimes' in the U.S.A. during this period. He could only discover one Ripper-style murder at the time that Klosowski was living in Jersey City. This was the stabbing and mutilation of a person, presumably a prostitute, described in press cuttings as 'a wretched woman', who was known by the name of 'Old Shakespeare'. She was murdered in a waterfront hotel in New York in 1891. Because of the similarity of this crime with those committed by Jack, New York newspapers asked in screaming headlines: 'Has Jack the Ripper arrived in U.S.A.?'

An Algerian named 'Frenchy' was arrested for the crime, but, because of lack of evidence, was eventually released and the murder remained unsolved. It seems probable that an echo of the New York newspaper headlines was heard in Britain and that this, and no more substantial evidence, was the sole basis of the rumours of Ripper killings in America.

American crime-writers also refute Adam's attempt to link Klosowski with the Ripper correspondence. They point out that Klosowski had not even visited America when the post-card and letter were sent to the Central News. How then did he, a Pole, acquire a knowledge of Americanisms, which were certainly not in widespread daily use in Britain as, to some extent, they are today?

Certainly Chief Inspector Abberline was convinced for some years that Klosowski was the Ripper. But the theory that he believed Klosowski found murder by throat-cutting too dangerous and consequently 'turned to poisoning as a safer mode of killing' is not plausible.

It seems unlikely that so experienced a detective as Abberline would put forward such a view, knowing, as he must have done, that sadistic killers do not react in this way. In fact, Dr. Dutton's *Crime Diaries* appear to contradict this.

'Abberline,' wrote Dutton, 'had long suspected Klosowski of being the Ripper and discussed the matter with me on many occasions. His original reasons for taking this view were that Klosowski had actually been seen with one of the Ripper's victims in George Yard on the night of her murder. Then, when he spoke with Lucy Baderski during Klosowki's imprisonment and trial, he was convinced that she, too, suspected her husband had something to do with the murders.

'Later, when Abberline checked his facts, he realised an important discrepancy in Baderski's statement. She spoke of

Klosowski being out until 3 or 4 a.m. at the period of the Whitechapel murders, when they were living in Commercial Street. But this period—and this is where Adam makes an error—was *after August 1889*—and there were no murders of the same type committed between July 1889 and February 1891 when Klosowski was indisputably in America.

'It looked as though Baderski (and her brother, too) were trying to mislead Abberline. The only other possible explanation is that Lucy Baderski, who was also a rather mysterious character, was the Polish woman who lived with Klosowski and his English mistress when he first came to London. That period would coincide with the Whitechapel murders. But, in front of her brother, Lucy Baderski always denied having known Klosowski before the early summer of 1889.

'Abberline could not be sure whether she was lying or not, as he never personally checked upon the identity of the Polish woman with whom Klosowski was living in 1888. But he was an honest man who faced the truth even when it was contrary to his theories. He admitted that there was not an iota of evidence linking Klosowski with any American killings, even if such murders were ever committed. If they were, then no one seems to have had any details of them.

'What finally convinced Abberline that he had made a mistake in thinking Klosowski was the Ripper was his discovery that the Polish barber-surgeon had a double in London and that this double, a Russian and also a barber-surgeon, sometimes posed as Klosowski for reasons which were not apparent. It was the Russian surgeon and not Klosowski who had been seen with the Ripper victim in George Yard.'

Could this be the same Russian surgeon hinted at by Sir Basil Thomson and others, the character named as Ostrog by Sir Melville Macnaghten? Or could it be the Russian named by William Le Queux as Dr. Alexander Pedachenko?

William Le Queux, who helped the British Government in Intelligence work in World War I, declared that the Kerensky Government in Russia handed over to him in confidence a great quantity of documents found in the safe of a cellar in Rasputin's house after the death of the strange *moujik* monk who had intrigued his way into the court of the Czar. The Kerensky Government were only too anxious that Le Queux should write a damning biography of the amorous charlatan they believed to be responsible for the corruption of the court.

'Among this mass of letters,' stated Le Queux, 'I found a manuscript entitled *Great Russian Criminals*, written in French, a language which he [Rasputin] knew slightly, typed under dictation.'

Long after he wrote his book on Rasputin Le Queux made use of some of this material in *Things I Know*, published in 1923. In it he alleged that 'the true author of the Jack the Ripper crimes was disclosed by a Russian in London, named Nideroest, who was a member of the Jubilee Street Club, the Anarchist Centre in the East End of London'.

According to Le Queux, Nideroest was given this information by an Old Russian Anarchist, Nicholas Zverieff, who declared that the Ripper was Dr. Alexander Pedachenko, who had been on the staff of the Maternity Hospital at Tver, but later went to London, 'where he lived with his sister in Westmoreland Road, Walworth'.

Zverieff's story was that Pedachenko sallied forth at night from Walworth, and walked to Whitechapel where he committed the murders. He was aided by a friend of his named Levitski and a young tailoress, Winberg. The latter would approach Pedachenko's prospective victim and hold her in conversation; then the murder was swiftly carried out while Levitski kept watch for police patrols. Levitski, alleged Zverieff, wrote the warning postcards and letters signed Jack the Ripper.

Le Queux quoted from Rasputin's manuscript:

'The report of Nideroest's discovery amused our secret police greatly, for, as a matter of fact, they knew the whole details at the time, and had themselves actively aided and encouraged the crimes, in order to exhibit to the world certain defects of the English police system, there having been some misunderstanding and rivalry between our own police and the British. It was, indeed, for that reason that Pedachenko, the greatest and boldest of all Russian criminal lunatics, was encouraged to go to London and commit that series of atrocious crimes, in which our agents of police aided him.

'Eventually, at the orders of the Ministry of the Interior the secret police smuggled the assassin out of London, and, as Count Luiskovo, he landed at Ostend and was conducted by a secret agent to Moscow. While there he was, a few months later, caught red-handed attempting to murder and mutilate a woman named Vogak and was eventually sent to an asylum where he died in 1908.

'After the return to Russia of Levitski and the woman, Winberg, the secret police deemed it wise to suppress them, and they were therefore exiled to Yakutsk. Such are the actual facts of the "Jack the Ripper Mystery", which still puzzles the whole world.'

This is a fantastic story, even more difficult to accept than some of the other theories which we have examined. Even Le Queux seems to have had some misgivings, because he omitted any reference to the alleged Rasputin manuscript in his book, *Minister of Evil*, published five years before *Things I Know*. He explained this earlier omission by saying that he had 'only recently discovered that a doctor named Pedachenko did actually live in Tver, and his homicidal tendencies were well known'. And he added that he had further ascertained that a man named Nideroest was a member of the Jubilee Street Club and was 'known in connection with the Anarchist affray at Tottenham and also with the Sidney Street affair'.

When this book was published *The Star* promptly ridiculed and denied it. Mr. Hall Richardson said 'the police availed themselves of *The Star* to deny it and I have every reason to believe that the account is semi-official'.*

The Star described Le Queux's account as a 'piece of nonsense'. 'We can believe many crimes of the Tsardom, but not that, and certainly not on the authority of a rascal like Rasputin. But Mr. Le Queux lets a large cat out of the bag when he reveals that the disclosure of the author of these atrocities originates with a Russian well known in London, named Nideroest, a spy in the Russian police. . . .

* *From the City to Fleet Street,* by J. Hall Richardson.

'The fact is that Johann Nideroest was not a Russian at all, but a Swiss. He was a member of the Russian and Lettish Socialist Club in the East End, but Chief Inspector McCarthy gave evidence in 1909 that Nideroest was not an Anarchist, but had been selling to newspapers information about bombs being made in Whitechapel, which the police had found to be "all nonsense".

'Mr. Le Queux says he did not include this Jack the Ripper yarn in his book on Rasputin because he wanted to verify the facts in it. He now adds this wonderful corroboration: "I have only recently discovered that a doctor named Pedachenko did actually live in Tver."

'The first fact proves nothing at all; the second, that Nideroest was known in connection with the Sidney Street affair, is pure fiction, and the reference to the Tottenham Anarchists in January 1909 is utterly misleading.

'Nideroest had nothing to do with the Anarchists, or the shooting, but when one of the captured men—Paul Hefeld—was lying in hospital, Nideroest arrived under a false name, pretending to be Hefeld's brother.

'As it was difficult to prove "felonious intent", Nideroest escaped with a reprimand from the Bench, but in June 1915 he was brought up at Bow Street and deported as an undesirable alien.

'In April 1916 he turned up in his native Switzerland with a story that he had been a passenger on the *Sussex* and, with other passengers, had been wrongfully coerced by the British and French authorities to swear that they had seen the *Sussex* torpedoed whereas in fact she was sunk by a mine.

'He was proved on that occasion to be an unscrupulous liar and the fact that Mr. Le Queux's theory rests on his testimony is sufficient for us to regard it as fiction, quite apart from the inherent internal improbabilities which we have mentioned.'

At this stage in the prolonged quest for the Ripper's identity, having experienced so many frustrations after seemingly being hot on his trail on countless occasions, one might be forgiven for wearily dismissing Le Queux's story without further investigations.

But Dr. Dutton's diary of 1924 contains this interesting observation: 'Another theory on the Ripper. This time by William Le Queux in *Things I Know*. It is a great pity that he did not follow up what is a useful clue. By failing to do so, and by taking the Rasputin MS at its face value, he has only made a fool of himself. Further examination might have shown that Pedachenko was Klosowski's double. The fact that Pedachenko was a doctor at a Russian hospital is neither here nor there. What Le Queux should have found out was that Pedachenko worked as a barber-surgeon for a hairdresser named Delhaye in Westmoreland Road, Walworth, in 1888.'

And for once a careful check of this statement leads one to something more than a negative conclusion. For in the *London Post Office Directory* of 1889 there is listed under 'Westmoreland Road, Walworth', the name 'Delhaye, Wm., hairdresser'.

15

The search for Dr. Pedachenko

Margaret Prothero in her *History of the C.I.D. at Scotland Yard* referred to the anarchist propaganda circulating among the poorer classes in London at the end of the last century. 'In 1894,' she stated, 'Anarchists and Nihilists from Russia were at work in England.'

In fact, as has been seen, they were active for at least ten years prior to this date, but it was a long time before Scotland Yard realised the extent of their machinations. Sir Basil Thomson declared that 'The East End of London ever since the Jack the Ripper murders had become a city of refuge for aliens whose countries had become too hot to hold them.'

Detective-Sergeant Leeson, whose work took him among the Anarchists of the East End, told how in 1908 occurred 'the great strike of Jewish dockers in the Whitechapel district, organised by one Perkoff, perhaps Russia's first *agent-provocateur* to operate in London. It was a strike organised on Chicago racketeer lines, a method to which the Anarchists were very partial.'

But Perkoff was not the first Anarchist leader to operate in London. Indeed, Perkoff was not really an Anarchist—not at least in 1908. He was a Bolshevik and belonged to the same revolutionary group as Stalin.

The years 1907–9 marked the gradual diminishing of the activities of the Anarchists and a corresponding rise in those of the Bolsheviks. For perhaps a period of ten years between 1903 and 1913 there was an overlapping of the activities of both sets of revolutionaries and this often led Scotland Yard to confuse Anarchists with Bolsheviks and vice versa. But long before this the situation had been further confused by the existence of a third organisation in London—a counter-revolutionary body, financed by the Czarist Government and aimed at discrediting and unmasking the Anarchists.

A typical example of the counter-revolutionary agents was Serge Makharov, alias Ivan Nikolaieff, who, according to Soviet sources, was the original 'Peter the Painter' of the Sidney Street siege. Makharov, who belonged to an aristocratic but impoverished family, first entered the Russian Army and then, following a duel with a brother officer, resigned his commission and served with the secret police. He was assigned the task of spying on revolutionary Russians in Paris, London and elsewhere.

Now the methods adopted by Makharov are of special interest. His instructions were to locate the revolutionaries, who were mainly in London, to compromise them and find some means of involving them in trouble with the British police. The object of this was to create a demand for their expulsion from Britain. That these were the permanent tactics of the Secret Police over many years is made abundantly clear not only in the records of the first Soviet Government, but in documents obtained from Czarist sources and from British police records.

Why did the Czarist Government not make representations to the British Government for the deportation of the revolutionaries? This would have been a simpler and less expensive procedure than relying upon secret agents. But the Czarist Governments were just as secretive and devious as Soviet Governments have been and just as reluctant to discuss their internal problems with foreigners. Apart from this, even unofficial representations to Britain had been unsuccessful. While the Czarist regime had succeeded in persuading European governments to ban Anarchists, London was still regarded as a sanctuary for them.

Thus London became the focal point of all Anarchist activities and the only chance of changing this situation was to discredit the revolutionaries and hope that public opinion in Britain would demand their removal. Makharov and other agents had so compromised certain Anarchists that the latter had to leave London to avoid arrest on criminal charges. The revolutionaries, who were men not usually engaged in criminal pursuits, were tricked by Makharov into lending their names to criminal enterprises in the belief that they were really waging war against the Romanoffs, and, in doing so, were providing the sinews of war for the revolutionary cause at the expense of the Czarist regime.

The perfect example of this counter-espionage technique was provided by the events which led up to the Siege of Sidney Street in London's East End. A police sergeant, investigating a report of 'strange noises' coming from a house in Sidney Street, called there and was shot dead. When other police surrounded the house and demanded that the occupants should surrender, they were met by a barrage of fire from automatic pistols. Winston Churchill (then Home Secretary) ordered the Scots Guards to assist the police in driving them out.

The relevant facts of the Sidney Street affair are still confused. It is definitely established that the Sidney Street gang was recruited from a small colony of about twenty Letts from Baltic Russia, but the identity of their leader was never officially confirmed. This mysterious character was known as 'Peter the Painter', but it is not proved that he was Makharov, as Soviet records state, and it is now considered certain that he was not Jacob Peters, who afterwards became one of the leading Bolsheviks in Russia, as the British police suspected at the time.

The immediate cause of the Sidney Street Siege was a burglary at a jeweller's shop in Houndsditch. Mr. Gerald Bullett, who delved into this story at some length, stated that there was a 'certain amount of corroborative evidence that Peter the Painter, so far from being the leader of the gang, was in fact an agent of the Russian Government, entrusted with the delicate and dangerous task of posing as a comrade of the anti-Czarist conspirators, and of persuading them to engage in criminal activities such as housebreaking, which would attract to them the attention of the London police, and ensure their ultimate deportation to Russia.

'This, I think, is by far the likeliest explanation of the mystery of Peter the Painter. . . . In all probability it was Peter the Painter, *agent provocateur* employed by the police of Czarist Russia, who by elaborate trickery encompassed the defeat and dispersal of the Houndsditch murderers. It was at his instigation, I suggest, that the jewel robbery was planned.'

It should perhaps be mentioned that an ex-officer of the old Russian police has stated that the jeweller in question had been entrusted with the safe custody of treasure belonging to the Romanoffs. That this statement is a distortion of the facts is more than likely. The explanation is possibly that this is the sort of story the Czarist agent would invent in order to incite the revolutionaries to burgle the jeweller's premises.

There are two reasons for this digression into events which have no direct bearing upon the Ripper crimes. In the first place they suggest a more plausible explanation for Le Queux's story about Pedachenko than that writer gives himself. Why Le Queux, with his background of secret service work, did not suggest that Pedachenko was used by the secret police for the purpose of discrediting the Anarchists is incredible. Surely an improbable story requires at least some degree of probability in explaining it. Instead Le Queux talked about exhibiting to the world 'certain defects in the English police system'.

But the second and more important reason is that the Sidney Street Siege reveals Nideroest in a different light from that suggested by *The Star* and this, in turn, brings to the surface a positive link between the mysterious Peter the Painter and Jack the Ripper.

The Star made play of the fact that Nideroest was not a Russian, but a Swiss, the implication presumably being that therefore he could not be a Russian agent. Yet an agent of another nationality would be far more useful to Russians in counter-espionage activities and less liable to be suspected than would one of their own people. In any case *The Star* admitted that he was a member of the Russian and Lettish Socialist Club in the East End, while at the same time mentioning the evidence of Chief Inspector McCarthy that he was not an Anarchist.

Now if Nideroest was a Swiss and not a Russian, a member of a Russian Socialist Club and yet not an Anarchist, what was he? The deduction surely is that he was a Russian counter-espionage agent. And of course the information he had been selling to newspapers about bombs being made in Whitechapel was 'all nonsense': it was part of his counter-espionage work to spread such stories.

It was Nideroest who helped the real Peter the Painter to escape to Australia after the Sidney Street affair, according to A. T. Vassilyev, one-time head of the Police Department in the Czarist Ministry of the Interior. 'On the orders of General Popov we searched Rasputin's dwelling for documents after his death,' said Vassilyev, 'and we found a vast quantity of intelligence reports. Protopopoff had made Rasputin one of his chief agents for gathering and assessing information and on one occasion ordered a sum of 1,000 roubles to be paid to him.'

Then Vassilyev went on to describe how among Rasputin's papers they found information showing that it was Nideroest who had helped 'Peter Straume, a Latvian in Whitechapel, to escape to Australia . . . later I was able to confirm from independent sources that this was indisputably correct'.

Now Peter the Painter has been variously identified as Jacob Peters, Serge Makharov, Fritz Svaars and Jacob Vogel. Who, therefore, was Peter Straume? The only British police chief to mention Straume was Sir Basil Thomson. In *The Story of Scotland Yard* he named Peter the Painter as 'Peter Straume, a Latvian living in Whitechapel, who, it is believed, escaped to Australia and died in U.S.A. in 1914'.

Detective-Sergeant Leeson, who was badly wounded in the Sidney Street affair, wrote afterwards that Peter the Painter 'fled to Australia'.

If anyone should have been able to identify the mysterious Peter it was Leeson. Sometime later Leeson went on a convalescent trip to Australia and when about to travel from Sydney to the Blue Mountains, 'whom should I see in the booking hall of the Central Station but Peter the Painter himself! You can imagine my surprise and discomfiture when the door of my compartment opened and in walked Peter.

'He could not, of course, guess that I was not in Australia on any official mission, or that my connection with the police force had been severed through my wound. To his way of thinking, I must have represented the long arm of the law stretched out to haul him back from that far continent.'

But nothing happened. Both men must have surveyed each other with apprehension, Peter expecting arrest at any moment and Leeson anticipating that the Latvian would produce a pistol. 'That was the last of him so far as I was concerned until I received a letter from his brother saying he had died in America in 1914.'*

Though the statements of Leeson, Basil Thomson and Vassilyev all tally, only the last-named asserts that Peter was a Czarist agent. Mr. Gerald Bullett, however, suggested a possible answer to the question of why Peter was not arrested—'that he escaped with the other inmates, *and with the knowledge of the police*, before the firing began'. The suggestion here is clearly that the British police connived at the activities of the Czarist counter-espionage in order to trap the real Anarchists.

The late Prince Belloselski, who spent the last quarter-century of his life in exile in Britain, corresponded with many leading figures in the Czarist Government and kept a scrap-book in which he pasted various newspaper accounts of pre-1914 Russian politics with his old handwritten comments on their veracity or otherwise. The Prince had this to say about William Le Queux's story on the Ripper:

'The MS from which Le Queux quoted would *not* have been dictated by Rasputin in French. Rasputin may have known the French language slightly, but he was certainly not fluent enough in it to dictate a narrative in that tongue. If he dictated this at all, it must have been in Russian. The subsequent translation into French probably distorted the original slightly, and by the time the French version was again trans-

* *Lost London.*

lated into English, the meaning must have been completely changed.

'I wrote to Le Queux, pointing this out, and suggesting he gave me the text of the French version. This he did, and my own view is that the following passage in Le Queux's translation should read as follows: "They actively aided and encouraged crimes in order to convince public opinion in Britain of certain defects in the English police system, there having been misunderstanding between our own police and the British."

'Though the wording is only slightly different, its meaning is now completely altered. It may, of course, be that the Kerensky Government had the text of Rasputin's original version "doctored" so that it would show up the Czarist Government in the worst light. Indeed, the only object for them to pass these documents on to Le Queux would have been for propaganda purposes.

'The man who could have thrown most light on this whole subject was Peter Straume, who, alas, is now dead. Straume was rather shamefully treated by his masters in Russia after he fled from Britain. I know nothing about Zverieff, but it was from Straume that Myednikov, head of the Moscow Ochrana (Secret Police), received the report about Pedachenko, whose real name, however, would appear to have been Konovalov.'

The Prince told me that Myednikov himself had told him this. To corroborate his statement he showed me a lithograph copy of the *Ochrana Gazette*, which he had been given by Myednikov. This was a confidential Secret Police bulletin which was issued twice a month to all chiefs of local sections of the Ochrana to let them know what was happening in revolutionary circles. One of the items contained therein read: 'KONOVALOV, Vasilly, alias PEDACHENKO, Alexey, alias LUISKOVO, Andrey, formerly of Tver, is now officially declared to be dead. Any files or information concerning him from district sections should be sent to the Moscow Central District of Ochrana. Such information, photographs, or identification details as may still exist might refer to KONO-

VALOV, PEDACHENKO or LUISKOVO either individually or collectively. If documents held by you do not contain these names, they should also be examined for any information concerning a man, answering to the description of the above, who was wanted for the murder of a woman in Paris in 1886, of the murder of five women in the East Quarter of London in 1888 and again of the murder of a woman in Petrograd in 1891.

'KONOVALOV's description is as follows: Born 1857 at Torshok, Tver. Height medium. Eyes, dark blue. Profession, junior surgeon. General description: usually wore black moustache, curled and waxed at ends. Heavy, black eyebrows. Broad-shouldered, but slight build. Known to disguise himself as woman on occasions and was arrested when in woman's clothes in Petrograd before his detention in the asylum where he died.'

So much for the Russian clues on Konovalov or Pedachenko. The document from which I have quoted was dated January 1909. Obviously the Ochrana wished to call in and possibly destroy all dossiers on this mysterious character. No doubt this wish was in part due to bureaucratic tidiness, but also because the Russians had no wish for embarrassing information to leak out as the truth of the Pedachenko story might have marred improved Anglo-Russian relations following the establishment of the Triple Alliance between Britain, France and Russia. It will be noted that the description of Konovalov tallies not only with that of the labourer, Hutchinson, but with some other descriptions of men seen with Ripper victims shortly before they met their deaths.

Mention of the fact that Konovalov was known to disguise himself as a woman recalls the theory put forward by Sir Arthur Conan Doyle, the creator of Sherlock Holmes. Sir Arthur, who was a keen amateur criminologist himself, believed that 'Jack the Ripper disguised himself as a woman in order to escape from the scene of his crimes'.

But what confirmation of all this is there in London? Before examining the London evidence further it is important to note two contradictory factors: first, that five of the nine experts mentioned assert that the Ripper was a Russian or Polish doctor; secondly, that while these experts imply that this was known immediately after Mary Kelly's murder, countless newspaper cuttings show that the police were continuing to arrest Ripper suspects for nearly a year after Kelly's death.

Abberline, who probably knew more than any other senior police officer about the investigations, still suspected Klosowski as late as 1903. Therefore one must conclude that while the police had suspicions about 'a Russian surgeon', their evidence against him was very scanty. Indeed, this to some extent is clear from Sir Melville Macnaghten's notes on Ostrog: '. . . whose whereabouts were not known exactly to the police'. In other words, if Ostrog was another of Pedachenko's aliases, he must have successfully eluded the police.

How much did the police know? And how much more did some of them pretend to know in the light of the wild assertions that the Ripper committed suicide by throwing himself in the Thames? It is a pity that Detective-Sergeant Leeson did not enlarge on his statement about 'a certain doctor, known to me' who 'could have thrown quite a lot of light on the subject'. Sir Basil Thomson categorically talked of 'an insane Russian doctor' who escaped arrest by committing suicide, but Major Arthur Griffiths suggests that the suspect who committed suicide was another doctor altogether. Though Griffiths' statements are inconclusive in that they mention three possible suspects, they are more palpably honest than the categorical statements of others as they frankly include the weaknesses of his arguments. True, one must assume that Griffiths is to a large extent duplicating the findings of Sir Melville Macnaghten, but the most interesting part of his narrative is: 'The second possible criminal was a Russian doctor, also insane, who had been in the habit of carrying about surgical knives and instruments in his pockets; his antecedents were of the very worst, and at the time of the Whitechapel murders he was in hiding, or, at least his whereabouts were never exactly known.'

This sounds very much nearer the truth than any other statements and it probably sums up the extent of the police's knowledge at the time. If they had been able to track down this man, they would at least have held him for questioning. But they must soon have had a shrewd suspicion that the Russian surgeon had left the country; perhaps it was because of this that they circulated the suicide story to placate public opinion.

There is no mention of a Pedachenko or a Konovalov in the *Medical Register* of this period, but if the Russian were a junior surgeon with qualifications not recognised over here, that is not surprising.* A Glasgow evening newspaper in 1947 referred to a statement by an amateur criminologist, Mr. Hector Cairns, who alleged that 'a Russian Secret Service man named Dr. Alexander Pedachenko . . . was a former surgeon in Glasgow'. But a lengthy search has revealed no confirmation of this.

There is no indication of anyone living in Westmoreland Road, Walworth, in 1888, who might have been the sister of the Russian surgeon. But, of course, she might have been married and using a British name, or she may not even have been a householder, in which case her name would not have appeared in the *Post Office Directory*.

But Dr. Dutton's notes on the Ripper cases give more information about the Pedachenko who 'worked as a barber-surgeon for a hairdresser named Delhaye in Westmoreland Road, Walworth:

'The witness Levisohn (in the Chapman case) told Abberline at the time of the Ripper crimes that he should look for a Russian who lived somewhere in Walworth, did a certain amount of illicit doctoring and attended barbers' shops to cut out warts and moles. Levisohn claimed to have seen this man in Commercial Street on the night of the Berner Street murder.

'Abberline thought that Levisohn was trying to mislead him, but I always urged the Inspector that he should follow up this clue. For I was quite positive that, while the murderer must be

* Nor was Klosowski in the *Medical Register*.

somebody who knew the East End thoroughly, he did not live there. But it seemed certain that he must live near to the East End and the area south of the river—Lambeth, Walworth and Camberwell—seemed a likely neighbourhood, particularly for a foreigner.

'An interesting aside on this theory is that Martha Turner, Annie Chapman, Mary Nichols and Mary Kelly all attended a clinic at St. Saviour's Infirmary in Westmoreland Road, Walworth, right up to the time of their deaths.'

This is somewhat more than an interesting aside when one considers another aspect of the Ripper cases to which no one else has alluded—that every victim, with the single exception of Elizabeth Stride, had links with places south of the river. Martha Turner was known to visit Rotherhithe and Walworth; Mary Nichols not only came from Camberwell, but lived at one time with a blacksmith named Drew in York Street, Walworth; Annie Chapman had a sister in Vauxhall, whom she visited just before her murder; Catherine Eddowes was seen in a public house in Walworth on her return from hop-picking in Kent (again, just before her murder) and she had a daughter living in Southwark; Mary Kelly used to visit the Elephant and Castle where a son of hers was boarded out.

How the four of the Ripper victims mentioned by Dr. Dutton should come to be visiting a clinic in Walworth is not explained. The doctor stated that he made this discovery from Dr. J. F. Williams, who lived in Camberwell, and attended the St. Saviour's Infirmary. 'I learned from Dr. Williams that a Russian barber-surgeon assisted him occasionally at the clinic, though strictly on an unpaid basis and largely as an observer of English methods. This man's name was Pedachenko.'

The *Medical Register* shows that a 'Dr. John Frederick Williams, M.R.C.S.' was attached to St. Saviour's Infirmary in 1888. He was then living at 6 Brunswick Villas, Brunswick Terrace, Camberwell Road.

'Dr. Williams understood that Pedachenko had degrees as a junior surgeon in Russia and that he was qualified "rather more than a skilled midwife and rather less than the average English G.P. But he was quick, intelligent and conscientious".

'It appeared that Pedachenko lived in the vicinity, though Dr. Williams could not say where. He also believed that he worked as a barber's surgeon at various establishments in the South of London, including that of a hairdresser named Delhaye in Westmoreland Road. He removed warts, treated skin diseases and was apparently a fairly versatile quack.'

This information certainly tallies with Levisohn's story. But Abberline for a long time thought that Pedachenko and Klosowski were one and the same person. There was some slight resemblance between the two men, if one is to judge from their respective descriptions. Probably, too, the similarity of their accents would make people liable to confuse the one with the other. But, according to Dr. Dutton (whose source one presumes was Dr. Williams), Pedachenko was a 'superior character, of medium height, with a dark moustache and sometimes side whiskers, well dressed in rather formal style'.

Dutton's suggestion that Klosowski 'posed' as his double, with the implication that the latter was Pedachenko, is not followed up by any explanation. It should perhaps be stressed that Dutton's *Chronicles of Crime* were not a single narrative, but rather a collection of impressions and theories which he noted at various periods. The answer to this puzzle is provided in the evidence which a Russian member of the International Workers' Club gave to the police. Lave, it will be remembered, was one of the last men who groped his way along Berner Street before the discovery of Elizabeth Stride's body.

Lave told the police: 'There was a stranger in the club earlier that night. He was a Russian, but he was not known to any of the other members. Yet he made me suspicious by claiming to be a Pole. I am quite sure he wasn't. He said he was a barber and that he had a business in a basement in George Yard. I should know him again all right. He could be perhaps between thirty and thirty-five years of age, with a dark moustache and a dark suit. I also remember that he had a rather heavy gold watch chain with some sort of stone set in a seal. Oddly enough, he wore a peaked hat, rather like a sailor's.'

But, according to Inspector Chandler, and confirmed by Abberline, when the police made inquiries at the dive basement in George Yard they found there not the Russian whom Lave had seen, but Klosowski. Lave admitted that Klosowski was not the man he had seen and there the inquiry ended. Shortly afterwards Klosowski disappeared to Tottenham.

Was Pedachenko posing as Klosowski? Did the two men know each other? And, more important, was the basement dive beneath the public house in George Yard, mentioned both by Dr. Dutton and Detective-Sergeant Leeson, the nocturnal hide-out of the Ripper? The first of the East End murders occurred in George Yard Buildings.

There is no complete answer to all these questions, but the fact that the *Ochrana Gazette* mentioned that Pedachenko was known to disguise himself as a woman and that he was in woman's clothes when arrested in Russia provides a possible explanation to the most baffling feature of the Kelly murder. For the police's task on that occasion was made doubly difficult because two women claimed to have seen Kelly at 8 a.m. —*after the time at which she must have been murdered.*

Had the inquest on Kelly been conducted at as great a length as the previous Coroner's inquiries, had the Coroner called more witnesses and cross-examined them, much more might have come to light. How would Mrs. Caroline Maxwell have stood up to cross-examination? Would she still have insisted that she saw Mary Kelly at the corner of Miller's Court at 8 a.m. and that half an hour later she saw her outside the Britannia public house talking to a man?

Certainly Mrs. Maxwell could not have seen Kelly, who was dead by that time. But the point to remember is that at that time in the morning it would still be fairly dark. Now if the person she saw was a man dressed up as a woman obviously he would pay no attention to any breezy 'Good morning' from Mrs. Maxwell. Possibly Mrs. Maxwell did not want to admit that she had been 'cut' by Kelly, for the latter was considered a superior type for Whitechapel and social snobbery was as acute in the East End as in the West. So, woman-like, she invented the story that she had conversation with Kelly. Possibly she may have thought 'Kelly' was drunk because the latter did not appear to recognise her.

A reconstruction of the Miller's Court murder now takes on a different aspect. Kelly had been to the clinic at St. Saviour's Infirmary. She would, therefore, possibly be known to Pedachenko. He may have found out her address and made a rendezvous with her. Hutchinson's account of the man he saw with Kelly coincides with the descriptions of Pedachenko even down to the 'big gold watch-chain' with a seal mentioned by the Russian, Lave. If Kelly knew Pedachenko already, she would have no qualms about taking him back to her room; she could reasonably assume that an assistant at a clinic would be respectable enough.

Now if Pedachenko killed Mary Kelly, he certainly did not escape wearing either her clothes, or those of Maria Harvey. Even Mrs. Maxwell admitted to Abberline that she couldn't 'rightly say that I had, or I hadn't seen her in those clothes before'. Yet she was quite positive that the maroon-coloured shawl was something she had seen Kelly wearing previously. Pedachenko may, therefore, have had women's clothing in the 'American-cloth parcel' which he was carrying. And the 'American-cloth parcel' may well have been the 'little black bag' which so many witnesses mentioned: a man with a bag or a parcel was invariably seen in the vicinity shortly before each crime.

If one assumed that Pedachenko discarded his own clothes and disguised himself as a woman with articles he had brought with him and wrapped Kelly's shawl round his head to hide his features, the two seemingly insoluble problems with which Abberline wrestled can be worked out logically. A fire fierce enough to ruin the kettle must have been stoked up with a purpose. Obviously the purpose was to destroy something and the unrecognisable ashes in the grate could have been some of Pedachenko's clothes. Then, to give the impression that he had destroyed only female attire, he may have thrown a few items of Harvey's clothes, including a bonnet, into the dying embers.

While some articles had not merely been burnt, but stirred around until they became ashes, the bonnet had almost been placed on the embers as an afterthought. And the burnt-out kettle? This must have been put on the fire for a purpose, too. Not to make tea as Abberline thought (surely no prospective murderer would waste time making tea?), but perhaps to boil water for Pedachenko to shave off his moustache.

The Times mentioned another woman who had been in Dorset Street between 8 and 9 a.m. and had 'seen Kelly walking towards Commercial Street'. Unfortunately the name of this witness was not given. But another newspaper account stated that this woman 'identified Kelly because she was wearing a horseshoe paste brooch on her bodice, an article which Kelly always wore'. Though Mrs. Maxwell did not mention this brooch, it is conceivable that, subconsciously, she identified the person she saw with Kelly because of the association of the brooch.

16

The end of the quest

At this stage of our quest for the Ripper it will perhaps be saluary to examine criticisms of my own findings by those authors who have most recently written on this theme—Robin Odell, Tom Cullen and Colin Wilson.

Mr. Odell writes that 'one of the greatest flaws in Donald McCormick's theory . . . came in his reconstruction of events in Miller's Court. He suggested that after killing Marie Kelly, Pedachenko exchanged his clothes for a woman's disguise, which he carried in the "American-cloth parcel" described by Hutchinson. He ignored that part of Hutchinson's statement which described the parcel as "a small parcel—a thin parcel about eight inches long". Obviously such a small parcel . . . could not have contained a bundled-up woman's skirt of the period, which was invariably made of heavy material in a voluminous style . . . the small size of the parcel completely invalidates McCormick's theory of how the killer escaped disguised as a woman.'

This is a fair enough point to make, yet if one examines Hutchinson's exact description it becomes somewhat of a quibble. Hutchinson said: 'In his left hand he carried a small parcel—a thin parcel about eight inches long. It was covered with dark American cloth and he held it by a piece of string.' Now one could submit that if the parcel was so very thin, if for example it was a narrow roll eight inches long and a couple of inches in circumference, the man would have gripped it in his hand, not dangled it on a piece of string. Hutchinson merely said it was eight inches long: he did not say what were its other dimensions. It might have been a thin flat parcel, eight inches long and four or five inches wide. It could still have contained a skirt rolled and wrapped tightly.

Mr. Odell also queries my theory that the kettle may have been boiled to enable the killer to have shaved off his moustache.

'Surely,' he writes, 'if the murderer had given sufficient premeditation to his plans to equip himself with a woman's disguise, as Mr. McCormick believed, then he would also have taken care of his moustache.' My answer to this is that a would-be killer who took care to provide himself with a disguise in which to escape would have taken care to retain his moustache until the last possible moment to prevent his being recognised.

Mr. Cullen, on the other hand, concedes that 'the Pedachenko theory is ably argued', but is critical of Dr. Dutton's statements. He argues that 'the good doctor time after time put forth statements without supporting evidence'. In particular he is critical of Dutton's assertion that four of the victims of the Ripper attended a clinic in Walworth where Pedachenko was an assistant 'right up to the time of their deaths'. What proof did he have for this 'wild assertion', asked Mr. Cullen?

Somewhat unfairly Mr. Cullen omits to mention that Dr. Dutton cited Dr. Williams as the source of his information. Both he and Mr. Odell seem to resent the testimony of Dr. Dutton, presumably because it does not fit in with their own findings.

Colin Wilson is an imaginative writer with almost telepathic gifts as an amateur detective. When he ventures on criticism he is on much firmer ground and he probes for the essential weakness. As he wrote in his review of the first edition of his book, 'Mr. McCormick and I would appear to have been pursuing parallel courses of research on the Ripper crimes. Consequently I can vouch for it that there are very few relevant details of the murder that he has missed.' But in his recent book *A Casebook of Murder* Mr. Wilson stresses the unreliability of William Le Queux as a source, asserting that Le Queux was 'a pathological liar' and stating that he had spoken at length to Rasputin's daughter, Maria, who assured him that her father never wrote about great Russian criminals because he was 'not remotely interested' in them.

Rasputin has been depicted as a sinister, two-faced scoundrel by many writers, but in the light of recent knowledge such a portrait seems to have been at the worst grossly exaggerated. I should prefer his testimony, if one had it first hand, to that of William Le Queux who, I willingly concede, overdramatised his case, probably embellished it in a ridiculous fashion in a manner which helped neither his own case nor mine. But my case rests not so much on Le Queux as on Dr. Dutton, Prince Belloselski and other sources. Indeed it might be true to say that my case would even be strengthened if the Le Queux testimony was omitted. Yet here again Colin Wilson claims that I offer 'no more evidence for the actual existence of Dr. Dutton than Matters did for Dr. Stanley, though he admits that Dr. Dutton actually existed'.

Well, this time I will offer some evidence for Dr. Dutton's existence. His biographical details will be found in various editions of the *Medical Directory* and the *Medical Register*. These will show that he lived in Bayswater in 1888–9 and that his last days were spent at Shepherd's Bush. I, too, fervently wish that Dr. Dutton's chronicles of his crime researches had been preserved for posterity. He allowed me to take notes from them as long ago as 1932 and they covered a number of other interesting cases. By a lucky chance my notes were safely tucked away, forgotten and then rediscovered after World War II.

When Dr. Dutton died in 1935 mention was made in his obituary notices of his links with and interest in the Ripper cases. The *Sunday Chronicle* published the following story:

' "I knew Jack the Ripper. I know why he committed the Whitechapel murders." This dramatic revelation in a secret diary of Dr. Thomas Dutton, the eighty-years-old specialist who was found dead at his home in Shepherd's Bush last week, was disclosed to me yesterday by a woman who had been one of his patients.'

The story referred to the doctor's 'three volumes of handwritten comments on all the chief crimes of the past sixty years', but the patient (Miss Hermione Dudley) did not reveal the name of the killer. Indeed it is doubtful whether she knew very much more than Dutton's claim to have established the identity of the Ripper, for her subsequent story (given in an interview) resembled very much the theory of Leonard Matters. Possibly she had read Mr. Matters' book and confused his version with that of Dutton. The only suggestion of any similarity between these two versions lies in this statement in Dutton's diaries:

'I have learned from a French doctor of a Russian junior surgeon, or *feldscher*, who was known to him in Paris about 1885–8. He was suspected of having killed and mutilated a *grisette* in Montmartre, but he left Paris before he could be arrested. This may account for Scotland Yard's search for a Russian surgeon they believed to be in hiding. At last there appears to be a hint as to motive. This surgeon, whose name was Konovalov, was said to have had a violent hatred of prostitutes due to a relative of his having suffered cruelly from contact with a woman of the streets. The description of Konovalov exactly fits that of Pedachenko and the final police assessment of what the Ripper looked like.'

The killer may have had male and female disguises. Though the various men seen with the Ripper victims shortly before each crime were physically alike, their attire was sometimes different. Yet the man Lave saw in the Workers' Club before Stride's murder and the man seen with Eddowes by the German near Mitre Square the same night were remarkably alike in description: 'a peaked hat, rather like a sailor's,' said Lave; 'a deerstalker's cap with a peak fore and aft,' said the German. The more one considers the possibility of the murderer disguising himself as a woman, the more probable it seems. It is significant that while many witnesses saw a man in the vicinity just before each murder was committed, no one saw a man immediately afterwards. The only possible exception is in the case of Elizabeth Stride, but even then it is not certain whether Mrs. Mortimer saw the man just before or just after the murder. People heard somebody leave Miller's Court after the killing of Kelly, but nobody actually saw who it was. Mrs. Cox heard someone shortly after 6 a.m., but she thought it was a policeman on patrol. If the killer left No. 13 as late as 7.45 a.m., she may have been correct.

Then there was the killer's halt at the close near Dorset Street to wash his hands in the sink after Eddowes' murder. It is feasible that he stopped more for the purpose of changing his clothes than washing his hands. Did he put on female attire on this occasion? Again, in the case of the Kelly murder, the delay in disguising himself as a woman may have accounted for a departure from Room No. 13 as late as 7.45 a.m.—that fact and the reason that it would be easier to slip off unrecognised when the streets were fairly crowded.

It is impossible to see how any man could have slipped through the cordon of police and civilian patrols, not to mention such passers-by as early-morning market workers and nightwatchmen, after the later murders. Even if it had happened on one occasion, it would hardly have occurred again with so many patrols about. It is true that nobody mentioned having seen a woman in the vicinity of these crimes, but the explanation may be that nobody was looking for a female and even had they noticed one, they would not have referred to her. There were more women than men about at this time of night in the East End.

Would the two women who claimed to have seen Kelly after she was murdered have invented these stories? It does not seem feasible. Mrs. Maxwell in her statement admitted she had 'only spoken to Kelly twice' previously; she could not have been able to identify her all that easily. Also she agreed that Kelly was 'all muffled up, as though she had a cold'; this would suggest that the 'woman' she had seen was trying to disguise her features. But the significant factor is that two women, quite independently, both thought they had seen Kelly and that Mrs. Maxwell was so sure of this that she embellished her story to try to convince the police. Doubtless Mrs. Maxwell, with an East Ender's fear of the police, was too scared to admit that she might have been wrong.

Dr. Dutton summarised the problem of Pedachenko as follows:

'Pedachenko was known to Dr. Williams, Levisohn, Joseph Lave and, presumably, to Klosowski [Dr. Dutton may or may not be presuming too much about Klosowski], though Levisohn does not appear to have known his name.

'He was never seen by Abberline, though the latter agreed afterwards that Pedachenko was probably a Russian surgeon, suspected of criminal activities in Paris, who was believed to be hiding in London. But Abberline was sure that Pedachenko was not the name he had used in Paris.'

Perhaps he had then used the name of Konovalov.

Pedachenko, according to Dr. Dutton, did not attend the clinic at St. Saviour's Infirmary after Mary Kelly's murder. Dr. Williams never saw him again.

'Dr. Williams described the Russian as having "a soft, low voice, rather like a woman's". He was slightly effeminate in manner, which Williams attributed to his being a foreigner [Victorians always ascribed effeminacy to foreigners, never to an Englishman!]. More important, Williams said he was ambidextrous: so was the Ripper.

'If, as seems likely, the Russian surgeon had made the acquaintance of some of these women at the clinic, this might be one reason why they would be unafraid to venture down dark alleys with him at a time when most prostitutes were terrified of meeting the Ripper and would be most likely to avoid strangers late at night.'

Shortly before his death Sir Basil Thomson was preparing a new series of articles on the Jack the Ripper story. As far as is known they were either never finished, or never published. But he wrote to a police colleague the following letter:

'In my book on Scotland Yard I made reference to the fact that it was generally believed that Jack the Ripper was a Russian surgeon who afterwards committed suicide.

'As you know, old as I am, I was not at Scotland Yard in that period: I wonder can you help? When I was in Paris recently I learned in talks with the French that they had always thought that the Ripper was a Russian named Konovalov, or some name like that. They did not, however, describe him as a surgeon, but rather as a barber's assistant. Odd that this should be the same profession as that of the poisoner Chapman, whom C.D.I. Abberline always thought was J.T.R.

'But the French discard the suicide theory. Their view is that this was a story put out by confederates of the Ripper and that we must have fallen for it.

'You know how the French, and especially their police, smell espionage in everything. Their somewhat romantic theory is that Konovalov was a counter-espionage agent for the Russian secret service, who was sent to London to spy on the Anarchists and, furthermore, that he committed the murders to discredit these terrorists.

'On the face of it, this is quite absurd. But my French police friends point to the fact that an anti-Jewish slogan, linking the Jews with the murder, was scrawled on a wall shortly after one of the murders was committed. They also stress that two of the murders were committed near clubs patronised by Russians, while alleging that the story of the Russian Anarchist surgeon was foisted on Scotland Yard. It is true that many of the early Anarchists and early Bolsheviks were Jews.

'Certainly part of the policy of the Czarist secret service was to discredit Anarchist organisations by means of trumped up charges of terrorism and robbery. The Peter the Painter affair proved that. But I should like to know whether you can throw any light on the matter, as I have undertaken to write a new series of articles on J.T.R.'

There is, of course, an alternative possibility: that the case against Pedachenko, or Konovalov, was framed by Russian agents and that he himself was innocent. But the evidence not only from the Russian side, but from France and Britain, would seem emphatically to reject such a possibility. There is no evidence that Pedachenko was an Anarchist, but some at least to suggest he was a Czarist agent and all the records of the Ochrana show that the Russian Secret Service employed criminals and even criminal lunatics as *agents provocateur*. Such agents may never have known in what way they were being exploited. If one accepts the story that the Russians helped him to escape, then one must assume that he was one of their agents. The only other possibility is that he was being used as a tool of the Czarist counter-espionage without his ever realising he was being exploited.

Since writing my previous edition of *The Identity of Jack the Ripper* I have discovered two other scraps of testimony which support the thesis that the Ripper may have indulged in his crimes in France and Russia. One of these scraps throws an entirely new light on the statement—as re-translated by Prince Belloselski—that there had been 'misunderstanding between our own police and the British'. If one could be exactly sure what this enigmatic statement really meant, one might be much nearer arriving at the truth. Guy B. Logan, writing in *Masters of Crime*, about the Ripper crimes, on which as a journalist he reported, stated: 'It is not generally known that Scotland Yard received a communication from the Russian police to which they were disposed to attach some importance. This took the form of a letter in which it was stated that similar murders had taken place in Moscow in, I think, 1885, that a man, whose name was given, had been caught red-handed and, since he was obviously insane, had been confined in a criminal lunatic asylum. He had made his escape from there in the early spring of 1888 and had never been captured; at one time he had been a doctor.'

This information is, unfortunately, vague and undocumented, but it does fit in with the other reports to some extent. Mr. Logan added that a description of this man was sent to Scotland Yard by the Russians and the London police were warned to look out for such a man—'the more so since he had spent three years in London and knew the English language well'.

Now while this story fits in with the rest of what we know about the search for a Russian of criminal habits, it does change completely the farrago of fiction which William Le Queux spun around his story. If the Russian police warned Scotland Yard, one must assume that this Russian was somebody they wished to catch, or that they were using this man as a pawn in some complicated counter-espionage plot. Thus the weight of evidence now swings one towards the possibility that Pedachenko was, if not an Anarchist, at least a member of one of the proscribed societies and sects which were the bane of the Ochrana.

When one reads on, this becomes clearer still. The letter from the Russian police, stated Logan, 'added that this man was a religious maniac, that he believed that only by killing them could the souls of "unfortunate" women enter into paradise and that there had been the same mutilations [presumably as in the Ripper murders] in the case of his victims'.

This might at first glance seem like the amateur theorising of a Russian Forbes Winslow, but if one studies the Ochrana records one finds that there existed on their proscribed list a strange sect which had such beliefs. A. T. Vassilyev, during his period as chief of police under the Czar, writing of the problems of keeping a watch on 'the plethora of religious sects in Russia' said that one sect, the Chlysty, had 'arrived at the dangerous opinion that man must sin in order to attain to God, for without sin there can be no repentance, and without repentance there is no redemption. This doubtful view of morals led them to all manner of extremely grave sensual excesses, which over and over again brought them into conflict with the authorities of both Church and State.'

The other item of information concerns the possibility of a Ripper murder in Paris. Dr. Dutton mentioned that a Russian junior surgeon, or *feldscher*, was known to have been in Paris between 1885–8 and that he was suspected of having killed and mutilated a *grisette* in Montmartre. I have examined *La Police Parisienne: Crimes Impunis*, by Gustave Macé, a former head of the *Sûreté*, as this book lists and describes all unsolved murders committed in Paris between 1871 and 1896. On 5 April 1886, between midnight and 5 a.m., a prostitute was found murdered on a pavement not far from the Church of Saint-Pierre de Montrouge. She had been severely mutilated; the body and arms were found wrapped in a green silk petticoat, while the dismembered legs, covered by oil cloth, were located in a public lavatory. The head of the woman was not found; nor was she ever identified other than as an unnamed woman known to have been plying her trade in that area. The dismemberment of the body was described as being unskilled, but, except for the complete removal of the head and the dismemberment of the legs, the killing, especially as regards the mutilations, was similar to those perpetrated by the Ripper. One of the significant details of the Ripper crimes was that the killer seemed to improve his technique and his skill with each murder. The early killings suggested a crude butcher with a slight knowledge of anatomy, whereas the later crimes revealed much greater skill.

I do not doubt that Dr. Dutton was anxious to prove his theory and that therefore he selected what evidence he could find which supported his case. But he did not put forward any wild theories, he was painstaking in his efforts to examine all the evidence and, while being quite emphatic that the Ripper was Konovalov, his summaries of the evidence are level-headed, cautious assessments of fact. He had nothing to gain from making sensational disclosures, for he made no attempt to sell them, or to have them published.

On the question of motive Dr. Dutton expressed no opinion at all. If I recollect correctly, when I asked him about it, he was inclined to the belief that the motive for the crimes was the most baffling feature of them, that it did not exactly tally with those of any other sex-mutilation murders and that to pursue the question of motive theoretically could blind one's way to the truth about the killer himself. I do not think he had heard of the theory that the killer might belong to a fanatical religious sect.

When one considers the allegations of murder as a weapon of counter-espionage, they do, as I trust I have indicated, lay one open to the charge of being decoyed by rumour and absurd premises. There can be no doubt that the killer himself murdered because he was a peculiar kind of sexual sadist. It has been impossible to find any independent evidence of the existence of the confederates of Pedachenko mentioned by Le Queux—Levitski and the young tailoress, Winberg. This part of the story is utterly uncorroborated. The suggestion that Levitski, who was 'born in London', wrote the post-card and letter signed Jack the Ripper might make sense if the Ripper correspondence contained any hints that the murders were done by Russian Anarchists. But they did not.

Colin Wilson in *A Casebook of Murder* mentions that after he wrote a series of articles on Jack the Ripper in 1960 he received two letters that made the same assertion: 'that Jack the Ripper died in a mental home somewhere near Ascot (or Windsor) a few years after the murders'. One writer alleged that the Ripper died in a mental home belonging to her father and that he was the son of well-to-do parents; the second letter referred to the Sickert theory already mentioned in this book, saying that the young man in Sickert's lodgings was 'taken away by his father and another man—a doctor who ran a mental home near Windsor'. The date given by the woman writer for the Ripper's death was 1892.

In further support of these statements Mr. Wilson also quotes from a letter he received from a retired brain surgeon, who believed that his suspect, 'a homosexual, died in a mental home near Ascot in 1892, of general paralysis of the insane'.

If there had been concrete evidence that this man was Jack the Ripper it is improbable that he would have been kept in a private mental home; the risks involved are almost too appalling to contemplate. He would have been consigned to a criminal lunatic asylum. There is also a discrepancy in the evidence concerning the Sickert story. There is no mention of Ascot, or of Windsor, in the Sickert testimony. In Osbert Sitwell's version it is quite clearly stated that the young man in question was fetched by his mother and taken 'back to Bournemouth, where she lived. . . . He died three months later.' This would have put the date of death as 1889, not 1892.

The theory that Jack the Ripper was a syphilitic lunatic is highly unlikely in the light of modern medical and psychiatric knowledge. It takes from twenty to thirty years as a rule for the final stage of syphilis, general paralysis of the insane, to develop. It is rare for such cases to be marked by maniacal violence; the great majority of such cases would be incapable of the cunning, skilled planning, precision in carrying out the killings and the ability to escape from the scene of the crime which the Ripper revealed.

In the previous edition of this book I omitted all reference to Robert James Lees because of its inherent absurdity. However, other writers since have seen fit to mention this man's claim to have discovered Jack the Ripper and within the last few months yet another book refers to it—*Ghost Detectives*, by Fred Archer. Lees was a scholar, philanthropist and medium, a friend of both Gladstone and Disraeli and is said to have arranged séances for Queen Victoria, trying to put her in touch with the spirit of the Prince Consort. It has also been suggested that Queen Victoria asked Lees to use his powers as a medium to try to locate Jack the Ripper, a story which is possibly true, but which gave place to an even more preposterous legend than any the Ripper crimes have yet produced. This was that the Queen feared that the Ripper might in fact be a future heir to the throne of England, none other than the Duke of Clarence. The Duke, who was the elder brother of the future King George V, died of influenza in 1892.

However, Robert James Lees undoubtedly had an obsession about Jack the Ripper and he dreamed on two occasions at least of murders which later were committed by the Whitechapel killer exactly as he described them. The police were told of his dreams, but remained sceptical until finally he forecast the murder of Mary Kelly. Then they took him to Miller's Court and had the pious, if unscientific, hope that he might lead them to the killer by playing the part of a psychic bloodhound. With detectives following in his trail, Lees walked the streets of London until he came to a large house in the West End and then solemnly informed the detectives that the killer would be found inside. The house was the home of a well-known surgeon and the police were not unnaturally reluctant to make inquiries. However, deciding that a desperate situation called for desperate measures, they spoke to the surgeon's wife. She made some remarkable disclosures. She said that one night she had found her husband torturing their cat, that he behaved abnormally and went out alone in the middle of the night. When he was out the Ripper struck. The story continues that the doctor, when questioned, admitted he had mental blackouts, that he was quietly certified as insane and put in an asylum.

Versions of this story vary, sometimes they contradict one another, but it is all third hand and totally uncorroborated. Lees was supposed to have been given a pension from the privy purse for his services to the police, but there is no record of this ever having been granted.

In the light of Sir Melville Macnaghten's notes one is tempted to ask whether 'Kosminski' or 'Karminski' was not Klosowski. The barber-surgeon from Warsaw used various aliases and 'Kosminski' or 'Karminski' may have been among them. Or Sir Melville may once again have got the actual name wrong. He says that 'Kosminski' resembled the individual seen by 'the City P.C.' near Mitre Square the night Eddowes was murdered. But the policeman on duty here declared he encountered nobody. Here again he may have confused the City policeman with the commercial traveller, Joseph Lawende, who saw a man and woman talking together in Mitre Square fifteen minutes before the crime was discovered.

The description of 'Kosminski' does not fit in with that of any other known suspect in the case. My own feeling is that 'Kosminski' is really a combination of Ostrog and one of Ostrog's associates, perhaps the double Pedachenko was said to have. Certainly Lawende's description of the man in Mitre Square was similar to descriptions of Pedachenko.

Indeed the more one considers the evidence to date the more it points to Pedachenko or Konovalov as the likeliest suspect. Sir Melville's statement about Ostrog tends to confirm this, especially as Ostrog was the only one against whom he advanced sound reasons for his being suspected. Ostrog's description is so close to that of Pedachenko that they must be one and the same man. True, Sir Melville does not give a personal and physical description of Ostrog, but he says that he was formerly a doctor, a Russian, and that he carried surgical instruments around with him. It is hardly likely that there were two mad Russian doctors both carrying knives and surgical instruments in the East End at this time.

That so little is known of him, whether his name was Ostrog, Pedachenko, Luiskovo or Konovalov matters little. Klosowski managed to remain in Britain for years under the name of George Chapman, even as a member of a police cycling club. More remarkably still, he actually managed to become the licensee of a public house without his true identity being revealed. So it is not surprising that the mysterious Russian for whom Scotland Yard was looking at the time of the murders was never, so far as one can ascertain, known by his true name. So well were his traces covered it is doubtful whether the police could have secured a conviction even had they been able to arrest him. Had forensic science been known in those days, had the evidence of fingerprints been acceptable, something might have been achieved. If the Ripper crimes had occurred today instead of in 1888, then the probability is that Konovalov would have been arrested and convicted.

The weakest link in the case against Konovalov would appear to be the vagueness of the views of the British police regarding the identity of the Ripper. This weakness might be removed if the original dossiers on the case were available. But they are not: they are not only incomplete, but it seems clear that certain papers were destroyed.

One has the impression that the majority opinion among the police hierarchy was that the murderer was a Russian surgeon, but that they knew very little, if indeed anything at all, about the man for whom they were looking. It should be noted that their opinion hardened after the death of Mary Kelly, and it is in the case of Kelly that the evidence against Konovalov is strongest. Konovalov had every reason to disappear after this murder; he had been seen with Kelly about the time of the murder and it could have been proved that Kelly had visited the clinic where he worked under the name of Pedachenko.

One might regard the Russian evidence against Konovalov as tainted, but it is formidable none the less. One might dismiss some of it, especially as espoused by William Le Queux, as being in the realms of fantasy. One can even rule out stories of plots and *agent-provocateur* tactics as inadmissible evidence, or irrelevant. But there is independent corroborative evidence not only from the French doctor, from Sir Basil Thomson and the French police, from Drs. Dutton and Williams, and not least from Sir Melville Macnaghten's own notes.

According to Dr. Tomaschewski, superintendent of the Nicolai Tchoudavorets Asylum in St. Petersburg in the 'nineties of the last century, Lord Snowdon's grandfather, Dr. Robert Jones, believed that Jack the Ripper was a Russian and in all probability to be found in a Russian asylum. In the archives of this hospital there is a note from Dr. Tomaschewski which states: '. . . the belief of Dr. Jones that the notorious London killer was a Russian was based on a description he was given by the English police. But he was more interested in the motives for the murder than in the killer himself and he asked many searching questions about the sadistic tendencies of the Chlysty.'

Helen Cathcart, Lord Snowdon's biographer, writes that Dr. Robert Jones 'had cause to take a special professional interest in the Jack the Ripper murders, for this was the very year [1888] he was appointed the first Medical Superintendent of the new L.C.C. asylum at Claybury in Essex'.*

The author goes on to say that the Ripper murders 'whetted Dr. Jones' all-absorbing interest in insanity. While other men went on fishing trips, Robert Jones spent his holidays abroad, visiting asylums. With the inquiring zeal of a reformer and a connoisseur's enthusiasm, he inspected mental hospitals diverse or distant as those of Norway and Italy, Poland, Switzerland, Austria and France. He once travelled far into Central Russia to see the advanded therapeutic workshops and tiled hygienic corridors of a model institution at Nijni-Novgorod.'

In the British Medical Association Library is a paper published by Dr. Robert Jones in 1890, entitled *Russian Retrospect: A Visit to Asylums in St. Petersburg, Moscow, Nijni-Novgorod and Warsaw*. It is clear from this paper that Dr. Jones met Dr. Tomaschewski in St. Petersburg, for he re-

* *Lord Snowdon*, by Helen Cathcart.

ferred to him in some detail, saying that 'he, in company with two of his colleagues, showed me over the asylum and I was much impressed with their earnestness of purpose, their interest in the patients and their genial kindness to all around'. It is true there is no reference in the paper to Jack the Ripper, but it is interesting to note that Dr. Jones visited Tver, where Konovalov was reputed to have lived, Nijni-Novgorod, where he was once said to have been detained and an asylum called St. Pantheleymon, which could well have been the institution from which he escaped. For Dr. Jones wrote of this place: 'It is an establishment for chronic cases of both sexes, and it is truly a colony, for an amount of liberty is practised here which I have never seen in England, Wales or Ireland, and the non-restraint shibboleth, as here understood, would cheer the heart of the most theoretical Scotch superintendent. There are no locks or locked doors by day, no airing courts, and no separation of the sexes when out of their wards.'

Perhaps the most damning fact is that Konovalov knew Martha Turner, Annie Chapman and Mary Nichols as well as Mary Kelly. Dr. Dutton not only confirmed with Dr. Williams that all these women visited the clinic at St. Saviour's, but that the Russian 'attended them'.

Yet the most convincing proof of the identity is the similarity of the descriptions of the man seen by Lave, Hutchinson and a commercial traveller named Lawende on three separate occasions. If Konovalov read the description given by Hutchinson in the press, he must have known it would lead to his being suspected by somebody. And Dr. Dutton asserts that 'Dr. Williams confirmed that Pedachenko wore a large gold watch with a heavy chain and unusual seal of a foreign pattern'.

One of the criticisms of Hutchinson's evidence has been that it was so minutely detailed that he must have invented it. I have already made clear that under severe cross-examination Hutchinson never changed a single detail of this description. But there is a more telling point. Hutchinson described how the man he saw pulled a red handkerchief from his pocket and gave it to Kelly. Lawende, the commercial traveller who saw Eddowes talking to a man ten minutes before her death, insisted that this man also 'wore a red handkerchief'. Major Smith was convinced that Lawende gave an accurate description 'as it was bright moonlight at the time'.

The differences in the three descriptions are only in relatively minor details. For example Lawende said the man he saw wore a peaked hat, while Hutchinson's man had a soft felt hat, pulled down over his eyes. But one would expect the killer to change some details of his clothing and headgear occasionally. The important common denominator is that the men described by Lave, Hutchinson and Lawende all tallied with the man described in the Ochrana's dossier.

The man described by Lawende resembled Konovalov (or Ostrog) as much as he was said to resemble the mysterious Pole, Kosminski. There was talk of Pedachenko having a double. Was Kosminski that double?

Police Constable Donald Rumbelow, of the City of London Police, showed me a knife, some ten centimetres in length, which he was given some time ago by a Miss Dorothy Stroud, who claimed it was Jack the Ripper's knife. When she first had the knife it was in a velvet-lined box, but as the lining was bloodstained she destroyed the box. Miss Stroud was given the box by the late Mr. Hugh Pollard, one-time partner of gunsmith and gun expert, Mr. Robert Churchill. From whom Mr. Pollard obtained the knife, or how the story that it had belonged to the Ripper arose, remain a mystery. But Mr. Pollard worked with the police on inquiries involving weapons and it is possible he may have obtained this souvenir in the course of such duties. The knife in question, it has been established, was of a type used for post mortems and manufactured sometime in the 'eighties. It was certainly the type of weapon which the killer could have used, though, as we know, he used more than one weapon on occasions.

I do not pretend to explain the riddle of the Ripper correspondence, nor do I claim to be able to probe the exact motives for the crime. It is doubtful whether the murderer himself could do so, unless he was a member of the Chlysty sect. But all the evidence points to the mysterious Russian as the author of this terrible series of crimes.

Bibliography

Adam, H. L.: *Trial of George Chapman*, Hodge, London, 1930.

Adam, H. L.: *The Police Encyclopaedia*, Waverley Book Co., London, 1920.

Anderson, Sir Robert: *Criminals and Crime*, J. Nisbet, London, 1907.

Anderson, Sir Robert: *The Lighter Side of My Official Life*, Hodder & Stoughton, London, 1948.

Brock, Alan: *A Casebook of Crime*, Rockcliff, London, 1948.

Cathcart, Helen: *Lord Snowdon*, W. H. Allen, London, 1968.

Cullen, Tom: *Autumn of Terror, Jack the Ripper, His Crimes and Times*, Bodley Head, London, 1965.

Dearden, Harold: Article entitled 'Who Was Jack the Ripper?' in *Great Unsolved Crimes*, Hutchinson, London, 1935.

Dew, Walter: *I Caught Crippen*, Blackie, London, 1938.

Griffiths, Major Arthur: *Mysteries of Police and Crime*, Cassell, London, 1898.

Halstead, D. G.: *Doctor in the Nineties*, Christopher Johnson, London, 1959.

Hyde, H. Montgomery: *Life of Carson*, Heinemann, London, 1953.

Leeson, B.: *Lost London*, Stanley Paul, London, 1934.

Le Queux, William: *Things I Know*, Eveleigh, Nash & Grayson, London, 1923.

Logan, G. B. H.: *Masters of Crime*, Stanley Paul, London, 1928.

Macnaghten, Sir Melville: *Days of My Years*, Edward Arnold, London, 1915.

Marjoribanks, Edward: *The Life of Lord Carson*, Gollancz, London, 1929.

Matters, Leonard: *The Mystery of Jack the Ripper*, W. H. Allen, London, 1948.

Mayhew, Henry: *London's Underworld*, William Kimber, London, 1950.

Moylan, Sir John: *Scotland Yard and the Metropolitan Police*, London, 1929.

Neil, Arthur F.: *Forty Years of Man-Hunting*, Jarrolds, London, 1932.

Odell, Robin: *Jack the Ripper in Fact and Fiction*, George G. Harrap, London, 1965.

Owen, Frank: *Tempestuous Journey*, Hutchinson, London, 1954.

Prothero, Margaret: *History of the C.I.D. at Scotland Yard*, Herbert Jenkins, London, 1931.

Reeves, John: *Recollections of a School Attendance Officer* (pamphlet).

Richardson, J. Hall: *From the City to Fleet Street*, Stanley Paul, London, 1927.

Scott, Sir Harold: *Encyclopaedia of Crime and Criminals*, Deutsch, London, 1961.

Sinclair, Robert: *East London*, Robert Hale, London, 1950.

Sitwell, Osbert: *Noble Essences, or Courteous Revelations*, Macmillan, London, 1950.

Smith, Lt.-Col. Sir Henry: *From Constable to Commissioner*, Chatto & Windus, London, 1910.

Stewart, William: *Jack the Ripper: A New Theory*, Quality Press, London, 1939.

Thomson, Sir Basil: *The Story of Scotland Yard*, Grayson & Grayson, London, 1935.

Vassilyer, A. T.: *The Ochrana*, Harrap, London, 1930.

Wallbrook, H. M.: *Murders and Murder Trials*, Constable, London, 1932.

Wensley, Frederick: *Detective Days*, Cassell, London, 1931.

Wilson, Colin: *A Casebook of Murder*, Leslie Frewen, London, 1969.

Winslow, L. Forbes: *Recollections of Forty Years*, John Ouseley, London, 1910.

Woodhall, Edwin T.: *Jack the Ripper, or When London Walked in Terror*, Mellifont Press, London, 1937.

Also consulted:

The papers of Sir Melville Macnaghten; the archives of the City of London Police Museum; *The Medical Directory*, 1888–9, 1889–90; *The Medical Register*, 1888–9, 1889–90; *Post Office London Directory*, 1888–89–90; Article entitled 'More about Jack the Ripper' by Professor F. E. Camps in *The Criminologist*, No. 7, February 1968; Article entitled 'A Ripper Handwriting Analysis' by C. M. MacLeod in *The Criminologist*, No. 9, August 1968, published by the Forensic Publishing Company; *The Times*, *Daily Telegraph*, *The Star*, *Daily Express*, *Sunday Chronicle*, *Murray's Magazine*, *Vanity Fair*, *Reynolds News*, *Empire News*, *Evening News*, *City Press*, *East London Advertiser*, *County of Middlesex Independent*, *Southern Guardian*; Notes taken from Dr. Thos. Dutton's privately compiled *Chronicles of Crime*; British Medical Association Library, *J. ment. Sci.*, *36*, 288–99: *Russian Retrospect*, Jones, R., 1890; Notes on the Jack the Ripper crimes by Sir Melville Macnaghten, in his private papers.

Index

Aarons, J., 52
Abberline, Chief Inspector, 34, 36–7, 48–9, 53, 59–63, 113, 116–17, 119, 121–6, 140, 144–51, 153, 168, 189, 190, 192, 195, 203–9, 211, 213, 226, 228–31, 237–8
Aberconway, Dowager Lady, 12, 174, 197
Adam, H. L., 115, 197, 207–12
Anderson, George, 177
Anderson, Sir Robert, 38, 56, 70, 73, 81, 97–8, 114–15, 140, 156
Andrews, P.C., 157
Angel & Crown, 18–20
Archer, Fred, 243
Arnold, Supt., 140

Backert, Albert, 88–9, 194–7
Baderski, Lucy, 203–4, 207, 211–12
Baderski, Stanislaus, 203, 213
Barnardo, Dr., 170
Barnett, Joseph (see also Kelly, Joseph), 132, 134, 138, 150, 184
Barnett, Rev. Samuel, 65
Baxter, Wynne E., 35, 49, 142–3, 158, 183
Belloselski, Prince Serge, 222, 234, 239
Bennett, J. R., 73
Berner Street, 75–7, 79, 84, 86–8, 95, 103, 114, 126, 226, 228
Birmingham, Walter, 200
Black Museum, 97–8
Blackwell, Dr. F., 77, 117
Blanchard, A. N., 123
Booth, General, 170
Bowyer, John, 137–40, 153
Brough, Edwin, 84
Brown, Dr. F. G., 96, 117–19, 141
Bucks Row, 31–4, 37, 39, 41–2, 66–7
Bull, William, 91
Bullett, Gerald, 219, 222
Burrow, Edward, 82

Cairns, Hector, 226
Camden Town Murder, 170
Camps, Prof. F. E., 118
Carson, Sir Edward, 206–7
Cass Case, 71
Castle Alley, 106, 157–8
Cathcart, Helen, 246
Central News Agency, 94, 101, 211
Chandler, Inspector J., 41–4, 47–8, 50, 54, 57–9, 229
Chapman, Annie, 46–9, 52–3, 56, 58, 61–3, 71, 117, 127, 130, 142, 155, 167, 183, 201, 227, 247

Chapman, Betsy, 204
Chapman, Fred, 46
Chapman, George (see also Klosowski), 204–10, 238, 245
Chlysty sect, 240, 248
Churchill, Robert, 248
Churchill, Sir Winston, 219
Clarence, Duke of, 243
Coles, Frances, 161–8, 177, 191, 208–9
Collier, George, 23
Conway, Thomas, 78, 128–9
Cooper, Elizabeth, 63
Coroner, Maria, 99
Cox, Mary Ann, 134, 151, 153, 236
Cream, Thomas Neil, 180–2
Cross, William, 31, 33–4
Crow, Albert G., 21, 23, 38
Cullen, Tom, 11, 12, 178–9, 195–6, 198–200, 232–3

Darrell, Mrs., 48, 61–2
Davies, Sir Alfred, 68
Davies, John, 42, 44, 49, 62
Dearden, Dr. Harold, 192
Deeming, Frederick, 180
Delhaye, William, 216, 226, 228
Dew, Inspector W., 108
Diemschutz, Louis, 75–7
Donovan, Timothy, 45–7, 58
Doyle, Sir Arthur Conan, 224
Druitt, Montagu John, 178–9, 195, 197–202
Dutton, Dr. Thomas, 103, 109, 111, 116–17, 122–3, 146, 148, 192, 211, 216, 226–9, 233–5, 237, 240–1, 246–7

Eagle, Morris, 76
Eddowes, Catherine, 78–80, 88, 95–6, 100, 117, 119, 128–9, 155, 167, 183, 227, 235–6, 244, 247
Ede, Thomas, 61, 67
Edwards, Frank, 172
Edwards, George Henry, 172–3
Evans, John, 48

Farmer, Amelia, 47–8
Farson, Daniel, 11–12
Fitzgerald, John, 67
Fleming, Joseph, 133
Flower and Dean Street, 53, 85, 134
Fraser, Col. Sir James, 82

George, David Lloyd, 68–9
George Yard Buildings, 19, 21, 212, 228–9
Gissing, George, 170
Godley, Inspector, 206, 208
Gold, Eliza, 78
Grantham, Mr. Justice, 206
Gray, Alfred, 168
Greatorex, Rev. Daniel, 92
Green, Emma, 34
Green, James, 42
Griffiths, Major A., 115, 175–6, 196, 225

Haine, P.C., 32–4, 37
Hall, E. Marshall, 181–2
Halstead, Dr. D. G., 169
Harvey, Maria, 134, 148–50, 188, 320
Hefeld, Paul, 215
Helston, Inspector, 66
Henage Court, 89, 104, 111
Herd, Richard, 190
Holland, Emily, 30, 34
Holland, Henry, 49
Hoxton Market Gang, 24
Hutchinson, George, 13, 134–6, 152–3, 189–90, 210, 230, 232, 247–8
Hyde, Montgomery, 207–8

International Workers' Club, 75, 87, 228, 235

Jackson, Elizabeth, 157
Jones, Dr. Robert, 246–7
Jubilee Club, 120, 213–14

Kay, Dr., 77
Keleene, Dr., 22, 27
Kelly, Mary Jane, 131–8, 142, 144–53, 155–6, 163, 167–8, 183–5, 188–93, 196–7, 208–10, 225, 227, 229–32, 236–7, 243, 245, 247
Kelly, John, 78–9
Kelly, Joseph, 131–2
Kent, James, 42
Keyler, Mrs., 151
Kidney, Michael, 86
Kirby, Col. Sir Alfred, 83
Klosowski, Severin, 121–6, 203–4, 206–12, 216, 226 fn., 228–9, 237, 244–5
Konovalov, Vassily, 223–4, 226, 235, 237–8, 241, 245, 247–8
Kosminski, 198–9, 244, 248

Lave, Joseph, 76, 228, 230, 235, 237, 247–8
Lawende, Joseph, 244, 247–8
'Leather Apron,' 40–1, 53, 55, 58–60, 94
Le Queux, William, 212–16, 220, 222–3, 233–4, 239, 241, 245
Lees, Robert James, 243–4
Leeson, Det. Sgt. (also P. C.), 120, 159–61, 191, 193, 208–10, 217, 221–2, 225, 229
Levisohn, Wolff, 122–3, 125–6, 226, 228, 237
Lewis, Sarah, 150–2
Llewellyn, Dr. R., 33, 35, 37–8
Logan, Guy B., 239–40
Long, P. C., 81
Long, Mrs. Elizabeth, 61–2
Ludwig, Charles, 67
Lusk, George, 96, 110

M'Carthy, John, 131, 133, 137, 139–40, 152
McCarthy, Chief Inspector, 215, 220
McCormack, John, 158
McDonald, Dr. Roderick, 143
Macé, Gustave, 240
McKenzie, Alice, 106, 156, 158, 167, 195
MacLeod, C. M., 110
Macnaghten, Sir Melville, 12, 24, 30, 37, 74–5, 84, 101, 155, 175–6, 178–80, 195–9, 201, 212, 225, 244, 246
MacWilliam, Inspector, 88
Maduro, Alonzo, 173
Mahoney, Mr., 19–20
Mahoney, Mrs. Elizabeth, 19–21
Makharov, Serge, 218–19, 221
Malcolm, Mrs. Mary, 86, 129
Marjoribanks, Edward, 182
Marsh, Maud, 205–6
Marshall, William, 86, 103
Matters, L. W., 111, 183–5, 187, 234–5
Matthews, Sir Charles, 166
Matthews, Henry, 65, 70, 83, 141
Maxwell, Mrs. Caroline, 13, 144–6, 229–31, 236
Mayhew, Henry, 65, 119
Miller's Court, 128, 131, 134, 137–8, 145, 148, 152, 176, 178, 183, 188–9, 195, 198, 229–30, 232, 236, 243
Minories, The, 67, 99, 109, 111
Mitre Square, 77–81, 88, 92, 95, 107–8, 114, 119, 198–9, 235, 244
Monk, Mary Ann, 30
Monro, Commissioner of Police, 70, 157
Montagu, S., M.P., 52
Mortimer, Mrs., 87–9, 96, 235
Moylan, Sir John, 195
Munn, Robert, 35–6
Myednikov, 223